White Magic

AN INSPIRING GUIDE
TO AN ENCHANTED LIFE

Lucy Cavendish

HAY HOUSE, INC.
Carlsbad, California
London • Sydney • Johannesburg
Vancouver • Hong Kong • Mumbai

• *Published and distributed in Australia by:* Hay House Australia Pty. Ltd.: www.hayhouse.com.au • *Published and distributed in the United States by:* Hay House, Inc.: www.hayhouse.com • *Published and distributed in the United Kingdom by:* Hay House UK, Ltd.: www.hayhouse.co.uk • *Published and distributed in the Republic of South Africa by:* Hay House SA (Pty), Ltd.: orders@psdprom.co.za • *Distributed in Canada by:* Raincoast: www.raincoast.com • *Published in India by:* Hay House Publications (India) Pvt. Ltd.: www.hayhouseindia.co.in • *Distributed in India by: Media Star:* booksdivision@mediastar.co.in

• *Edited by:* Serene Conneeley • *Cover Designed by:* Rhett Nacson
• *Author Photo:* Suzanne Maxim

ISBN 13: 978-1-4019-1803-3
ISBN 10: 1-4019-1803-4

09 08 07   7 6 5 4 3 2
1st printing in Australia, September 2006
2nd printing in Australia, March 2007

Printed in Australia by Griffin Press

Thank You

Deepest gratitude and lots of love to Leon Nacson, my champion and hero, Heidi Sullivan, my sister and friend, and Serene Conneeley, my light and guide for this book, and possibly the sweetest person on the planet. Hugs and tickles to my darling Thomasina, and to the wonderful Jo Mitchell: I treasure you. To the very inspiring Suzanne Maxim. To my beloved birth family (Mum, Dad and my brother Mark), for their care and the spiritual foundation they continue to give me, to my other family at Hay House, Eli, Rhett, Lauren and Candace. To the beautiful Rachelle Charman and the magnificent Stella Yfantidis. To the Goddess Temple in Glastonbury for keeping Avalon alive, and welcoming seekers with such open arms and loving hearts. To my online friends at the Grove, aka www.lucycavendish.com. You are all appreciated and loved so much. To the Goddess and the God, for the truths that we are never alone, and that we are born blessed.

Most of all, to all my sisters and brothers who walk the mist-filled path and dance to the light of the moon. You, who keep the wisdom and knowledge alive for when this sacred planet most needs our help and our love, I thank you.

Contents

Beltane's passionate rites.
Litha's midsummer madness.
Lughnasadh's harvest help.
Mabon's autumnal treasures.

So, my beloved friend. Why are you reading White Magic?

Are you curious? Perhaps this book fell into your hands in a coincidental way? Or are you finally taking action and answering a call that you can barely admit to yourself you've been hearing for years... perhaps lifetimes?

In some ways it doesn't matter why you picked up this book. It only matters that you have. Because there is a message for you here.

Don't stop now. Because you will soon discover that you are never alone.

What do these words, White Magic, mean?

White Magic is MAGIC focused on loving thoughts, acts and intentions. It is practiced, and developed until we create such beautiful changes in ourselves, and on this planet, that we feel a state of heaven within, and heaven in our environment.

You feel the power of White Magic when your heart soars when you begin to understand the deeper meanings of the seasons, when you feel a beckoning to the ancient sacred ways, when you know that something in your ancestry is calling you to explore this path.

There are many things we are. White magical practitioners have been many things. We were present when the sea rose and the earth came forth, when the first fires sprang up around humanity. We were there to care for the first crops that were planted, to sing into being the new seasons, to change, to hide, to hunt, to call out the names of the animals, to be at one with all the elements. We have always been here, from the legendary times of Atlantis and Avalon to the resurgence of our kind, now flourishing. When we say White Magic is returning to the planet, we also say to those who came before us – the ones who hid their magical selves, who cried from the pain of denial and persecution – "We are here. We never left. You were never abandoned. And we never forgot you."

All some of us need is one outstretched hand to help guide us to who we are.

Let this book be your guide, and enter a magical realm. The realm of White Magic.

White Magic and Me.

I was born Lucy Cavendish, but that did not become my name until some time after I'd become an adult.

You see, as in many magical paths – shamanism, yoga, and martial arts – it is common to take on a new name once you have passed your tests, both inner and outer.

It is traditional in White Magic to be an apprentice, if you like, for a year and a day. In this time you study, and work, and are tested, in ways direct and indirect, and after that time, you may have earned for yourself a magical name. This magical name represents your essence, and assists you in focusing on who you are becoming through your study, through your peeling back of conditioned layers, through living in magic.

Even to this day, some orders require one's magical name to be kept secret. Years ago this was a matter of life or death to the coven, to your fellow magical beings, to the people who needed your help. But those days have, blessedly, gone. My name is not a secret. It is out in the open, and that's how I chose it to be.

My name is Lucy Cavendish.

But Lucy was not what I was called for many years.

I was born in Sydney, Australia, with a different name. I have two very lovely parents and one very wayward, wonderful brother. I had a sunburnt country kind of childhood.

Nothing at all remarkable, really.

Except for a few things.

Maybe it's best that I tell you my story, starting from the middle. Because that was when I began to remember the magic of my childhood.

In London – young, alone and far, far away from home, friends and family – I wandered through Covent Garden's cold and narrow cobbled back streets. I knew I had come to England to find something, but exactly what it was I didn't know. I certainly didn't think I'd be wandering around in circles, feeling the pull of something, in a busy, touristy section of this massive city. But here I knew I was getting closer and closer to what felt like fate.

It seemed to be a spiritual quest, although I wouldn't have put it in those terms – not then, not out loud.

You see, from an early age I had been in touch with spirits. I'd seen ghosts, had prophetic dreams, felt presences, sensed atmospheres change, had told the future with startling accuracy and could see what was "really" happening in a situation. But it didn't make me much wiser in my own life. And for years I'd felt strange, somewhat embarrassed by these abilities, which I'd walled up more and more thickly over the years, until a crisis brought them pouring forth into my life again. The career I'd chosen had also made me feel even more estranged from this essential part of myself, until finally I reached a place where I could examine the truth.

For many of us, this takes a wake-up call of monumental dimensions. For some of us it is cancer, death, a personal life in ruins. For me it was a lost baby and a relationship that scored and burnt which made me question everything. Terrible things often happen to people for no reason at all, but sometimes the side effect of a traumatic event is that the person is shocked out of their… not complacency exactly, but the comfort zone so many of us have sealed ourselves into.

My comfort zone was where I felt I should be. I'd done my best to deny all otherworldly impulses, had struggled to fit in and live the normal version of life we all get sold. But whether it was where I was meant to be was another matter entirely.

The events that chased me away from home and across the sea to London were actually leading me back to myself. I felt that to rediscover who I truly was, what I was meant to be, I had to get away from everything and everyone who could project preconceived ideas onto me. I knew with absolute certainty that unless I found out for myself who I was, I risked being permanently cast in the roles others saw me in. In the role I felt would most please others.

I had to be alone in order to work out who I could be. And I could feel that something was getting closer – it seemed that just beyond my outstretched hand was another world altogether. I just had to find my way through. I knew in my bones that it was there.

When do we start to repress our intuitive selves? We know why – that's the simple part. It's to fit in. To avoid being different. To feel safe. To avoid punishment. But when does the negating of special, sensitive abilities finally do its work, leaving us so far from our inner selves that there seems to be no hope of reconnection?

For me, it had been so gradual that it seemed impossible I could ever really lose that girl I'd been. She'd been so strange. Yet surely the disguise I covered her in would never truly become a part of who I was? But when I thought about it, the mixture of shame and denial told me that yes, I had disowned the girl I once was. It was time to seek her out. To reclaim my magical self.

I recalled that when I was young I'd seen a ghost in my bedroom. Its long pale hands, disembodied, had floated through the air before me then, inexplicably, had taken clothes out of my wardrobe, hanging and re-hanging them. I had sat, small hands clenching my sheets like they were my only anchor to reality, eyes wide open, staring out into the dark, at the white marble hands, trying hard not to blink in case they vanished into the… into wherever they must have come from. Did something so inconsequential as going through clothes signify something?

They were gypsy hands, I'd thought. And they were rifling and re-ordering, putting things back together, but why? Why would a ghost bother to show me something so mundane?

I never discussed this with my parents, although "the hands" came back again and again. They started to move around my room at night, sometimes batting a book off my shelf and across the room, at other times restful, composed. I even felt them stroking my forehead occasionally, so my fear of them dissipated over time.

I couldn't talk about them though because, well, you have to understand my family. They're very down to earth. It was football, the beach, physical fitness and report cards that were big in our house. There was an enormous amount of love and laughter, but it was not at all an esoteric kind of household. We were Catholics of the confused kind – we believed in something profound and sacred at the core of our lives, but we'd given up going to church when we all figured we'd rather be at the beach or at swimming club on Sundays. We felt instinctively that we could worship spirit as effectively when we were under God's heavens as under a church roof. So even though we were respectful, and spiritual, we were hardly aware of psychic phenomena - we were more likely to be cheering on the Australian swimming squad at the Olympics. While I was an avid reader, no-one else in my family shared my passion. In fact there wasn't a single book in the house at that time that didn't belong to me – it was just the newspaper, textbooks and a golf manual. So why these night-time experiences? And day experiences too, later.

One night I overheard my mum talking to Dad about the land we'd built the house on. Apparently it had "belonged" to gypsies, Mum was saying, and the council had taken a long time to get them to move from the land. I wondered if the gypsy hands were connected.

That night they were back, messing with my clothes again and pulling drawers open. I wasn't frightened, but I knew they were annoyed. I lay in bed, wondering what to do. Finally I sat up and explained that my family and I had not known that they felt this was their land. We were sorry, and hoped they were okay. The hands stilled. Stroked my head. Waved once then faded into the air.

All I had left was a messy room. Which I knew I'd better tidy up before my dad saw it.

Other nights I would lay in bed for hours, watching the incredible washes of color flooding across my internal vision. Clearest, purest purples and azures, exploding into constellations and reforming as clear bright spheres. Sometimes they were moving abstract designs, geometric and perfect, like a secret code for the universe. I could gaze and gaze at my own world within. I lay with my eyes closed for hours, loving this incredible show, having no idea what it was but experiencing pure joy and happiness that something so simple – closing my eyes – could bring me such happiness.

These weren't my first "experiences" either. When I was tiny, and I know I was tiny because I can remember the weight of my plastic toilet training pants, I flew out my bedroom window. Now, I may have been astral traveling, I may have been flying, I don't know. But I know I was flying along above the narrow garden at the side of the small house we lived in, with its flowers and rockery, and I was amongst them all. I flew right to the end of the garden, which joined the front yard, then quickly turned around, flying back in the window. I was scared! I mean, how many kids flew about – in their toilet training pants?

But it happened many times. Gardens have always fascinated me. I used to stare for ages at bluebells and hollyhocks, but the flowers I loved most of all were the ones with the fairies in them. I could see tiny beings floating around the top.

One morning just a few years ago, my daughter told me that angels had gathered at the foot of her bed, and that they had woken her up to tell her their names, and asked her to remember them. She was annoyed when her father suggested she was dreaming. "Daddy," she stated in her firm five-year-old voice, "it was not a dream."

When I related this to my mother, she said I had told her the exact same thing when I was the same age. Could this be an inherited quality? Or was it simply so natural, so simple, that it occurs to many of us when we are young, before the discord of reason begs us to stamp out intuition?

As a child and a devout Catholic, I went to a convent school where there were many statues of Mary, the mother of Jesus – who I now realize was also Mary, his loving soulmate. There was one divine statue I adored, carved from wood. She sat on the steps we climbed on our way to assembly, clattering past in a schoolgirl mob. I would often stop and gaze at her. I loved her face, which was so gentle and serene, tranquil and kind.

One day I felt her gaze move to me, and I stopped on the stairs and spent time speaking with her silently, within my head, as everyone rushed by on their way to class. Her bare feet in particular moved me deeply. I became fascinated by her and painted her image over and over again in art class. I attended chapel for the feel of it.

But the nuns, bless them, did not feel sacred to me. When they made us get right inside the enormous skips at school to clean them out as punishment, when I was told I was a slattern for whistling (I'd been feeling happy – so proud of being able to produce such a clear bright sound), when my hair was tsked at and described as a mess, I did not feel love. I felt fear.

So on the surface I was a normal schoolgirl who had a sunburnt nose, was a pretty good swimmer and student and was teased by my brother. But at night I had a totally different life. Every night when I was growing up a spirit visited me around 3am – and it accompanied me over the water to London, until a final showdown separated us.

But until that time it was virtually a secret. I did tell my mother once, and she, understanding more than I ever gave her credit for, wanted to take me to see a psychic. But I was frightened, feeling that if I unlocked the door The Visitor could be with me all the time, and I didn't want that.

If it had visited you too, you would understand. Maybe it has. Plenty of sensitives have received this kind of energy into their psyche. Heavy and relentless, it would bear down on me, crushing the air from my lungs, making my childish self cry out helplessly at night. I learned to cope with it, and fight it off, but never enough to make it leave.

But my talents to sense The Others wasn't only troubling – sometimes these undeveloped, raw skills brought me great pleasure and happiness. By 10 years of age I began to study. I read and I read – myths, legends, history. The Gods and the Goddesses were more real to me than any of the saints and other figures at my Catholic church, although I knew their tales held echoes of the Gods and Goddesses I loved.

I did not love the church, or the priests or even the nuns, but I adored the statues of Mary, and I devoured the histories of the saints. With their visions and ecstasies, they seemed to be in touch with another realm, unlike the dry, austere interiors of my church. I learned the myths and legends of the Irish, the Greeks, the Celts, the Maori and the Polynesian peoples. And slowly, looking around me, I began to notice – and to be able to articulate – that the spiritual was everywhere.

Once I saw something move within the depths of a huge Moreton Bay fig, and I knew that trees had spirit. The Moreton Bay figs truly come alive when in groves, because they need to be together to speak to most people. Plumeria trees are magical too, as are the bushes and the shrubs and every blade of grass. But the trees, the really old ones, resonate with spirit and magic. They gave me a sense of being attached to the land, and I felt myself forge a kinship with nature.

Near my home when I was growing up there was a waterfall I used to go to alone, not breathing a word to another soul about where I'd been. I considered it my secret. I'd ride my bike, taking an apple and a book, and lie there on the black rocks, feeling the heat seep in to my skin, looking at markings on the trees, listening out for something that I couldn't have put into words if I tried. I felt it was also trying to reach me. Again the bridge to another plane, another kind of place, seemed to be there, I just didn't know how to pull away the veil between the worlds that kept us so separated, so alone.

One night I crept out and went there during a full moon, and lay on the rocks and soaked up the moonlight. I adored the moon and felt even then that its silvery light had magic in it. An incredible feeling of peace would stay with me for two or three days after going to my secret waterfall. I knew magical beings came out to play in the darkness. I was certain I saw bush fairies dancing in the sunlight. It was a hidden place, a sacred place, a spirit place.

Maybe it was – I never saw another person there, and years later I couldn't find my way back. It was as if I'd imagined the whole place into existence. Maybe I had imagined it – or maybe I'd lost the path back because I'd lost touch with that part of myself that could discover such secrets. Whatever the reason for its disappearance, my inability to find my way back to my secret grotto made me immeasurably sad, and an emptiness that I'd only sensed before now seemed painfully apparent. I felt shut out.

And the path, the way to finding out what it was that would help me on my journey, remained as misty as the streets I walked through every night. London's lamp-lit romance fed my soul. I'd escaped a life where I'd felt condemned by the brutal, hard people around me, whose ethics disturbed and jarred my soul – but who was I and what was I meant to be doing?

I was haunted by these thoughts. I knew that in coming to this place I'd freed myself from a deadening, meaningless, shallow life – but where was this freedom going to take me?

I used to walk the city's ancient streets for hours, thinking about these things. I'd had some strange experiences since arriving in England, and a recurring dream that made me sure I was in contact with another realm.

Then, on a day that became a turning point, I came to a halt outside Mystery's – a shop drenched in soft light and sweet incense and crowded with mystical tools and gorgeous guys with pointy beards. I loved it, but I hadn't intentionally been heading there on this day. But I was working up the courage

– and saving up the money – to have a reading.

Inside, I wandered around, warm and comfortable after the cold and frost of outside. My eyes trailed over the shelves with their mystic titles. I wanted in to this world, but how? Did you need a sign? Some kind of permission?

Among the shelves were stacks of tarot decks – modern takes, one with horror film metaphors, one called the Witches Tarot, a few Celtic variations. They fascinated me and they held my gaze for longer than usual. One deck was loose from its packaging, and I stared longingly at the delicate cards.

"You can pick them up you know – have a look," said a friendly guy hauling packing cases.

Almost hesitantly I picked them up, waiting for a sudden feeling to come over me. Nothing. But there was no denying I was spellbound. The images were beautiful, yet strange and peculiar, and some were even a little frightening. I could feel that they had something to say to me. But could I learn to speak with them?

I shook my head. I wasn't skilled enough for this.

I ran my gaze over them, and then a smaller set caught my eye. It was a thin deck, a variation, I know now, on the Marseilles deck from 16th century France, made up only of what I came eventually to know as the major arcana cards. Their beautiful, medieval images spoke to me. They made me feel connected to what I know now is my own magical history.

Devils and angels, ladies and lords, children and planets and plants and flowers – all seemed beautiful and exotic. And desperately desirable.

I had just enough money for the deck, as it was a starter pack. I took them carefully to the counter, where the gorgeous man served me with a friendly grin.

I felt like I'd just entered a club. No, that wasn't the word. An order. A history. An enchanted realm.

That was my entrance to the world of the tarot, which led me to the world of magic, and to meetings with people who called themselves Witch. I explored bookshops after that, and spent the little money I earned at the time on works like A Feminist Tarot and old hardbacks with handwritten notes in them. I discovered occultist and magical writer Dion Fortune in the esoteric section of national book chain Waterstone's.

And at night I worked with the cards. I would light a candle and an incense stick in the tiny, freezing, shabby bedroom which served as my home and gaze upon the images, committing their meanings – the myriad of meanings and variations – to my memory with far more enthusiasm than I'd ever applied myself to mathematics tables, although the meanings were infinitely more subtle and complex, more akin to the perfection of chaos theory than predictable outcomes.

I progressed to a complete deck, and began to read for friends and the neo-family that grew slowly around me. I hand-stitched a black silk wrap for them, which I still use to this day. I did not go a single day without them. I read for myself and I read for strangers and I read for friends.

The beautiful images of every tarot deck I saw became my home, my fantasy, my country and my self.

I also devoured stories about magic and kept a journal where I outlined my thoughts and my readings. Slowly my life began to take shape. It was as if the story of the Witches was helping me find the meaning I knew had been there, but which I'd lost along the way – just like thousands upon thousands of other seekers have done before me on discovering the beguiling nature of magic.

Then I traveled extensively. In Spain I read the cards, worked spells, chanted and meditated, spoke and studied. I stayed with teachers who all revealed so much to me, sometimes through practice, sometimes through example, sometimes through silence. I practiced with the Breton Witches on the coast of France. I lived in Paris for a while, and read tarot for friends and people who wanted me to prove to them that there was something to the cards. In cafes in Amsterdam I spoke to people who told me their family's magical secrets. At the edge of Africa, looking out to Morocco, I learned about the mystics of that country and their craft. In the city of Bath in England, where the Romans hid the past, I learned of Goddesses that bridged cultures. Further north, the Lake District, home of the Romantic poets who were all deeply mystical, revealed more again. Stonehenge, the magical stone circle of Wiltshire, and the beautiful forests of Wales taught me their songs. I read and I read. I meditated, thought, contemplated and studied, because that is the way to learn. And I loved it.

As I read the tarot, cast a spell, chanted the remnants of a ritual, greeted the moon and observed the sacred seasons, I became more and more my self. My life became more and more about white magic – high magic, intuitive magic, magic that soothes your soul, helps to heal, and uses energy in its most sacred ways.

Years later, back home in Australia, I eventually arrived at the grove of Moreton Bay figs that I think of as one of my own sacred spaces. It's near a massive main road, with a beautiful hill. It looks over the city lights and yet you can see the stars. There are possums, there are leaves, and damp smells and earth. During the day massive flocks of screaming white cockatoos dangle from branch to branch. There are lorikeets and precious birds amongst the pigeons and the possums and the ibis.

I believe I am closer to Them when I am there. As you will be when you begin to learn the magical secrets. The laws of the Goddess. The lore of the land.

The secrets of white magic.

Chapter One ~
The Ancient Path that goes Forever

WHAT IS WHITE MAGIC?

White Magic is the ancient and eternal spiritual path of creating and manifesting by conducting and directing the power of Light. Through white magic we connect to nature, her cycles, her people, her animals, her creatures, her spirits and we reconnect and develop wonderful connections to the sacred continents and places on this earth. Atlantis, Avalon, the heartland of Australia, Greece, Ireland, the Scottish highlands, Brittany in France, Egypt. Through white magic we learn of the Universe, and the heavenly bodies and their energies and influences, their healing powers and wonders.

White magic is as old as life itself, yet it is eternal and ever-evolving. But how did the white magical path start?

When life on this planet was young, we honored all that was around us, all that created life. Earth, air, fire, water and spirit.

White magic is like a tree with its many roots. It has one

strong trunk yet many branches, leaves and fruits – likewise we are all one, but we have a multitude of beliefs. Being a white magic practitioner involves walking a road of ancient and divine learning that includes wisdom, enjoyment, magic, laughter and light – and creating a better future for us all. White magic is a term that embraces many paths and traditions, but essentially it is a belief in the sacred qualities of nature, in ourselves as spiritual beings, in deities, fairies and divine magical creatures who are utterly real and who can help and inspire and teach us.

To practice white magic is to practice the healing and psychic arts. White magic gathers together the fruits of the earth and the five elements, it draws down cosmic energy and magical earth energy via connections to divine beings and to this beautiful green and blue planet Gaia.

If you feel drawn to this path, you are a being of white magic.

You have nothing to prove. No test to pass. No knowledge to learn that does not already dwell within you. No initiation can validate you more than you can, by simply acknowledging your own sacred nature. I am not here to tell you that you are magical. I believe, as you do, that you already are practicing white magic. You don't have to have red hair and white skin, be able to trace your roots back to a stone circle in Scotland, or have heard voices in the night speaking a magical name to you! But you may be a Witch and yet have had no sign you consider concrete. All of those things may have happened – or the signs may be infinitely more subtle, or perhaps you have been taught to dismiss them, repress them, smother them in order to fit in.

I ask you again, why are you reading this book?

I thought so.

You see, you knew the whole time.

White magic, you see, is simply a tool for reawakening what you may have half-forgotten – the magical being who you are at your very core.

The path of white magic is highly ethical, positive, healing and beautiful. As with any path, it is the intent of the individual that makes all the difference. White magic can be used to heighten psychic power, draw love and affection, heal past life issues and create wonder and joy in the everyday moments we all experience.

It is also a path that walks gently on the earth, and to embrace white magic is to love, bless and heal the planet. It is to take care of your physical body while transforming your spirit. It is to become as healthy as possible, for your body is the sacred vessel through which divine magic can be made manifest. It is to respect people of all appearances and of all ages, for we are all part of the glorious Goddess and her cycle of birth, creation, death, rebirth, ascension.

Since the written word became the way in which we keep our knowledge, there have been records of white magical practitioners. Some of this written historical information has been, and continues to be, fed and fueled by ego, fear, misunderstanding and intolerance. In other words, it does not come from love. In Britain before the spread of Christianity in the Middle Ages, to use just one example, many white magical practitioners were active members of their communities, respected as healers, midwives, herbalists and medicine men and women. They kept in touch with the land, its secrets and all our ancestors, and communicated within the void where the veils between the worlds were lifted. The elementals joined them for communion, to talk of how to share this planet and to assist in our human evolution.

However when the Burning Times came, from the mid-1300s onwards, people began to view their magic and healing skills with fear, and the wise women and wizards became one of the many scapegoats targeted by an inquisition that saw many white magical practitioners killed. Others hid, storing their energy and knowledge for a safer time. Many of us today carry a bloodline or spiritual bloodline, or past life memory, of these times, and even now we fear to exercise our powers, knowledge and speak our truths, as we hold in our cellular memory the fear of being punished.

Some of us have swallowed the historical and present day propaganda, and the result is that we are torn – denying who we are for fear of what will happen to us when we claim our birthright, but suffering from that denial.

And yet everywhere I can see signs of the return of white magic. Everywhere. It is in every movement of the moon and sun, every change in hue of the vivid sky, all the mysteries of the planet's seasonal shifts. It is in the force that binds new lovers together, in the strength and friendship that keeps us companions and soulmates. White magic is in the kindness we show a stranger, the magic we feel when we face a significant task or test in our lives. It is in the mother bringing forth her child, and is present when that child speaks to imaginary friends. Its secrets are shared and spoken even when we know little about what we say, or the sacred origins of our words.

Yet our words are spoken even by those who do not follow the way of white magic. Do people know they are speaking the language of white magic when they say harm ye none? When they speak of the power of three? Or greet each other with love and light? All of these beliefs and laws are summed up in The Wiccan Rede, a poem which is attributed to Adriana Porter, and was written early last century but not published until 1975. It captures the sacred traditional greeting between white magical practitioners, the code of behavior they have lived by for centuries and the ancient and eternal beliefs that encompass white magic – a path of self-responsibility rather than strict

rules laid down for all to follow without question or thought.
There are several versions of The Rede – the one I feel most
inspired by is this one:

> *Bide within the law you must*
> *In perfect love and perfect trust*
> *Live you must and let to live*
> *Fairly take and fairly give*
> *Light of eye and soft of touch*
> *Speak you little listen much*
> *Honor the old ones in deed and name*
> *Let love and light be our guides again*
> *Merry meet and merry part*
> *Bright the cheeks and warm the heart*
> *Mind the threefold laws you should*
> *Three times bad and three times good*
> *These eight words the rede fulfill:*
> *"An' it harm none, do what ye will."*

Those magical words, "An' it harm none, do what ye will,"
is considered by white magical practitioners to be similar
to the golden rule, a belief found in nearly every religion,
which forbids harm to others – and which we broaden to
encompass ourselves as well. This is why white magical
practioners, the wise women and wizards of this path don't
cast spells on people to affect their behavior – they believe
that all people have free will, and that it is wrong to inflict
their will on another, no matter how kind the intent. Many
also believe the implications of this rede, or creed, go further,
that it means not just to do no harm, but to actively do good
for one's fellow humans, including oneself.

And when we say love and light be guides again, what do
we mean? I believe that it means that we are re-embracing
our path. Rediscovering our selves, and old secrets. How

many of us know the shores of Britain were kept safe from invasion during World War II by a group of wise women and wizards working in the New Forest?

How many of us are aware that the wisdom of Atlantis was kept alive for us by the white magical practitioners of Avalon? Indeed, how many of us understand the sacred truth that a white magic is the path of the priestess, the healer, a midwife, a keeper of the sacred ways both ancient and modern, both of the earth and of the stars?

How many of us know this? Too few. Perhaps that is why so many of us still fear who we are.

History tells us why, in explicit and saddening detail.

Ancient societies had their priestesses and priests – the women and men of the temples of Artemis and Diana in ancient Greece and Rome, the Oracle of Apollo at Delphi, the Celtic priestesses of Britain, and those whispered of in the legends of the lost lands of Atlantis and Lemuria, which are slowly becoming accepted as real. All were white magic practitioners – wise ones and wizards who were the keepers of arcane, sacred knowledge.

They had many skills, including the sacred observance of seasonal customs, healing, starcraft, divination, seeing the future and understanding and recognizing the roots of that future in the past and the present, and they held sacred the spiritual lives of the communities they served.

This wisdom developed through groups of men and women who worked with each other, sharing skills and testing their practices and experiences. Between them was built, stored and kept safe an immense body of sacred knowledge, most of it passed on through the oral tradition, through words and song, committed to memory not books. Now, our white magic is spreading forth from the shadowlands where we took refuge, back out into the brightness of the spiritual mainstream in a way that the community can slowly, gently, begin to accept.

In the past, knowledge was shared without competition or fear, and with great love and respect. We all had different skills, which we pooled together to gather up and keep safe and grow from. This occurred from Europe to Africa to the Americas and everywhere in between – in all countries we were close to the Goddess Gaia, our beautiful earth.

Before the rise of Christianity, the current mainstream western religion, with its dominating political culture that contradicts its sacred and beautiful philosophical message, white magicians practiced a faith which was centered around the belief in a God and a Goddess – balance, sacred and divine.

But with the rise of religions with predominantly masculine figureheads, the hereditary line throughout clans and cultures became male. Men are beautiful and wonderful, sacred healers whose energy has been distorted and compromised as much as the female energies of this planet. We do not need to replace men – not at all! It is the energetic imbalance and the misuse of all of our powers that we need to address so that our beautiful planet can survive and be loved. She has been abused, raped, insulted, overlooked, feared, bound, controlled, strangled, cut and burnt. So we must love her back to full health. Men have been cruelly corralled into appearing emotionless, mechanistic and controlling.

We play an immense part in the future of the universe, and our future depends on these energies rebalancing both within ourselves, and within our cultures, and within the earth's etheric blueprint, which in turn has a ripple effect across the cosmos.

The stamping out of the religions of the Great Goddess and her beloved consort, the God, was carried out in many ways, some of which were cruel and terrible. Some of us still carry a blood-echo of fear, shame and confusion within us from this time. The Celtic priestesses were tortured and killed, hung by their hair from the oaks they worshipped, their feet weighed down with heavy stones. The conversions to Christianity which were wrung from Goddess worshipers were not of the heart, but driven by the urge to survive and stay safe. Today, some of us still fear that we will not survive if we turn to our true divine expression.

This is not a modern condition. The fear of feminine power and fertility and of our innately sacred nature has deep, deep roots. Well before the Romans attempted to destroy the druids and the Witches in the common era, the Temple of Diana in Greece was burnt to the ground by the followers of the sun God Apollo who, wishing to see his ascendancy, destroyed the temple of the most revered Goddess.

When people were forced to turn away from nature and the earth, the Goddess, the giver of life, they began to fear the symbol of the serpent, which is actually the symbol of rebirth, healing and all that is sacred. When the missionaries swept through the Celtic lands in the 400s and 500s CE, our sacred seasons were blurred into Christian celebrations – perhaps, ironically, ensuring their survival. Beltane became May Day; Samhain, the day of the dead, became All Saint's Day; Ostara, the ancient festival celebrating the fertility goddess Ostara, became Easter; Yule, and the birth of the sun, became Christmas, and the birth of Jesus, the son.

But it was when the plague cut its dreadful swathe through Europe in the 14th century that Witchcraft became blamed, then feared, then hated, and the inquisitions, torture and deaths began in earnest. In 1484 a Papal Bull was issued by Pope Innocent VIII, based on the Bible statement: "Thou shalt not suffer a Witch to live." (Exodus 22:18.) It described the supposed activities of Witches, and gave the church authority to find them and kill them. All rights to a fair trial were denied.

Soon after came the publication of fear, The Malleus Maleficarum, or The Hammer of the Witches. It was initially written to lend credibility to, then justify, support and enforce the Papal Bull. It acknowledged the existence of demons (an inversion of their true nature – daemons are animal spirits who guide us and sometimes teach us sharp, harsh lessons) and devils, of evil spirits that haunted, taunted and cursed the populace. It claimed white magical practitioners made pacts with them and called on them for help with crops, with birth, with curing ailments, with preventing conception and with killing their enemies. And God, The Malleus Maleficarum said, was angry, and thus He had sent the plague. Other versions of the same story say that it was Witches, or the psychics, healers, starcrafters and herbalists, the midwives and the knights of the old ways themselves who created the plague.

The belief which underpinned these accusations was the church's interpretation of Christianity. The theory went that, as Eve had brought evil into the world, she and all that was feminine was the cause of all that was still wrong with the world. Thus all of those who worshiped the feminine, especially those who were daughters of Eve (i.e. all women) were directly responsible for bringing more evil into the world.

A terrible, terrifying distortion began to take root in an exhausted, ill, starving and fretful population: hysteria had fruitful ground in which to flourish.

We now know only too well what the devastating first plague

was caused by. An outbreak began in China, and it wasn't long before merchants brought it back to Europe. Called the Black Death because of the black spots it left on the body, it spread rapidly through misinformation, confusion, a lack of medical knowledge or supplies and superstition. Within five years 25 million were dead. The Crusades, which had drained money from the coffers of local landholders, had decimated the male warriors of the population. This was swiftly followed by a fierce winter that caused crops to fail and people to starve. These factors, combined with religious upheaval left the population, serf and lord alike, fearful and all too aware of their mortality. The powers that be were at a loss to control the population. But there was a solution to a mass returning to the old ways.

They just needed someone to blame.

The history of The Burning Times is so frightening in its irrationality, fear and methods of torture that to recount it even in this bare-boned style is to risk reawakening many memories within us. Women who were healers, who refused a man's advance, who didn't conceive or who inspired sexual desire were often labeled a Witch, and thus doomed, as whether or not you were "innocent" didn't matter – once accused you suffered. In Scotland women accused of Witchcraft were tied up, hands to feet, and thrown in a lake. Those who didn't drown were declared Witches and burned to death; those who drowned were deemed innocent – but being dead, this wasn't very useful!

Many women who inspired lust in men were accused by those same men who wanted them. Sex was such a sin that the men's guilt could only be appeased through punishment of the inspiration of their lust.

No one was safe. The Old Ways went to ground.

The accusations became ridiculous. If you had a cat. If you spoke to animals. If you were skilled in herblore. If your neighbor disliked you. If you knew the secret meanings of numbers, cards, stones and the future. If you knew how to birth a baby, ease a woman through childbirth or prevent conception...

The fact that sexuality was stifled and seen as evil created a ripe environment in which women could be harmed. When we stifle our natural inclinations they do not leave us. Instead their repression can lead to guilt, anger, blame and the denial of beautiful, natural feelings.

The burnings were beyond counting, and horrible. Some say 100,000, others nine million. Many deaths went unrecorded. Anne Boleyn, the mother of Elizabeth 1 of England, was called a Witch and accused of enchanting the king with sexual wiles. She was slain too.

Epileptics and sufferers of Huntington's chorea were also put to death, their twitching symptoms said to be evidence of their dealings with the devil.

There is no need for fear when reading of these times – there is only a need for understanding why fear is still present. When we understand its roots we can draw it forth and let it go. In case we feel detached from this past, please consider that as recently as March 1995 an Anglican vicar in Lincolnshire, England, called for female priests – Christian priestesses – to be burnt at the stake, calling them witches. In the US today there are extreme religious leaders calling for the army to napalm Wiccan communities. In parts of Africa you can still be murdered if you are suspected of practicing Witchcraft.

But fear cannot stop love. White magic is returning...and nothing can stop the outpouring of love and light.

Hidden though the knowledge was, it was not forgotten, and was not lost.

Anthropologists like Englishman Gerald Gardner first began documenting the living, tattered remnants of white magic in the early 1920s in England, throughout Somerset, Wales, Cornwall and the New Forest. Not coincidentally, these were the very areas where the Celtic priestesses hid when escaping their persecution and the destruction of their sacred groves. These brave souls passed on their knowledge, keeping the white magical teachings alive.

Gerald wrote down what they told him of their teachings, and began researching the connections between the pre-Christian Goddess religions and these women of the New Forest. He is known as the father of Wicca and credited with bringing modern Witchcraft to life and paving the way for those practicing today.

Gradually the slumbering form of the divine feminine wakened. In 1951, by an act of parliament, the English law banning Witchcraft was repealed. After centuries of fear and oppression, white magic began to stir again.

It is uncertain exactly how we wove our white magic in ages past; unclear how we survived in the face of such opposition and fear; and I am not sure exactly how we will continue to develop and contribute.

What is certain and clear to me is that this ancient, new and beautiful knowledge is now being revived with wonderful, healing results. We honor ourselves as the keepers of the sacred feminine flame, of the masculine light, the keepers of enchantments throughout all the dark sad times when the Goddess was forced to hide her face.

But she survived, and can shine again.

Let love and light be guides again. Blessed be the return of white magic.

Chapter Two ~ The Making of White Magic

BEING A WHITE MAGIC PRACTITIONER

Often when people discover I'm a white magic practitioner, they wonder what I actually do. Some brave souls, who usually gulp a bit when they first ask, although I'm hardly scary at all, tend to nervously blurt: "What do you, um, do... exactly?"

I can't tell you how hard it is to resist the temptation to tell them I fly off on my broom and dispense love and healing throughout the neighborhood, realm, universe. (Which I do!) That I wiggle my nose. I try very very hard not to be naughty. You see, you can definitely work white magic, and love to laugh!

But when it gets down to it, there are some basics I can talk to people about. It may not sound as fun as broomstick joyrides at midnight and nose wiggling feats, but this is what I do. And it's so much a part of my life that sometimes it's wonderful to be asked what it is that I do – because it reminds me of what it is that I sometimes take just a little for granted.

We are healers. We use the natural energy of the planet and of the heavens to heal. How exactly?

Well, we are assisted by the loving deities. We call upon male and female deities: the Gods and the Goddesses. There are many faces, or aspects, of them. The Goddess is revealed in deities such as Aphrodite, Pele, Isis, Ishtar, Kali and Hecate. The God is the Horned God, Lugh, Merlin, Apollo, Zeus, Pan, Ares and many many others. This is why there is such diversity and opportunity for self-exploration in this path – we acknowledge that there are many manifestations of divinity, including those that lie within, which is where true white magic resides.

Some worship the Goddess exclusively. Sometimes called Dianic Witches, after the Goddess Diana, they offer their spellworking and their rituals and set up their covens to explore the Goddess, both without and within. Others see divinity as being within themselves, and being manifested in all other people and beings – thus their form of worship is inwardly directed, and outwardly manifested. Some do not worship Gods and Goddesses at all, but focus on nature as the manifestation of all that is sacred. It is up to you to find the belief system that is most meaningful to you.

All of us revere nature. If we worship anything, it is the earth, known also as Gaia (pronounced Guy-ya). Through the earth we can hear the words of the God and the Goddess. In the sunrise and the sunset, in the moon and stars and the change of seasons. In the food we eat and the love we make. In the cities and the buildings and the trees and the volcanoes and the fires and the cries of human beings when their hearts break – it's that true feeling of being alive. Awareness via the senses, awareness via the elements.

But the earth has so many forms and faces, so many creatures and people and beings. Even the stones, in fact very often the stones, have a language that's magical. (Think of gems and crystals!) That's why I say the earth articulates the God and the Goddess through all of the elements, in all of their myriad forms – the wind and the rain, the sea and the sky.

And we take care to treat the earth with respect. We may live in the city or in the country, we may wear a suit or flowing gowns, we may eat meat or take only raw foods into our bodies. But we respect and acknowledge Gaia as the source of life, and her connectedness to the universe is what keeps us alive, connected, well and growing.

And the question I'm most often asked? "Do you practice your magical rites naked?" Well, yes and no. This is a matter of personal preference. Working skyclad can be beautiful and empowering, as we embrace our bodies for the sacred temples that they are. Working without clothing in my experience is not about sex, although it can be about our sensuality – after all, feeling the air on all of our body, or swimming naked while doing a water blessing, is a divinely sensory experience.

For me, working skyclad has helped me to bare myself to the Goddess, and to the elements – disrobing in order to be who I truly am. It took me some time to even contemplate working in this way, as my own body issues were very much triggered by disrobing. I also confronted my own deep mistrust of others – why would people gather together, naked? And I feared, I think, an angry God's punishment, no matter how much conditioning I felt I'd stripped away – no pun intended!

However, by starting alone, and in safe areas, I discovered the power of working skyclad to heal, and the extraordinary connection it creates with your entire self to all of divine nature. You must experience this at least once. Even the simple act of swimming alone, naked, bathed in moonlight, in a natural body of water, will become a profound and holy act that sanctifies and heals our body issues, helping us move through our maiden/ mother/crone aspects, our hunter/father/sage selves, to a new understanding of ourselves as truly divine.

White Magic Workshop

White magic practitioners live by example. We practice love, compassion and understanding, and live with pride, courage, strength and self-mastery. We don't preach or try to convert people, we simply help others develop respect for our path by living it well, with strength, beauty, laughter and dignity.

Always feel strong and able to be who you are – you do not need to twist and turn in order to fit in. You are who you are. White magic will assist you in expressing the pure essence of your unique and divine true self.

When you create the workings suggested here, you will begin to activate your innate energetic white magic, and as you move forward through this series of magical tasks you will integrate these revived skills into your new self. Keep a journal – your Book of Shadows and Light – about what you do and what happens when you do it. Record your feelings, your thoughts, and any ideas that come to your mind.

Walk Your Talk

White magical practitioners care for the planet and its people. They are also aware of their surroundings at all times. It doesn't matter where you live either – white magic can be created in the biggest city or the most remote country hideaway. Connect to the place you live and learn its secrets.

Exercise: Take one hour (or more!) each week and devote it to healing the earth. Pick up rubbish, recycle, use environmentally-friendly products to clean your house, grow your own food, eat organically, find alternatives to pesticides for your garden, and educate yourself about the karmic history of your area. What has happened where you live? How can you be part of its healing?

Take Responsibility

White magical practitioners engage in responsible white magical work to integrate our energy with that of the earth and the universe. We explore our magical selves and respect the privacy and wishes of others at all times – we never interfere with another's free will. When thinking of how you are expressing yourself magically and thus energetically, always come from the position of what would be best for all concerned, for the highest good of all.

Exercise: Consider times in your life when you may have crossed a personal boundary. Ponder how you can respect others yet still express yourself in powerful, sacred ways. Could you have done anything differently? How did the other person feel? What would you wish others to do for you?

Respect all People

We honor men and women, at birth, as children, as young adults, as mothers and fathers and as wise ones and crones. We understand and honor every path of life, knowing that each step of our journey is a unique lesson.

Exercise: Connect with an age group you rarely have contact with. Ask them about their lives and listen to what they have to say. Consider their experience and see the world through their eyes. What can they teach you?

Spellcasting

WHITE MAGICAL SPELLS FOR HEALING AND TRANSFORMATION

A spell is a prayer in action. It is an active way of manifesting. A SPELL is Sacred Purposeful Energy using Love and Light.

We can also manifest whatever we don't want, because it is where we put our thoughts and our energies that we manifest. If ever we want a snapshot of the state of our mind, we simply need to look at our lives. What have we created? We can either use the magic of our creative power for our good, to improve our lives and create happiness and health, or we can remain stubborn and insist that it is simply the way life is, and create our own downward spiral.

Life can be challenging. That is the nature of incarnating and being alive. We are here to learn lessons, to become who we are meant to be, and we go through tests. Just as white magical practitioners are tested, your entire life can also be viewed in this way. Once we shift our attitude however, what we once saw as terrible, unfair and harsh circumstances can be viewed as lessons, teachers and opportunities.

We are human, and being human is a beautiful gift. Which is the difficulty. We always manifest. We are always spellworking, every second of the day, whether that is our intention or not. Every word we speak is a spell. Spellworking for the highest good of all is our mission as white magical practitioners.

The Magical Law of Three times Three

The law of the threefold return is perhaps the most important ethic of working white magic. The number three is very powerful. It symbolizes the sending out, the manifestation, and then the returning karmic influence – the three important steps of casting a spell.

This means that whatever you send out in spellwork will come back to you to the power of three. This is a natural law that is a basis of all life – the law of cause and effect – and it's a wonderful incentive to keep your intentions as high as possible. By obeying this natural law, you will be creating positive experiences for yourself and others.

And be assured that positive magic brings about the most powerful results of all. When you wish for fulfilling, loving experiences, and are mindful of your thoughts and actions, always seeking to go for the highest possible choice, for the greatest good of all, you will reap far more benefits than if you are thinking in old, negative patterns.

So what is a Spell?

A spell can be as simple as sitting somewhere peaceful and wishing something – sending your desire out into the universe – or as complex and beautiful as you want. Some spells are worked over a month (one moon cycle), and involve a long list of magical ingredients, like herbs, incense, essential oils, colored candles, ribbons, a rhyme or written invocation and the blessing of a certain God or Goddess.

If it is a major spellworking, choose the day appropriate for the outcome (listed later in this chapter), the ingredients you are most drawn to, either intuitively or by their properties, and the tools, like candles, ribbons or a chalice. Then write your own words for what it is that you are hoping to manifest. You can also dress in the color that most fits the type of spell, anoint yourself with a corresponding essential oil and pick a tarot card to help guide you if you feel that way inclined. When you are ready, cast your circle, call in the God and the Goddess and the elements/directions, then allow your white magic, your love and your light, to flow. Don't forget to thank and farewell all the beings, deities or angels you called in and close circle when you are done.

Remember though that a spell can be just as powerful if you simply sit in a park in the sunshine or in your car in peak-hour traffic and whisper your hopes to the universe. It's all up to you!

How to Work Magic

* Take loving responsibility for your spellworking.
* Center and ground your energy prior to spellcasting, using meditation, releasing, cleansing or physical exercise.
* Cleanse your auric field and chakras. Bathing by blue or white candlelight, burning in a circle of salt, will cleanse your energy field and that of the room you are working within. Breathing in a color can work too. Imagine that with each breath you take, the air you are inhaling is beautiful, white and purifying, or pink, the color of unconditional love, or blue, that of balance and harmony and grace, or

green, for healing, abundance and prosperity, or violet, for spirit and psychic power, and so on.

* Nurture yourself. The purpose of spells is to bring about positive change for the good of all – ALL! The universe itself is included in that, and so are you. As everything is connected – as above, so below; as within, so without – it is necessary to care for yourself in order to create the most beneficial outcome for all. This means gentle regular exercise, healthful organic foods, eating consciously and avoiding foods and substances that can lower your energy (fast food, alcohol and coffee for example).
* Sleep well.
* Allow your body to receive and be healed by some sunlight and moonlight each day. But don't get burnt.
* Trust in your inner self. Claim your power for yourself, and know you are the ultimate source of love and authority in your life.
* Actively create love in your life. Smiling at people, patting a dog, meditating and sending love to the planet will all raise your own personal vibration.
* Breathe fresh air. Every breath we take is a gift from the planet's trees. Please contribute by planting trees, nurturing plants or simply sending them love. When you do this you are also supporting the elementals and their realm. And if you smoke, try to stop – there are many other ways to use the element of fire in our lives, in far more healthful ways. You need the vibrational energy of fresh clean air – polluted air is hard for sensitive people like us to cope with without respite.
* Finally, before casting circle, simply visualize a beautiful circle of white light which you are standing within. It has no breaks, no place where it can be penetrated. Around

this, if you wish, you may place a circle of blue fire, added protection for those of us who feel we need it.

Casting Circle

Before a white magical practitioner casts a spell, does a ritual, performs divination or does any other kind of white magical work, he or she casts a powerful circle of protection. This keeps your magical energies within the sacred space, and keeps any other energies out. Because you are often working between the worlds, you want to make a statement of intent that your actions are for the highest good of all, and prevent anything else affecting your work.

Like a spell, this can be a simple or elaborate ritual. You can simply use your finger to trace the line of the sacred space around you, or you can visualize a circle of white light surrounding you, or you can mark out a physical circle with salt. If you have more time or prefer to go deeper into this sacred art, you can use your athame or wand to draw the circle, chanting your intent as you go.

When casting a circle or raising power you move deosil – with the sun – which in the northern hemisphere means clockwise but in the southern hemisphere means counter-clockwise. When closing a circle or banishing power you move widdershins – against the sun – which means counter-clockwise in the northern hemisphere and clockwise in the southern.

Invoking the Elements

White magical practitioners consider that there are five sacred elements, these being earth, air, fire, water and spirit. Each element has a particular quality. After casting circle we welcome each element to the circle to support us in our spellcasting, meditation and sacred work. Some of us simply welcome them in, others "invoke" the elements, some say they "summon" them. What is most important is that we treat each element with love, respect and honor.

It's important to note that the five element system is by no means universal – some work with earth, air, fire and water only. Some who work strongly in the Celtic traditions tend to work with earth, sea and sky. However most commonly we work with earth, air, fire, water and spirit, spirit being the unifying force, the element in which all the others are unified, and thus the element where transformation and transmutation takes place.

Elements are associated with the directions, and often follow this pattern: air in the east, fire in the south, water in the west and earth in the north – however it does depend in which hemisphere you live. In the southern hemisphere earth is usually in the south and fire is in the north, as that is where the sun is. It can also vary depending on your geographical location, for instance if you live south of a major lake or ocean you may wish to put water in the north. If you are calling in the elements, I feel it is of most value to follow your intuition and the features of the region you are working in.

Represents: Intellect, the cognitive functions, the mind. Truth, mental and psychic work, intuition, knowledge, philosophy, creativity, wind, breath, clouds, inspiration, detachment, what we hear, past lives.
Direction: East.
Colors: White, pale blues, gray, the colors of clouds.
Time: Dawn.

Season: Spring.
Starpeople: Aquarius, Gemini, Libra.
Altar tools: Athame, incense, feathers.
Energy: Reaching, external, outwards, searching.

Fire

Represents: Passion, sexuality and the sacred expression of both. Fire magic is strong, powerful, purifying and primal. It transforms and changes us forever. For many of us, fire is the element we have most issues with, as its sacred nature was misused during the Burning Times, thus many of us fear working with its energy. It can be useful to draw fire into your circle and work with it for good once again, healing that relationship, so we can be strong and empowered again.

Direction: South.
Colors: Red, crimson, orange, yellow, blue flame.
Time: Midday.
Season: Summer.
Starpeople: Aries, Leo, Sagittarius.
Altar tools: Wand, candles, paper.
Energy: Reaching, external, physical, active.

Water

Represents: The underworld, the feminine, the fluid emotions, intuition, emotions, fertility, blood, ancestry, cleansing, merging, healing, sadness, all bodies of water on the planet.

Direction: West.
Colors: Blue, blue-green, green, gray, indigo, aquamarine, white.
Time: Twilight, dusk.
Season: Autumn.

Starpeople: Cancer, Scorpio, Pisces.
Altar tools: Chalice, cauldron, mirrors, scrying bowls.
Energy: Inclusive, emotional, psychic, feminine.

Earth

Represents: This is the element that is practical, tangible, substantial, solid, grounded. It is that which helps us to create and sustain food, wealth, jewels, and is beloved of artisans and craftspeople. It heals, gives birth, manifests, is strong, practical and material.

Direction: North.
Colors: Brown, ochres, greens.
Time: Midnight.
Season: Winter.
Starpeople: Taurus, Virgo, Capricorn.
Altar tools: Pentacle, stones, sea salt, images, magnets.
Energy: Internal, mysterious, transformative, feminine.

White Magic and the Energy of the Days of the Week

Each day of the week has different energy, which can assist us in manifesting our desired outcome. If you wish to time your spellworking to great effect, make use of the energies most appropriate to that spell.

Sunday: The day and the night governing shining at an activity: birth, praise, acknowledgment, children, ambition, power, control.

Monday: For psychic development, intuition, dreams, visions, hunches, detective work and home – the reason we so often get "Monday-itis" when we have to leave for work.

Tuesday: For courage, action, sexuality, conflict,

confrontation, travel, progress, determination, self-protection, training and physical workouts.

Wednesday: For communication, discussion, flirtations, impulsive action and the written word. This is the day when gossip is most likely to flourish! We need not indulge this though – instead simply and lovingly turn your thoughts and words back to that which is true, and for your highest good, and that which comes from love.

Thursday: For legal matters, politics, wealth creation, prosperity and abundance issues, strategic thinking, practical planning and development of business plans.

Friday: The day of compassion, matters of the heart, love, both friendship and romantic love, creativity, sensuality, sending word of love and declaring love.

Saturday: For past lives, karmic issues, financial issues (borrowing, lending, committing to see a financial planner) the ending of relationships and closure of all kinds.

Essential Oils and White Magic

Essential oils have profound energetic benefits in white magic. They can be used to anoint and bless candles and cords, they can be burnt on your white magic altar or added to baths for powerful healing results. I have found them to be of enormous benefit, and to be very pleasurable and sensual as well as natural mood shifters.

Here are some of the white magic uses for essential oils.

For love: Rose, ylang ylang, jasmine.

Warming the heart: Cinnamon, rosewood.

Abundance and prosperity: Bergamot, mint, clove.

Healing: Rosemary, sandalwood, orange, rose geranium.

Protection: Lavender, sandalwood.

Good cheer: Lime, grapefruit, lemon myrtle, neroli.

Success: Bergamot, ginger.

Happiness: Clary sage, peppermint.

Strength: Cedarwood, frankincense.

Sleep: Marjoram, chamomile, lavender.

Herbs and White Magic

Many herbs have magical properties too, and they can be eaten, infused in oils, used in spells or simply grown on your kitchen windowsill so you can smell them. One simple but effective herb is rosemary, which helps with past life issues and assists with memory lessons. Basil is also common and easy to grow, and is good for clarity and focus, while thyme will attract fairies. By simply hanging some up to dry or growing it about your house, and added to with your loving messages, fairies will know they are in a "safe area" and begin to visit regularly. They are cautious though, so this may take time!

For love: Apple, jasmine, frangipani, rose, honeysuckle.

Prosperity: Cedar, comfrey, bergamot.

Protection: Bay, clove, pine.

Health: Nutmeg, oak, ruse.

Fertility: Geranium, mustard, patchouli, poppy.

Happiness: Marjoram, lavender.

Some herbs are multi-purpose, like chilli, which is wonderful for use as both a herb of love and a herb of protection. As always the intent fuels the power of your spell. Be creative with your use of herbs, and do your research. Lemon verbena, for example, is wonderful for healing the pain of a previous relationship's breakdown, and is also wonderful for soothing worry. There are many applications, some of them traditional, and some which will be uniquely your own.

White Magical Color Vibration

Each color has a unique vibration, and by utilizing the magic of color, you charge your spell with beautiful energy and power. As you have your own unique energetic vibration, the colors you are drawn to reveal much about your magical talents and preferences. You can wear clothes in a certain color while casting a spell, write it on colored paper, change the shade of your altar cloth, use different hued candles or tie up a scroll with the relevant colored ribbon.

White: This purifies, cleanses and energizes your etheric nature, your clairvoyance and your connection to God and Goddess (the druids wore white).

Pink: For love, friendship, self-love, confidence and gatherings.

Red: For sexual desire, passion and love of the romantic and sexual kind. Red raises your energy and determination, and increases sexual desire.

Orange: Attracts good cheer, happiness and optimism and allows you to radiate attractiveness when used in small quantities. It's a wonderful color to help raise physical energy, so it is very beneficial when your healing is established, but can be a little too strong when you are unwell or feeling depleted. In this case, using a small amount, such as burning an orange candle, can gently raise your energy levels.

Yellow: For mental focus, clarity, concentration, renewal of mental vigor and breakthroughs in thinking patterns. Use sparingly if you tend to be a little obsessive; use more frequently if you tend to be a little vague.

Green: Aids growth, abundance, prosperity, renewal of life force and healing of the heart chakra. It reflects nature and its beautiful healing energy.

Turquoise: For happiness, spirit connections, mental balance, physical wellbeing, strength in your happiness, inner self, sovereignty and strong, grounded psychic ability.

Blue: For grace, divine intent, the healing energy of the Goddess, the strength of persistence, clarity mingled with compassion, being able to do the right thing for self under all circumstances, independence from another's energy.

Purple: For the ability to create your own world, strength and wisdom from your inner self, understanding your own king or queenship, serious intent, victory, loyalty to a great cause, devotion to sacred matters.

Violet: A gentle change facilitator, it aids perceptiveness, communication delivered with love from the realm of the Goddess, gentle delivery of psychic knowledge and messages and honorable and spiritual intent.

Gold: For confidence, abundance, strength of purpose and unshakable inner belief in a positive outcome.

Brown: Represents the deep wisdom of the planet, the ancient knowledge of stones, the power of wisdom that is ageless, the understanding of how to create wealth for the long term, stability and balance. This is a wonderful color too often dismissed. Brown can be rich and vibrant, full of the beautiful hues of the planet. Explore its subtle and wonderful power.

Black: Is protective, healing and wonderful for those of us who wish to go within for a time. Combining its power with inky purples and indigos adds depth and dimension – think of a black crystal and its variations in color and you'll get the picture. Black is traditionally attributed to Witches, as it was worn throughout the time of danger when we hid our names, our path and our physical selves in the forest during gatherings. Black was, and still is, a wonderful camouflage.

White Magic uses of Candles

White magic using candles is a simple but effective spell technique which uses the element of fire to activate the white magic. It can be as simple as lighting a colored candle as you speak aloud your intent, or as elaborate as anointing it with essential oils, carving symbols in its side and burning it for an hour a night for a week as you say a lengthy spell. For a spell requiring a candle to burn down, you may wish to use a smaller one. Some people develop such a fascination with this type of magic that they make their own candles, a wonderful craft.

White Magic Spell for energetic clearing

A simple candle spell for room cleansing is to anoint a tall white candle with sandalwood, gently sprinkle a circle of salt around it in a clockwise direction (counter-clockwise in the southern hemisphere), light it, then allow it to burn down. This is wonderful for any room or area of your home that may have some need of energetic rebalancing.

White magic candle spell for passion

This is found in my Magical Spell Cards deck, where there are 44 spells for many situations and occasions.

On a Friday night, take one deep red candle, and breathe on it as you gently roll it between your hands. Then into your candle carve the words Passion and Beloved. You can carve specific words or names, but it is often best to leave it open to the universe to deliver passion to you in its own way – although if you are in a relationship you may wish to carve your beloved's name entwined with your own into the candle.

Anoint your candle with seven drops of rose oil and seven drops of patchouli. Light the candle for seven minutes a night at 7pm for seven consecutive evenings. Allow it to burn down on the final night, then lovingly scatter the wax into a moving body of water. As it moves away, see it bringing joyful passion to all lovers everywhere, and with this intent your spell's power, threefold, will return to you.

White Magic using Ribbons

Ribbon (traditionally called cord) magic is the tying together of thread, ribbon or cord for white magical spells – the act of tying off the knot in the ribbon is usually the moment in which the spell is forged. I tend to use ribbons, but you can use embroidery thread or any other kind of cord.

A simple white magical ribbon spell is to write a wish upon a green ribbon at the new moon and tie it to a tree, either a living tree or a symbolic tree on your altar. As I tie the knot three times, thinking my intent, I whisper, "So mote it be" upon the final tying.

You can braid different colored chunks of thread together, forming a cord, and chant your spell as you work. This can then become an altar tool and be used throughout the year.

You can also incorporate essential oils into this form of magic by anointing your ribbon or cord to infuse it with the oil's magical qualities. The color of the cord or ribbon can also influence the spellworking, so simply check the list of colors for their meanings and choose ribbons of the color or colors most appropriate for your desired outcome.

Chapter Three – Your Magical Home

CREATING YOUR SACRED SPACE

Wherever you live, wherever you go, you can take safe, beautiful, enjoyable and simple magical steps to create a harmonious, loving, energetically balanced and creative home. By rebalancing your environment, you will draw more love, prosperity, joy and friendship into your life.

Your surroundings are a kind of map, showing others who you are and where you are going. The furnishings, colors, accessories and objects you surround yourself with say so much about you, so much about how you feel about yourself and what you feel you are worth.

Your home is a reflection of your awareness, an enhancer of your vibrational field and even if you never say a word, it tells the story of your desires and dreams, and your ability to create wonderful new ways to live. If you are unhappy with aspects of your home, please attempt to put these feelings aside and look at your home through detached but loving eyes. This is not a time for self-criticism but for self-knowledge. Is your home chaotic and dirty? Do you feel this way in your life? Is it out of date and worn looking? If so, chances are you could feel similarly.

Refreshing your home does not require money, but it does take time and attention, all of which will benefit you enormously. Whatever you spend, money and time-wise, on creating a beautiful home will return to you, as the universe will reflect back to you your own self-love by helping you co-create a beautiful life, prosperous employment and deep and strong supportive friendships with like-minded people.

The first thing to do is spring clean, physically clearing space to symbolically clear your mind. Put up photos of your favorite place, your family and friends or your happiest moment. Bring in some pot plants, either herbs, flowers or leafy ferns, or fill a vase with gorgeous blooms. Change the color of your curtains if you feel inclined, or move the furniture around. If you have room, dedicate a sacred space where you can go to meditate, do card readings and work magic. It might be a whole room, or simply a cushion on the floor in a corner of the lounge room.

When we change our home, it is a powerful statement to the universe that we intend to recreate our lives. Sometimes when we do this there is an initial period of instability as we shed what no longer works for us – what we are no longer actively in the process of attracting with our subconscious, our conscious thoughts and our actions.

Please remember this if there is change at home, in your workplace and in your love life, because actively tuning in to what you want and actively seeking out what is for your highest good will activate change immediately.

Altared state

The most powerful exercise is building an altar. Every person working magic would benefit from having an altar in their home. White magicians use it as a place for spellcasting and ritual, meditation and contemplation, to burn oils and incense, write new moon wishes and place food for cleansing and offering up before eating. It is the physical center of your craft. I read my tarot cards, scry and communicate with the Goddess at my altar. We are connected to her at all times, but this act of sitting with her in a place dedicated to her seems to work extremely well for many friends and for me.

Caring for an altar is simple and profound, a ritual which focuses your mind on spiritual matters and on what you want to create in your life. Its beautiful appearance is a symbol of the respect you have for yourself – respect and love for yourself for being who you are, right now, just as you are. The Goddess adores you simply for being alive. You do not have to do anything else other than breathe in the knowledge that she loves you, for simply being here on this beautiful green and blue planet.

Your altar will bring this meaning into your home simply by being there. When you work with it, set it up, change it or use it as a space for creating your magical work, you remind yourself that you are a beloved child of the Goddess. She never leaves you. She is with you always. You are beloved, for simply breathing in and out. Nothing else is necessary for you to have her love.

What to make your altar from

Traditionally, a magical altar is made from a low wooden table, but any surface can be used for your act of loving meditation. One of my many altars at present is a low box, a sort of clothes chest that belonged to my grandmother. Another is an inbuilt mosaic altar I built myself into my courtyard. Both are only two amongst my many spontaneous altars within my surrounds, and they are beautiful, however, a simple slab of wood on two bricks would also suffice, as would a small dressing table, an upside down milk crate with some chipboard on top, a chest of drawers – you can even set it up on the floor. What is most important is your intent in building your altar.

Magical tools for your altar

Athame (element of air): The athame (ath-ah-may) is a double bladed knife used for energy work – it is never used for cutting anything on the physical plane. Priestesses often wore theirs strapped to their legs, and worked with them to heal. They are especially powerful for casting circle and cutting etheric cords – think of them as being a little like the sword of Archangel Michael. I have a beautiful brass athame. Most metal moves too quickly for me to feel I am directing it efficiently, but brass is perfect. It has a beautiful rose quartz in it and is very rounded at the top, which gives it a feeling of femininity that I adore. It is heavy in my hand. My young daughter often wanders in, picks it up, gently draws a circle in the air above her head with it and says softly: "In perfect love and perfect trust." If you don't have an athame though a feather works just as well, and you can also use your finger to cast circle and direct energy.

Wand (element of fire): Wands are also used to work with

energy, however they primarily direct and send it out. They also strongly connect us with the fairy realm. I have two wands at present. One is amethyst, which I use when it feels right – it is stronger, more protective and more psychic, solid, powerful and commanding. The other is rose quartz and crystal, and is more loving, romantic, feminine and sweet in its energy, although it almost has a "naughty" energy at times. I also use wooden wands, ones I gather myself and activate with crystals and found objects, but you can also use a small candle to represent fire if you are keeping things simple.

Crystals/stones: (element of earth): I have a collection of crystals that is constantly evolving. Rose quartz, gathered under moonlight. Healing smoky quartz. Gifts from a valued friend of crystals they mined ethically in Brazil. Stones found at the seaside, tumbled over and over until they're smooth. Rocks that simply "ask" to be collected and worked with. They are all an articulation of the Goddess and the grounding element of earth, although you can also use a small dish of salt to represent this element.

Chalice: (element of water) In my chalice, or bowl, I keep water. Over the years I have collected water from the sea, from the sacred wells of Glastonbury, and from rain, but all water is blessed when you bless it. By simply doing this you change its structure. A bowl of clean, clear water on your altar represents this powerful, cleansing element. Sea shells, a picture of a dolphin or mermaid or a simple glass of water will also activate the water aspect of an altar.

At Chalice Well Gardens in Avalon, the element of water and a water sign

Other Magical Objects

Once the four directions, or five elements are represented, you can add anything you like to your altar – the most important factor in your choice is intuition and that the object speaks to you. Most white magical practitioners like to have a statue or drawing of the God and the Goddess – it could be an elaborate stone statue, an inexpensive brass figurine, the Empress from the Oracle Tarot or something you draw yourself. It is whatever is meaningful for you – perhaps a sun candle represents the God for you and a moon candle the Goddess.

Many magical altars also include a pentacle, or the five-pointed star in a circle, to represent the five elements coming together. Again it can be a picture, a piece of jewelry, a large pewter plate, a stick drawing – whatever is meaningful for you.

You can choose to drape your altar too, with anything

from a specially bought altar cloth to a piece of beautiful fabric or material cut from a favorite old skirt, or something sentimental that holds great meaning, and thus energy for you. Its color also contains magic, so you can change it daily, with the seasonal festivals, when the mood takes you or not at all. Perhaps if you are working a major spell you could choose the color that most corresponds to the desired outcome.

A cauldron is another popular choice. While it is probably the most stereotypical of all the altar tools, it's also very practical. Burn a spell once it is cast and leave it to smolder in your cauldron. Grind up incense or other magical brews. Cook a sacred feast in it. It is also the three-legged symbol of the triple goddess (maiden, mother and crone), and our wonderful ability to create and give life.

Most magical of all however are the "found" objects that resonate with you. These things, which have actually been looking for you, are very powerful magical tools. For example, I have a small, delicately spun bird's nest, which I found outside my back door. When I work on spellcrafting for my home out it comes, as it represents the creation of home and hearth. A stone you find in your favorite park, a shell you pick up on a birthday beach wander, a crystal you are gifted with, dried flowers, a snake's shed skin that you come across – all are magical.

Your altar is your own sacred self symbol, so choose objects, images and symbols that are personally activating to you. There is no need to purchase expensive tools – simply placing a sea shell, an image of an angel or Goddess aspect you wish to connect with and some clean, clear water on your altar is a profoundly magical thing. When I look around me, my tools are everywhere, because everything is a tool to me.

The act of gathering what speaks to you is in itself a sacred act, and will reveal much about you. Your altar and its objects can be as complex, as ritualized, theatrical, simple, masculine, feminine, angelic, earthy, sexy and pure as you wish. It is your sacred space. What do you want to ask for?

You may wish to keep your candles and ribbons, cords, incenses and oils in special boxes or drawers, and only bring them out when you intuitively feel the time is right for their energy to be activated on your altar. You may also like to keep specific supplies on hand, like a pelican feather for Mabon, swan feathers for Imbolc, red cloth for Beltane, pink candles for a love invocation on a Friday night, moonlit water in a silver scrying bowl to speak personally with Arianrhod, the moon Goddess of the Celts.

The most potent magic of all is to revere your home as a living altar that is unique and personal and divine, as you are. When we think of everything in our home as being magical, a tool, a spell at work, our home becomes a sensual manifesting zone. Experiencing its magic is deeply moving and very fulfilling, and connects us deeply with the Goddess Vesta, the original Domestic Goddess, who teaches us of the honor of having a home we love and which loves us back. By working with our homes in this way, people will feel its healing energy when they walk through your door – bringing them back again and again, and bringing you good fortune and prosperity.

May your home be blessed, as are you.

Chapter Four ~ The Crystal Moon
~ The Ultimate White Light Magic

LUNAR CYCLES AND THE TIDES OF LIFE

I first fell in love with the moon when I was very very young. She always seemed so magical, so amazing to me, and I often sent her wishes without knowing anything formal about her significance or meaning. I called her Diana, without knowing of the Roman deity, the moon Goddess of the same name. That came later. My intuitive knowing that she was magical, crystal, divine came to me from the first time we connected.

Later, I learned that cultures throughout time and across the world have worshipped the moon as the Goddess. I love that Diana, the huntress, is one of the deities related to the moon. Others include Isis, Selene, Artemis, Arianrhod (pronounced Ahr-ee-AHN-hrod) and Mawu. I also understand now that part of my connection to the moon is because of her physiological effect – moonlight allows us to see under a different light. Magical and new, silvery and ethereal, she teaches us to recreate our ideas about how things seem. By simply bathing in the moon's light, her healing rays enter our body, and can manifest as increased psychic power, wonderful insights and a gentle, tranquil new love of our feminine side – be we male or female!

The moon changes all the time – yet her changes are regular, harmonious and in tune with all that is around her, revealing to us the secret of our selves – that we too have time to shine, to go within, to be reborn. Working with her phases can reawaken our own natural energetic flow, and give us insights into the divine timing of events in our lives. When we connect with her cycles, we relax and stop forcing – we literally go with her flow. Life becomes more magical, and seems to have its own magical pace.

I'm a Cancerian, so the moon has special significance to me, as Cancerians feel changes in the moon more than other signs. But it will still have an impact on every single person, and you will be able to create your own magical relationship with her and her cycles.

Moonlight is essential for activating our physiological cell's health. But did you know that moonlight also activates our etheric body's cells? Our aura (or our EMF) is "washed" and cleansed under moonlight, and the moon's light activates our psychic abilities and intuitive power, for the good of all.

Standing under moonlight is one of the most powerful ways you can activate and link your psychic self, and recharge an exhausted etheric body. Just as crystals are charged and cleansed under moonlight, so too are we, which is what the Priestesses of Atlantis and Avalon knew, and practiced. It traditionally took 13 moons of study for a woman to be initiated as a Priestess of Avalon, and for a Druid to pass through the first initiatory stage. To become a fully attuned Priestess of Avalon took 19 years – the cycles of the moon. So attuned were the Ancient peoples of Britain and Ireland to the moon that their calendars were based around the cycles of the moon, with 13 "months". Moon cycles are a powerful way of re-linking to sources of ancient wisdom, such as the Avalonian tradition. Moving with her natural course, this enormous crystalline celestial power source goes through different phases and astrological signs, with a particularly potent effect on magic. Each cycle of the waxing and waning crystal moon spans several days, and by being aware of each phase of the moon, you can add power to each ritual you perform or spell you cast.

Dark of the moon

From the time the moon is no longer visible to the naked eye until the new moon shows herself is the most useful time for divination of all kinds.

The new moon

When you first spy the slim crescent moon it is an exceptional time to do spellcraft for new beginnings, and for the conception and initiation of new projects. It is also a powerful time to make wishes!

Waxing moon

The waxing moon – when it is growing towards full – is appropriate for spells that involve growth, healing and increase. Focus your magic on bringing the qualities you want into your life.

The full moon

Known as the high tide of psychic power, the full moon represents culmination, climax, fulfillment and abundance. The day of the full moon and a day either side is a potent time for spellworking.

Waning moon

The waning moon – when it is shrinking back down towards the dark moon – is the best time for cleansing, banishing and completion. If you want to bring something into your life at this time, focus on banishing its opposite, as that is supported by this moon phase.

Eclipse alerts!

Eclipses are powerful events that coincide with full moons and new moons. They are energetically wonderful times to recreate ourselves, to shift energy and to change our lives. They are the powerful cosmic makeover power points, and we can work with their energy to move on to the next stage of our personal growth, inner lives and external selves. If we are not on track, an eclipse has an almost uncanny way of removing all obstacles to growth, making them a little daunting at times! However, just think of them as literally the hand of the Goddess – working with you to get you on track. As such, there is much to be grateful for, and nothing at all to fear from her loving assistance.

Solar eclipse

This is the day when the moon overshadows the sun, meaning that feminine energy is in full flow. It's a great time to celebrate with the girls and throw an all-woman celebration of the divine feminine. It's also a perfect time to get back in touch with your feminine side, and to remember that you can be feminine and powerful at the same time. Solar eclipses, be they total or partial, provide us with an opportunity to go within and discover more about our inner lives. Dreams, visions and psychic powers are all heightened during this magical time.

Lunar eclipse

It's not just the moon that affects us magically – throughout the ages the sun has typically been worshipped as a God, with the moon most usually revered as a Goddess. Not only does the sun sustain life by making crops grow and providing warmth and light, but when it eclipses the moon it creates an opportunity to integrate who you "secretly" are with who you appear to be. For example, a lunar eclipse can be a wonderful time to tell the truth about who we are, gently and powerfully. The energy at this time enables others to see who we really are, as opposed to who they believe we should be, making it a wonderful time for new understanding. Consider what it is about yourself that you need to bring out in the open, and gently begin to integrate this aspect of yourself into your persona.

Moon Power

The Full Moon's Magic

The full moon is especially significant to white magical practitioners. For each of these pinnacles of the power of the moon, we have for thousands of years gathered together and danced our joy at the crystal moon's fullness. We raise our arms to the starlit sky and draw into us her beautiful healing rays, her silvery light reawakening our powers, healing our physical bodies and dissolving any energetic imbalances we may have accumulated over the past 29 days. By her crystalline violet white light, our etheric body is charged with energy and power and love.

Full moons are holy. When we gather to celebrate them, or simply stand under her rays alone, we are joining together in a sacred moment not only with others walking their magical path on this planet now, but with the animals, the elementals, the tides, the sea creatures, the dolphins and all of nature. We attune ourselves with her energy, and we are cleansed and reborn each month in her magical rays. It is a powerful magical act of the present that reconnects us to our ancestors, to all other creatures, and helps us create a sacred future together.

Dancing, standing, leaping and bathing under the full moon in circle or alone can also help us to have powerful visions. This simple act of worshipping and acknowledging the Goddess will create so much wonder and joy in your life – partake of it and be blessed.

Harnessing the magic of the new moon

The moon moves through an astrological house, or star sign, every two and a half days, and covers all 12 each month. This affects us all in subtle but very significant ways. Our moods, reactions, emotions and even our health are all influenced by the ebbs and flows of the moon's cycle, as well as the astro-house it is residing in at any given time.

Each new moon has a particular quality, depending on the star sign it is in, as you will see below. Every month it is in a different astrological house, and you can time your new moon wishes to coincide with these special influences. For example, when it is a Cancer new moon, you may wish: "I want a committed, loving relationship with a wonderful partner," or "I wish to conceive a child this month," as stable relationships and fertility are favored under a Cancer new moon.

The most important task for you is to complete a list every new moon. Make all your wishes positive and for the good of all involved, and watch the magic of the moon unfold each and every month. Ensure you make your new moon wish list within the first eight hours after the new moon. Simply take a piece of paper and a pen, and write down 10 wishes around the energy of that particular moon.

It usually takes around three moon cycles for goals to reach fruition, so be patient!

If the new moon is in your own sign, be sure to work with

and acknowledge its magical energy – your own sign's new moon contains the seeds of your own personal rebirth. It is your annual chance to start afresh in an important area of your life. Don't miss it!

New Moon Energies

Aries: This is a great time for new beginnings, action, fast bursts of energy and starting and completing demanding short-term tasks. Sometimes we can be more impetuous and daring during the influence of an Aries new moon. Harnessing this drive can add much energy to our projects and dreams.

Taurus: Use this time to establish new situations, make commitments, sign papers and make long-term changes, especially regarding love, possessions and your home's decoration. Be sure though – projects begun under a Taurus new moon are very difficult to change and tend to be a little inflexible.

Gemini: This is a whimsical, fun and intellectual new moon – perfect for deep and meaningful discussions, making new friends and having flirtations, both of the sensual and the mental kind. It's fabulous for first dates and reviving the spark of desire in a long-term relationship, as we can discover a new connection via sparky communications at this time.

Cancer: This is a wonderful moon for conception, entertaining friends at home, telling someone how you feel about your future with them, and for mothers and daughters to grow closer to each other. It is a time to make a commitment to exploring the qualities of the moon cycles themselves, and to reconnect with the Goddess within via moonlight.

Leo: This is a great time for presentations, job interviews and any situation where you have to "strut your stuff" or impress someone! We are all much more charismatic under the influence of this moon, which also sees us able to perform under pressure, claim our own sovereignty and stand in our power for all to see.

Virgo: Under the focused quality of this new moon, organizing details, practicalities and massive spring cleans are favored. This sweet yet very practical new moon has a great deal of can-do energy, meaning that many of the housekeeping details of your projects can be tended at this time, enabling you to be clear and on track.

Libra: Hold off on making difficult or challenging decisions at this time – instead use the social, harmonious energy to have warm catch-ups with friends or to choose a first date venue that will ignite your passions. It's a great time for a makeover too, as Libra new moons are influenced by Venus, the Goddess of love and beauty.

Scorpio: This intense new moon creates opportunities for profound insight, as Scorpio is a sign that penetrates the veils, and sees past our social masks and the smokescreens of our personas to the truth of who we are. It is a new moon to make wishes for authenticity, and is very powerful for creating sexual bonds between lovers, due to Scorpio's pure sensual magnetism. Mysteries come to light at this time, making it a profound time for divination.

Sagittarius: This cheerful new moon is wonderful for loving, laughter-filled family get-togethers, for increasing the humor you see in your life, and for being able to laugh about situations you once cried over. The archer's moon can also help you build self-confidence and solid friendships based on trust.

Capricorn: This new moon is a powerful time to be able to easily take on new responsibility and challenges. Its strong and courageous energy can also help us deal with power – both personal power and the power struggles we may have with others – and make tough decisions about our plans for the future. This new moon helps us to soar career-wise.

Aquarius: If you have felt out of touch with your inner creator, this new moon will fill you with new inspiration. All forms of eccentric and unusual behavior, creative endeavors and lateral thinking – including spontaneous breaks in your routine – are favored by this individualistic moon.

Pisces: This moon captures wonderful dream states and brings them to life, empowering us through our dreams, fantasies and imaginations. It is a wonderful time to learn a new skill and to investigate our own psychic talents. Water is especially favored at this time, so emotions may flow, and we will be able to feel deeply.

Magical moon power blend

Here is a beautiful essential oil blend which will enhance any new moon wish list you make. Blend it on the night of the full moon and leave it out – stoppered tightly to maintain its potency – under the rays of the full moon. Then on the next new moon, when you make your wish list, burn this oil in a vaporizer as you write your list, and pop a little on your pillow before you sleep. Burn it throughout the month, and each time you smell its aroma you will be reminded not only of your goals, but will be even more determined to achieve them.

Combine:
10 drops of sandalwood oil
7 drops of vanilla oil
3 drops of jasmine oil
3 drops of rose oil

Chapter Five ~ Invoking the Goddesses and the Gods

HEALING THE WOUNDED MASCULINE AND FEMININE, REBALANCING THE INFINITE'S SACRED ENERGIES

White magical practitioners are attuned to a masculine and feminine aspect of the divine. Some see this as an all encompassing Goddess and God without name or limit. Others worship specific faces of the two, such as Artemis and Apollo or Isis and Osiris or Brid and Lugh or the moon Goddess and the sun God. Some believe in a pantheon of Gods and Goddesses and call on several, depending on the occasion or need.

There are many aspects of the Goddess and the God, which are determined by our personal path. Some white magicians are more inclined and able to easily connect with the Celtic divinities. Others resonate with the Egyptian – Ra, Osiris, Isis, Nut (pronounced Newt); the Greek – Aphrodite, Artemis,

Apollo; or with Middle Eastern deities like Ishtar. Others connect with deities from many cultural systems, working with the ones they feel most called by at the time, and those they feel an affinity with. These deities all have complex social histories and representations, and are manifold and varied in their cultural relevance. Others fly further afield, dealing with interstellar beings, otherworldly cosmologies and inter dimensional crossovers. We all have our individual paths and talents!

Many people, including White Magical practitioners, are adamant about "their" version of the God and the Goddess. While it is natural to feel strongly about our own path and what has been revealed to us through study, magic and contemplation, it is also wise to acknowledge the sanctity of other people's experiences, and to choose to see most variations as fascinating reminders of human diversity.

Whatever your beliefs, for every significant life moment you experience, there's a Goddess and a God, an aspect of divinity, who can assist you in reaching your goals, finding the wisdom in a difficult life test or challenge, and guiding you through the heartbreak that we humans can be heir to, via manifestation, karmic imbalances and attitudinal errors. These beings are living entities, as real as you or I. Through them connecting with our own inner divine spark, we understand our themes, our magnificence, our lessons.

White magical workshop

To gently introduce yourself to working with God and Goddess energy, choose an aspect of both the God and the Goddess, and honor him and her via your altar, your thoughts, your dress, your behavior and your will. Make this ceremonial acknowledgment as simple or as complex as you wish, but do it to connect with what you consider to be God and Goddess energy. How our energy interacts with deities determines how they will manifest – we will each have a unique experience when we work with divinity. The lessons they teach us are in many ways a mirroring, reflecting to us what we are sending out.

However their energies have also been collectively "agreed upon" already, thus we may all work with Aphrodite for love, with Merlin for an increase in psychic powers and with Ganesh to help us with abundance. How each of these manifest for us will be different though. It is important for us to remember this, and not attempt to determine a narrow, prescribed vision of how an individual's experience of the divine should manifest, emerge and be translated into action. Remember too, it is as valuable and valid to call on them for assistance with supposedly mundane issues as for those of spiritual knowledge and the quest for understanding.

Which deity to call on

Would you like to be stronger? Able to fearlessly defend yourself? What about having the power to attract the perfect love? Or the strength to deal with your own power? You can actively work on all of these sacred areas, and much much more, with the guidance of the Goddesses and the Gods, who can be called on for help with any issue.

For career change, abundance, financial flow

Call on Dana: Dana is the Celtic Goddess of alchemy and deep change. She can assist you in honoring yourself, considering yourself worthy of assistance and finding helpful, strong and powerful mentors to guide and support you. Call respectfully on Dana to assist you with issues around finances, deserving and prosperity. She can also help and support those of us who experience confusion regarding our purpose in life – what we are meant to be doing with our time and our career. She stops us prevaricating, self-sabotaging or talking ourselves out of following a wonderful idea through to fruition.

Invocation to Dana: "Beloved Dana, allow me to permit others to help me. Allow me to dissolve all bonds to poverty, to transform my self-denial into self-love, and to create myself anew as an abundant, beloved child of the Goddess and the God, able to create prosperity and positive change, care for myself and others and make a contribution to the universe in its material form that makes a strong difference. Allow me to break through conditioned thinking and be enabled to manifest exactly what I need at the perfect time."

Other divinities who will help with this issue: Ganesh, Brigit, Thoth, Hermes, Lu Hsing.

For happiness, joy, lifting depression

Call on Isis: Isis is the beautiful Egyptian Goddess of the moon, who enables us to be happy while seeking our own truths and paths – helping us shed guilt, worry, ambivalence and fear. She worked with a magical wand, and you may wish to incorporate that into any work you do with her. She can lift heavy, depressed energy by helping you direct the wand to the place or person or issue that most needs healing. She is extremely intuitive, and able to help you see the bigger picture in all situations, which can immediately lift the perceived burden. In ancient times her temples were places of wisdom and teaching, and a deep and abiding joy in simply being alive and able to perceive this wonderful physical world with our six senses.

Invocation to Isis: "Beloved Isis, may your protective wings lift me up and beyond the troubles I now believe myself to be experiencing. Help me show gratitude for all my gifts, and help me create magical solutions to these challenges. Allow me to laugh with compassion, cry with empathy and detach enough to be of assistance. Allow me to play while I learn and to remember that lightness of heart is the sacred lesson of life itself."

Other divinities who will reconnect you to joy: Lakshmi, Maitreya, Aphrodite, Buddha, the fairy elementals.

For better health

Call on Apollo: The Greek God of the sun, Apollo helps us heal ourselves using natural means, as everything that lives, lives due to the sunlight on this planet. He is a physically impressive God, and helps those of us who are aiming for higher and higher levels of fitness, sports, health, eating and better feeling and looking bodies, as well as anyone simply wishing their bodies to be more comfortable and healthy. He also assists with weight training, weight loss and dissolving weight and food issues to bring your body to a state of balance. He is especially helpful to those in harsh climates such as Australia, as he assists us in benefiting from the sun without being harmed by it. It is best to communicate with him in the light itself, at safe times of the day for exposure. Working with Apollo skyclad (naked) is very healing, but not necessary.

Invocation to Apollo: "Divine Apollo, help me see my body as perfect, whole and complete. Guide me to the correct foods for my body, the right mineral combinations, and allow me to work with my body to experience my magical self more wholly. I understand that the body is a divine source of wisdom and knowledge, and I know I am guided to the perfect exercise, health, fitness and beauty program for my own needs. Please assist my body to heal to its highest possible state. Thank you."

Other divinities who will assist with health problems: Devi, Archangel Raphael (the healing archangel), Green Tara, Kali, Krishna.

For magical abilities and psychic powers

Call on Merlin: This is the collective term many of us working with magic use for the druids, the great sages of pre-Christian Britain, but when we speak specifically of Merlin we are usually referring to the druid Taliesin, the legendary leader of the druids in the Arthurian era. The wise druids read the stars, the trees, the animals and the stones and protected these natural things because they saw them as they truly are: sacred. To the druids, everything on this planet – everything – was a repository of consciousness, and we too can be so connected to the natural world and our own innate psychic abilities. Merlin can help you with this, and can also turn your power up or down – if you feel bombarded with messages, respectfully ask him to make them simpler, clearer and to turn them down a notch! It is hard for those on the etheric plane to work with us unless we are absolutely clear. Also be ready for communications with the plant kingdom after connecting with Merlin.

Invocation to Merlin: "Honored Merlin, great sage wizard of the Celts, dissolve all blocks which prevent me from seeing, hearing, smelling, tasting and in all ways experiencing my psychic powers. Allow me to see the signs which are all around me, and to read them with clarity, courage, detachment, compassion and for the highest good of all concerned. Allow me to know that it is now safe to be fully functioning clairvoyantly, clairsentiently, clairaudiently and through my dreams and every aspect of the natural world and the etheric plane. Help me trust the messages when they come, and pass them on without becoming involved in the message itself, and to know that this process is sacred, safe and for the highest good of all concerned."

Other divinities who assist with psychic and magical gifts: Horus, Quan Yin, Diana, Maeve, Artemis, Oonagh.

To find your soulmate

Call on Oenghus: This is the Celtic God of deep true love, commitment and passion, and of communication between lovers. Oenghus has many parallels with Aphrodite and Cupid, so he is wonderful to call on to assist you in your search for a lover who will ignite your soul, your passion and your deep love. He delights in carrying messages between people who have never met, in this life anyway, so if you have dreamed of a soulmate who has yet to materialize, Oenghus can sing an energetic message between the two of you on the etheric plane, which will draw you closer and closer until meeting is inevitable. You will know when you meet this person, because the recognition will be so strong it cannot be denied by either party. He also protects lovers who are being vilified or separated by people who do not approve of their union. He himself has experienced this with his love, the Goddess Caer, and understands the longing to be one with your soulmate. Thus he stands as a strong guardian of those who are meant to be together.

Invocation to Oenghus: "Beloved bard Oenghus, please sing to me through your message of my love. Help me to understand who it is, and to bring us closer to each other.

Allow this person to be seeking me, as I seek them. Allow them to know me, as I will know them. Allow us to be together, without strain or impediment, for all the days of our lives."

Other divinities to call on to find true love: Aphrodite, Hathor, Isolt.

For grief, separation issues and difficulties with children

Call on Demeter: Grounded, nurturing, protective and unrelenting, Demeter teaches us to maintain a relationship while allowing others their independence – to let go. While she aids us in seeking out, helping and protecting others, particularly young women, she also assists us to learn to trust others in relationships. She is of great help when parents and children are experiencing battles of wills, fearful thoughts and mistrust, and where thinking has become obsessive, inflexible and untrusting. She helps transform such thoughts into ones that are tenacious, bountiful, fertile, imaginative and brave.

Invocation to Demeter: "Demeter, help us heal this family rift, and bring peaceful communication and love, for the highest good of all concerned, to all of our interactions. Allow my child to express themselves and their growing independence with grace and honor, and help us parents nurture ourselves by putting our needs concerning ourselves and our next life change first. I trust that when my needs are met, everyone benefits. I trust. I trust."

Other divinities who will help with these issues: Artemis, Quan Yin, Horus, Diana, Hathor.

For freedom and independence

Call on Artemis: The Goddess who is the Virgin Huntress,

Artemis is fiercely independent, and thus can be of enormous assistance to us when we fear separation, are ready to move out of home and into our own lives, or are ending a relationship and want to be strong as we let go of the pain and move on. She can be contacted easily by casting circle and invoking her presence. She will come whenever she is needed, although Mondays are a particularly strong day for calling on her.

Invocation to Artemis: "Blessed Artemis, help me to be wild and free, to know who I am within and without myself, in all directions of time. Help me to create friendships which support my independence and my becoming who I am meant to be. Help me choose my partners well, have strong relationships, and leave them without pain if that is for the higher good. Help me learn to choose well to whom I give my body, and when, and how, and to allow myself the transient joys and ecstasies of the flesh without fear of reprimand, punishment or suffering. I am wild and innocent."

Other divinities to call on for working with issues of independence: Quan Ti, Forseti, Maat, Athena, Lugh, Ganesh, Tara, Pele.

A White magical working

In the following ritual you can invoke any God or Goddess, elemental, angel or archangel. It can also be of great assistance in reaching your personal spirit guides. And it can be done alone or in a group.

When you have chosen who to work with, think about how best to approach them. If it is Aphrodite, perhaps hold a rose quartz crystal or perform the ritual in a pretty outdoor garden. If it is Hecate, you may have better results in a darkened room, or with a scarf over your head and around your shoulders to facilitate journeying within.

If you are working in a group, you could simply ask everyone to hold hands. Then, sitting barefoot with feet resting firmly on the ground, chant the name of the God or the Goddess over and over again. As you chant the energy will naturally rise, peak, then eventually fall. Let it trail away as it comes to a natural end.

Sometimes during this process a person will channel a message directly from the entity you are working with. Allow them to do so, and have someone else recording it should this happen. This message will be very clear and strong and powerful, as well as healing for all concerned.

Solitary white magical practitioners can also do this, simply by casting circle, chanting the name of the God, Goddess or entity they want to work with, then allowing the messages to come. They may come through in a physical way, through your voice or your vision, or mentally, with ideas and solutions to dilemmas you have given over to the deity. Always have pen and paper handy to write anything down or draw an image that comes to your mind, or a tape recorder to catch any message you may channel.

Quiz

Finding your Inner Goddess

We all share traits with the God and the Goddess, and we can call on them to help boost the qualities they represent within us. Are you articulate and fearless, but with a tendency to overpower others and create conflict unintentionally? If this rings true for you, you may be unconsciously working with the goddess Hecate, a powerful deity who gives the gifts of undaunted assertion and strong will, but who also has a tendency to be seen as overwhelming and controlling. Or do you identify more with Demeter, a Goddess who loves deeply and passionately, but fears betrayal? Or are you more like Aphrodite, the loving, beautiful party-girl Goddess who adores all things sensual, but who can also find herself in trouble due to her inability to commit – and to resist her own appetites?

No matter which Goddess you are most like, you can balance the energy and begin to create more strength, love and commitment in your life by understanding the strengths and weaknesses inherent in her. Take this quiz to learn about which one you resonate most strongly with – and how you can collaborate with her to create a wonderful life.

1. You prefer…
a) Twilight and the rising moon.
b) The entire day – you love daylight.
c) Any time after 3am.
d) The night sky sparkling with stars and planets.
e) Sunrise, and the start of something new.
f) Sunset, with its soothing flush of beautiful color.

2. Your favorite colors are:
a) Silvers and soft metallic pastels.
b) Golds and yellows.
c) Deep blues and greens.
d) Lush, impenetrable black.
e) Violets and pale blues.
f) Deep reds and hot pinks.

3. Which of the following animals do you most identify with?
a) A deer.
b) A snake.
c) A cat.
d) An owl.
e) A bear.
f) A dolphin.

4. Your idea of love is…
a) Being completed by another person.
b) Finding someone you can care for.
c) Creating an indestructible bond with your soulmate.
d) Being challenged by a stimulating partner.
e) Painful, as possible betrayals and deceit frighten you.
f) An amazing sexual relationship, romantic and wild.

5. You most wish to develop…
a) Your spiritual side.
b) A beautiful, loving home to protect you from the world.
c) Power in your workplace.
d) Strong relationships and friendships.
e) Peace and tranquility.
f) Your allure and attractiveness.

6. The image that most moves you is…
a) Full moon on snow.
b) Bright sunshine on a field of buttercups.
c) Lightning across the peaks of spectacular mountains.
d) Perfect waves on a golden seashore.
e) Gentle rain on green meadows.
f) A balmy, sensual tropical paradise.

7. The human trait that most troubles you is…
a) Loneliness.
b) Vindictiveness.
c) Mental aggression.
d) Stupidity.
e) Betrayal.
f) Cold-heartedness.

8. The human trait you are most attracted by is…
a) Spirituality.
b) Fulfillment.
c) Peacefulness.
d) Power.
e) Kindness.
f) Desire.

9. Your favorite place is…
a) A beautiful, serene lake.
b) An amazing home.
c) A super-slick luxury hotel.
d) A temple in an ancient city.
e) Forests and fields, areas that live and grow.
f) A bedroom that is rich with luxury and sensuality.

10. You admire people who…
a) Are creative geniuses and succeed in their vision.
b) Who are rich, and powerful with it.
c) Live their own life, whatever the consequences.
d) Are fiercely intelligent and inspiring.
e) Are loving parents and trustworthy people.
f) Are beautiful and delightful.

Which Goddess is with you?

Mostly As – Selene

If you answered mostly 'A's your inner goddess is Selene.

You are ethereal, intuitive, feminine, sensitive and psychic.

You are here to assert yourself and retain your femininity.

Your challenge is in overcoming the tendency you have to let others take advantage of you and leaving decisions to others – to trust and act on your intuition.

Your strengths are enormous psychic power, being a light and inspiration to others, gentle leadership and spiritual connection.

Your stone is moonstone.

Your oil is sandalwood.

Your magical affirmation is: "I am a divine example of the sacred feminine. I am perfect, whole and complete."

Mostly Bs – Vesta

If you answered mostly Bs your inner goddess is Vesta.

You are just, wise, clear and calm.

You are here to learn how to protect yourself as well as you protect others.

Your challenge is to stop putting yourself last, working for other people's benefit with no thought for yourself, thus ending up exhausted and taken advantage of.

Your strength is that when balanced, you are able to nurture yourself, and be a beloved and loyal mother, sister, friend and wife.

Your stone is citrine.

Your oil is geranium.

Your magical affirmation is: "I create a beautiful environment wherever I am. Everyone who comes into contact with me benefits from this wonderful energy. I love myself."

Mostly Cs – Hecate (pronounced Hec-Ah-Tay)

If you answered mostly Cs your inner goddess is Hecate.

You are ages-old, instinctually wise and able to withstand great tests.

You are here to pass on your wisdom and support others when they are going through similar tests and challenges.

Your challenge is that you can seem bitter about the past, unable to learn your own lessons and disconnected from younger people – you need to release this.

Your strength is that, when balanced, you are wise, compassionate, truthful and a wonderful example for younger people of female strength.

Your stone is black obsidian.

Your oil is patchouli.

Your magical affirmation is: "It is safe to be a powerful woman. I express myself compassionately. Peace begins with me."

Mostly Ds – Minerva

If you answered mostly Ds your inner goddess is Minerva.

You are analytical, intellectual, academic – brilliant!

You are here to see things as they are, which can be painful and enlightening, and to learn to bring compassion without judgment.

Your challenge is that you may be considered cold, judgmental, condescending and over-critical. Allow your inner warmth to show.

Your strength is that you are courageous, a born teacher, an ethical politician and an astute keeper of knowledge.

Your stone is clear quartz.

Your oil is clary sage.

Your magical affirmation is: "I fearlessly show my intelligence, and make my own decisions. I am an intelligent being and I appreciate my wisdom."

Mostly Es – Demeter

If you answered mostly Es your inner goddess is Demeter.

You are grounded, nurturing, protective and unrelenting.

You are here to maintain a relationship while allowing others their independence, to learn to let go, to seek out, help and protect others, particularly young women, and to learn to trust others in relationships.

Your challenge is that you can be obsessive, inflexible and untrusting, so you need to learn your lessons!

Your stones are smoky quartz and onyx.

Your oil is vetiver.

Your magical affirmation is: "I nurture myself and put my needs first. I trust. When my needs are met, everyone benefits."

Mostly Fs – Aphrodite

If you answered mostly Fs your inner goddess is Aphrodite.

You are physical, alluring, charismatic and sexual.

You are here to respect the sacred vows of enduring love, to renew romantic love at any stage of life and to explore your sensuality and create great physical joy.

Your challenge is to overcome a tendency to be selfish, thoughtless, faithless, chaotic and hurtful.

Your strength is that you are delightful, light-hearted, humorous, loving and a lover to conquer any heart.

Your stone is rose quartz.

Your oil is rose absolue.

Your magical affirmation is: "I honor my sexuality. I am a divine expression of perfect desire. I respect my body."

White Magic Workshop

Now that you have established the Goddess whose energy

you are most aligned with, you can begin to work with it to improve your life and draw on her wisdom. When I teach this exercise in a group or workshop situation, I divide the group – yes, the men too! – according to their Goddess affiliation, so all the Minervas are in one group and all the Aphrodites in another, and we discuss how the deity appears to us in our lives and share ideas about how to bring this energy into balance and into its most positive aspect.

If you do this on your own, simply write down your Goddess archetype, what she means to you and what having contact with her brings up for you. Chant her name too if you wish.

Below are some starting points for the discussion.

Aphrodite: The lesson of Aphrodite is faithful love, romantic attraction and passion.

Minerva: The Minerva lesson is how to combine wisdom with compassion and intellect with love.

Demeter: Is about separating from the past and learning to be a partner. Doing what you wish to do despite disapproval.

Selene: The lesson is in being magical but staying grounded.

Hecate: This lesson is about being fearless but being loved.

Vesta: Is about being a domestic goddess without compromising your self.

And remember, always ground yourself afterwards with some cakes and wine – the Witches way of coming back to earth. Of course it can be fruit and water, or mead and banana bread, whatever you wish. The point is to reconnect strongly with your body and the physical realm after interacting with the Goddesses.

The Goddess chant

This chant is one which many earth-dwelling Goddesses and Gods work with to vibrationally connect with deity through the powerful magic of song, sound and the spoken word. Chanting the name is powerful, evocative and extremely magical – it can raise energy and power for spellcasting, transport you to the world between worlds and help you connect with these divine Goddesses. Let all the names run together and flow – amazing things will happen!

The chant is: Isis, Astarte, Diana, Hecate, Demeter, Kali, Inanna.

Who are these Goddesses?

Isis The Queen of the Heavens is the Egyptian goddess of magic, fertility and motherhood, the lady of Ten Thousand names, and her name means "throne". She speaks to us of our own authority in our lives. She assists with maintaining a positive outlook, inner strength, courage and dignity, and reminds you that you are worthy of great things.

Astarte (pronounced As-TAR-tay) The Phoenician goddess of love and fertility is also a warrior woman of great power. She is helpful whether you want to bear a child, plant a garden or grow a project. She is invoked for wisdom and protection, and you can call on her to resolve arguments, for protection and for sacred sexuality. She is sensual, sexual, expressive and outspoken.

Diana The revered Roman moon Goddess combines strength and beauty, power and love. She shares traits with the Greek Goddess Artemis (there is debate over whether they are one and the same), but in her Dianic variation she is mother to her culture and to civilization. She is the feminine influence on the world, and is incorporated into our own selves through us respecting the women in our lives. She protects women and is a huntress, remaining independent but not without sex!

Hecate The ultimate crone energy, Hecate is the wise and respected queen of the underworld and Goddess of the crossroads – the turning points of our lives. She is compassionate and kind, fearless and fierce, and helps souls make the transition from life to the afterlife. Wise and powerful, you can call on her for manifestation and protection. She brings death too – not literal death, but change – and new beginnings.

Demeter The Greek Goddess of the harvest, you can call on her to help grow literal or figurative crops in your life. She is the mother who loves her children passionately, and who keeps the balance in the world – when she is in balance, the earth itself is in balance. It is said her grieving for her daughter caused winter, and the girl's eventual return brought spring.

Kali This Hindu Goddess of destruction is the face of all that needs to go in order for creation to come about. Without Kali's intervention we can stagnate and fail to reach our potential. But with her assistance we push through barriers, and literally are able to give birth to our projects or ourselves. Change, her métier, is not necessarily easy, but it is natural.

Inanna A Sumerian fertility Goddess known for her protective qualities, she is a fierce, protective mother to her children and her people, who fearlessly went into the underworld to bring back souls whose time had not yet come. While she had no fear of the underworld, she is now said to dwell in heaven as its queen, with a sparkling crown of blue-white stars.

Variations on the chant

The Goddess names are said, spoken or sung as a repetitive chant – as loudly or as softly as you wish. Some sing it as a kind of bedtime blessing to themselves or their children. What also works wonderfully is thinking of which Goddesses and Gods you feel drawn to working with, and working their names into the chant. For example, I created an Avalonian version: "Bride, Rhiannon, Blodeuwedd (pronounced Blod-EYE-weth), Arianrhod, Branwen, Cerridwen."

Bride, also known as Brigit, is the Goddess of wells and holy waters, flame and fire and new beginnings. Rhiannon is a Goddess of love, fertility and creativity. Blodeuwedd is a Goddess of transformation, beauty, hunting and sexual power. Arianrhod is the Celtic Goddess of the moon and her cycles. Branwen is the Celtic Goddess of the land and compassion for its people and beings. Cerridwen is the keeper of the cauldron, from which we may learn to drink fearlessly and fully when we explore our authentic selves. She also governs creativity.

You could also construct an Egyptian version, a Greek version, or simply be eclectic and work with the Goddesses who call to you.

Or you can work with the maiden/mother/crone aspect of the Goddess – here I was inspired by the legendary priestesses of Avalon, all faces of the Lady of the Lake.

Nimue (maiden) (pronounced NIM-ooo-way)

Morgan (mother)

Viviane (crone).

The popular God chant is: Dionysus, Cernunnos (pronounced KER-noo-nus), Uriah-Mazda, Manatu, Loki, Ra, Brahma.

Another version is: Pan, Poseidon, Dionysus, Cernnunos, Mitros, Loki, Apollo.

An alternative for men, again inspired by Avalon, could be:

Arthur (student)

Uther Pendragon (father)

Merlin (sage).

Another masculine, eclectic version could be:

Cupid (young lover)

Cernunnos (Horned God)

Chiron (wounded healer, pronounced Ky-ron)

Chapter six ~
White Magic for Romance

UNLEASH YOUR BEWITCHING INNER FIRE

Being magical can give you, well, an erotic edge. Being magical can also cleanse you of old hurts, reignite your self-love and help you see yourself as the beautiful, powerful sensual being that is the truth of your essence. But back to that erotic edge. The erotic frisson of magic just cannot be denied. Aren't you just a little curious? Remember, we're powerful, innocent, wise beings. So let's embrace the bewitching power of erotic love, and explore its wealth for our bodies and souls.

The rites of love and true white magic have long been intertwined. Just think of the fires of Beltane, which celebrate fertility and the honoring of our bodies and the beautiful expressions of love of which we are all capable. In many people's minds of course this healthy, beautiful expression of physical desire became something "darker" – those who practiced white magic were maligned, said to be seductresses hell-bent on enslaving men with their beguiling sexuality and irresistible wiles, not to mention their sinister potions and the help they had from mischievous fairies and spirits.

It certainly is a powerful trait, this loving of your own physicality – but it doesn't mean we use sensuality as a weapon, oh no, for that would be far from wise, and bring us no true pleasure. Instead we use it as the Goddess intended. For pleasure, expression and procreation.

White magical practitioners' image is often perceived as one of kinky and over the top sexual practices – helped by sensational Hollywood films and folks who claim they're practicing magic but who really... well, never mind. In the 21st century, sex and sensuality are often openly spoken of, which is good, but simultaneously they have been bought and sold and commercially utilized. Airbrushed perfections masquerading as flesh and blood figures exclude so many of us. We wobble. We change. We age. We go from maiden to mother to crone, all in the one lifetime, all in the one day at times. And it is all good and beautiful that we do. So because of sex's denigration – from being a sacred act to now being treated as an item for sale – when we speak of sex magic are we not being sensational, a little lurid and, well, unevolved?

Not at all. To marginalize the beautiful power of loving sexual union is to deny an incredible source of magical transformation and healthy enchantment, and to deny ourselves a natural source of self-esteem building exercise! The side effects of magical sex can include intimacy, strong relationships, ecstasy, beauty, self-esteem, body confidence (no matter what your individual shape!) and past life healing. So now is the time to reclaim bewitching sex magic, for the many ways in which it can empower and pleasure us all.

Sex is a merging, and in merging we combine who we are and increase the energy we can send out. As in yoga, where many poses are performed with a partner because the effects are not achievable alone, sexual magic allows us to achieve different and more extensive natural interplay with the elements, with our partner and with our own capacity for joy and harmony.

We also raise safe, magical power when we work together – on any level! – but when we do it sexually we raise our individual vibrational levels holistically and immensely. Now, if you're thinking, "Hang on, all this and orgasm too?" Why yes! Please consider the physiological effects sex creates. Heart palpitations. Erections. Breasts actually growing – nipples lengthen and reach out. Our skin becomes exquisitely sensitive to touch. Our breathing changes and our bodies open, like tropical flowers in the heat.

If we accept that we are bewitching enchanters and enchantresses – which you are! – we accept that we have an energetic body as well as this physiological one. Imagine what your auric field and your etheric body resemble during sex! Add to that the possibilities of sex and love-making – the variety and emotional repertoire that can be created in that amazing exchange of energy. There are so many ways of directing the energy that is raised during sex. Should we not consider being aware of it, and of how it can help us to evolve, transcend and work magic in our day-to-day lives?

If we intentionally, with good motives and true hearts, set out to achieve magic through sex, our individual vibrational level can shift to the extent that we can attract different circumstances into our lives – our very consciousness at a cellular level can be altered through magical sex! We can even more closely contact ourselves, our own past lives, the Goddess and her manifestations, the ascended masters, beings of light and the angelic realm. And it is of course extremely elemental to make love, so the fairies are always with us when we do! Even deceased loved ones can come through – in the most compromising moments. (Even if sex is magical, I'm not sure I want my grandma watching! Sorry, Gran! Come back during meditation!)

It is desirable to be very focused and disciplined so we do not attract inappropriate energies during sex – and especially during magical sex. All that is necessary is to always act for the highest good of all! I know, it seems a rather tall order. But intent is what matters – intent is exactly the discipline we are required to be aware of, as our intent will set in action the magic that creates manifesting results – sometimes almost immediately.

Being aware of the power of love has become even more significant now. In June 2004, the planet Venus occulted the sun – astrospeak for a planetary equivalent of an eclipse. In other words, the power of Venus overshadowed the sun, quite apparently and literally. On an energetic level, this introduced a host of new energies to our planet. It signified the resurgence of the Goddess, divine love and sexuality – especially female sexuality and feminine power.

Now we have an amazing opportunity to integrate sex and sexuality into our lives in a way that is loving, powerful, strong, free, joyful and completely void of the old energetic patterns of shame and struggle. Feminine power will rise and rise over the next phase of human history.

In the late 16th century, when Venus similarly occulted the sun, there was a Queen in England, a Queen in Scotland, Catherine de Medici ruled Italy and France, and in Ireland another Mary, known affectionately as The Pirate Queen, ruled and challenged English domination. At this stage feminine power was supreme but inharmonious, with all sources of feminine power battling each other.

In the 1800s, another Venus occultation heralded in the Victorian era, and the rise of feminism and the suffragette movement.

This time around we will see large political changes, with the politics of power shifting as strong female leaders move to center stage. In our personal lives and our spiritual development, female pleasure and power will become stronger and stronger forces, creating fast yet gentle changes in personal relationships. Force will no longer be acceptable. Corruption neither. The Goddess principle coming into full force will see us all enjoying our love and romantic lives more freely, and will also see feminine role models in churches and in even the most traditional patriarchal religious systems. The current imbalance we are healing is affecting us all, men and women alike.

When this imbalance of male and female energies is healed we will all have a beautiful background against which to work loving sex magic, based on desire and healthful needs, respect and pure intent. Our loving relationships will be sensual, and the sacred and the sexual will no longer be considered separate.

True sexual magical unity is a matter of free will and individual choice as to how you manifest your romantic and sexual magic. On a practical level, it can be practiced by a couple in a long-term loving relationship, with partners of both genders or of the same sex; it can be worked alone, in a guilt-free and beautiful way to bring you pleasure; and it can, if this works for you, be practiced in groups. However the most healthful way to experience romantic magic is with a person with whom you are meant to be, in whose arms you can experience the physical ecstasy that reminds us of the magic of our own beautiful bodies – healthy, alive, tingling with sensation, revering every touch and word.

Magical sex and love comes about when we are aware of our intent and focused in the moment. Slow things down – experience what is taking place. Make time for love. Turn off all phones, faxes and even your laptop. Give yourself space to become Love.

There are various techniques that can be worked during sex to release your own desires into the work, making manifest your dreams. Intent plus thought plus action creates opportunity, and dreams have a habit of coming true. Personal ritual, when shared between two loving partners with the same intention, can be a beautiful, magical working, invoking trance-like states during which we can experience ourselves on a level so rich and divine that coming back to earth, so to speak, can be almost another level of experience entirely.

Invoking the Goddesses

It is often customary – and often absolutely instinctual – to invoke the Goddess and the God during romantic physical situations. Sex, however, can have many and varied qualities and colors. Aphrodite has a certain energy, Isis another. Calling on the energies of the elementals can also be thrilling, inspiring and (third) eye opening during romance. Dragons, unicorns and mermaids all have great sexual allure and energy, of different hues and varieties. Fairies adore sex, and love bringing people together in myriad forms of joyous liaisons, especially around Beltane, the ancient fertility festival of sex and love that is celebrated on May 1 in the northern hemisphere and October 31 in the southern. At this sacred time of the Wheel of the Year, you could experience the exquisite pleasure and innocence of a fairy king or queen as lover.

To be fearlessly sensual, contact the beautiful, wild-hearted Goddess Ishtar. Judgment does not alter the essence of her behavior. She experiences no guilt. Her lovers taste exquisite joy, and she partakes of sexual love without traditional attachments.

She is also a Goddess of fertility, so if you are wishing to conceive, Ishtar will assist you in achieving that dream. Children born with Ishtar's help have a very special destiny, and many twins are born of her intervention. If you do not want to conceive but you would love her help in other ways, simply let her know. She is a wonderful deity to invoke for brief physical liaisons which can be immensely healing despite their non-traditional brevity and lack of attachment, as they will be full of honor and honesty.

The formidable and fascinating Goddess Pele can be a powerful and loving ally to call on when you are working on healing yourself from the trauma of sexual abuse. [Please see the section on the centaur for help with sexual abuse issues too.]

She can also lovingly assist you if your libido is diminished. As the Goddess of volcanoes, she helps with "flow" of all kinds – communication, the exchange of energy and honest power communications. Anger and sexual issues often go hand in hand. Sometimes a diminished libido is covering up anger with our partner, a previous partner or poor sexual experiences. Pele will assist you to explore what lies beneath all such issues. Simply light a red or orange candle and ask for her assistance.

Another quality Pele brings to all sexual relationships is courage – she can be very helpful when it comes to having the courage to ask for what you want in bed, and in attracting the lover you want.

The Goddess of love

Many of us have benefited from the beautiful stream of energy that merges with us when we connect with Aphrodite, the Greek Goddess of love. In mythology she is notorious for creating havoc via romantic love, but this is a distortion of her true self, and is more about our own reaction to love. When we are hit by the wave of energy known as love it can create pandemonium in our lives or utter contentment, satisfaction and erotic joy – both of these are created from within us. But asking for her help and intervention can create bonds of flesh and soul that outlast time.

She is very gracious and nurturing in energy, and will assist you in overcoming any insecurities you may have about your body. She also governs bodies of water, having been born of the sea, and thus romances on a beach, in the bath and in pools and waterfalls are very blessed by her tangible presence.

She loves to assist people in relationships to maintain their passionate physical connection, and also helps single people who are looking for love. You can work with her to improve the quality of your sex life, in being attractive and feeling loved as a woman or a man. She wants you to be blessed and admired in innocence and love.

When we are communicating from a place of love and pure intent she will aid us in recharging our own belief in our attractiveness – thus making us attractive! – and help us feel respected and acknowledged as Gods and Goddesses.

To establish a relationship with her, here is a sacred Mysteries ritual to bring you close to her, so you can ask for her help from a sacred place of love and respect for her and for yourself.

Cast your magic circle, call in the elements and directions, then welcome Aphrodite to your rite. Disrobe gently, without fear or harm. Anoint your body with essential oil of rose: on your legs, your arms, your forehead, the top of your head, above your pubic hair, on the base of your spine and under your feet. Gaze deeply at yourself in a mirror and allow your eyes to unfocus slightly – she may appear to you in a guise that is for you alone.

Respectfully ask for her help and loving assistance in loving yourself more. You will know when she is with you, as you will be filled with a lightness of being that is beautiful, strong and gentle. You will have her presence confirmed when you begin to see yourself as more and more beautiful, more and more desirable. A deliciously warm feeling, an opening of the heart chakra, will also occur, and spread throughout your body. This feeling will spread throughout your every cell, cleansing away pockets of darkness and grief, the remnants of disrespect and hurt regarding sexuality, relationships and worthiness.

You will feel it is complete when the warmth has spread. Thank her, re-robe, open circle, and be gentle with yourself for the rest of the day. This ritual is especially powerful if worked on a Friday. This is the day of love, and thus the best and most popular day for dates and romance – and, if we are not conscious, the potential pandemonium of love.

With sensual white magic, you can do trance work and communicate with the elementals and spirits to heal and re-balance chakras, body image issues, emotional issues, trust issues and past life issues.

Healing past life issues is an area of spiritual development we are all working on. Consciously or unconsciously, we are exploring our lessons and soul contracts in every moment. What can accelerate the process of healing, of learning and of experiencing healthy closure, is romance, relationships and our sexuality.

Many of us exploring white magic have past life issues due to our previous incarnations as healers, midwives, heretics, priestesses of the old ways and wizards of the wise who were persecuted, tortured and cruelly executed during the Burning Times. But our past life issue may be from any era, and our relationships and the nature of our sex life can reveal the dilemmas of our other lifetimes. We can then choose healing therapies or processes, or healthier relationships, that assist us in moving onwards and literally upwards in our divine purpose of reconnecting to the source, of which the white magic is just one road by which we travel back to who we really are.

We may be re-experiencing our own incarnations when we experience the following in our romantic lives – although these can also be the result of events from this lifetime that we need to heal from.

Chapter Seven ~ Past Lives
DISCOVERING WHO YOU ARE NOW

You have dreams that make no sense to you at all. You have fears and phobias that you don't understand because nothing happened to you to cause them. You may be sensing the cellular residue, and karmic imbalances of a past life.

Past lives – more accurately, dimensional lives are a part of us – they are who we are, and unless we understand and clear certain issues, as we incarnate again we may keep working on the same old lesson, sometimes seemingly forever. Here's how to identify who you may have been, who you may be in the future, and how to identify the issues you may still be living with – then take steps to clear them, and see how much your life improves.

Please remember that there is nothing to pay for in any lifetime, simply lessons to learn. Sometimes we spend more than one lifetime perfecting a lesson before we move on. We may have several lessons or life themes occurring simultaneously, and until we release the old issues in our current lifetime, we will carry them through again and again.

Use this quiz to gain insight into your current life issues and relationships, and if you do have things to face, past life regression can be a very powerful healing therapy. If you wish to explore PLT, there are many wonderful CDs and books on the subject, and many wonderful healers. A hypnotherapist can help you regress and literally re-experience past lives, as well as counsel you as you deal with the aftermath, while a psychic can pick up information regarding your past lives and relay that to you to give you some insight.

But you are your own best guide – a white magical practitioner simply needs to begin noting the signs to discover the truths about the path of your soul, in all directions of time.

Have you lived before?

Answer yes or no to the following questions to discover whether you may have lived before.

* You have peculiar food allergies or health issues that don't seem to be at all environmental – they just rise up at times of emotional stress.

* You are drawn to the look and feel of another era, for example, the knights of Arthurian England, the Egypt of the Pharaohs, the classical philosophers of Ancient Greece.

* You are frightened of something for which there is no rational basis (ie no experience in this lifetime), such as drowning, strangulation, burning or food poisoning.

* You are sometimes surprised at your own appearance – you don't look or feel at all at home in your body.

* There are certain people you just feel drawn to, even if they make you feel uncomfortable or strange. There's something about them that makes you want to be with them, no matter what.

* You sometimes feel like you've "done all this before" in situations which are totally unfamiliar to you.

* You know things about other cultures, places or languages that you haven't learned in this life. Some children have started speaking in a language they have never heard before, that they can have no way of knowing, which does lend credence to the possibility of past lives.

* You've visited another country or place and felt that you had come home after being away for a long time.

* You can't stand certain things – some foods, smells, colors and people – for no real reason. They somehow just repel you.

* You've had repetitive dreams featuring a place or people that has always seemed to be important, but it bears no relationship to anything currently happening in your life.

If you answered yes to three or more of these questions, you can be assured that you are not living your first lifetime. Now, this is where you need to do your own detective work – investigate your own home, interests and hobbies, and note which themes come up. Is there a tendency to be attracted to Ancient Egypt? To the time of cowboys and Indians? To the magical England of Arthurian times? To a time when we all lived in harmony with the earth? Noting this, you will start to see which lifetime is attempting to get your attention, and by figuring out what and who you were, you can start to do some work.

Quiz: Who were you in a past life?

1. Your friends would call you:
a) Dynamic and strong-willed.
b) Sweet, a true friend.

c) Smart, clever and ahead of your time.

d) Confidant, you go after what you want and expect to get it.

e) Flirtatious and attractive.

2. People who don't like you would describe you as:

a) Aggressive.

b) A victim.

c) Cold, you use your head rather than your heart.

d) Bossy, demanding, spoilt.

e) Trampy and untrustworthy.

3. If you could have been born in another time and place, where would you choose?

a) A battlefield in a glorious war, with you leading the winning side.

b) A time of peace and beauty, where you lived in harmony with the land.

c) A time of change, when great discoveries were made.

d) An era when kings and queens ruled with absolute authority.

e) A romantic medieval court filled with lords and ladies.

4. You prefer music that:

a) Gives you strength – hard rock.

b) Calms you down – ambient, New Age tracks.

c) Makes you think better – Mozart and experimental music.

d) Celebrates your achievements – marches and film scores.

e) Evokes passion – romantic pop songs and power ballads.

5. Your favorite colors are:

a) Bright hues, strong tones.

b) Metallic silvers and pastels.

c) Blues and greens.

d) Purples and indigo blues.

e) Reds, pinks and crimsons.

6. You are attracted to people who are:

a) Kind and loving.

b) Exciting and dramatic.

c) Innovative and intellectual.

d) Worship you and treat you like you're someone
very special.

f) Are romantic, sexy fools – just like you.

Which one are you?

Mostly As – warrior

If you answered with a majority of 'A's your strongest past life influence is that of a warrior. You may need to learn how to meditate and be more diplomatic to balance this energy. You tend to want to solve problems quickly, and you sometimes wish you could simply fight it out rather than talk it through. Other people may find you brash, forceful and even aggressive at times, but you're not violent, simply trained to fight and use your body as a weapon. Re-channel that energy into athletics, for example, and learn to listen to the other person's point of view.

Mostly Bs – homemaker

If you answered with a majority of 'B's you have had a lifetime where you were an extremely timid and gentle person, who nevertheless had to deal with a certain amount of upheaval. It would be helpful to investigate ways to become more balanced – by learning a martial art, becoming fit or taking an assertiveness class so you can have more influence over your own life. In a past life, you were a peaceful homemaker or farmer, but this time around you have to learn to defend what's yours without compromising your ideals.

Mostly Cs – innovator

If you answered with a majority of Cs you have had a life where you were a great scientist, inventor or innovator, someone who always thought of a new and clever way to solve problems. This time around you're still solving problems, but you are at risk of becoming so "in your head" that you can turn other people off. Take up a hobby that brings out your inner fire and learn why romance, dancing and laughter bring people together in magical ways. Use some of your clever brain to help people, and you'll be amazed at how attractive you become – and how much you begin to feel.

Mostly Ds – royalty

If you answered with a majority of Ds you have been royalty in a past life – and this time around you may be struggling with the fact that you're not super-rich, adored by millions and considered perfect by everyone around you. Your credit card may often be maxed out and you probably crave the good things in life, without actually wanting to work to achieve any of them. You love making decisions for other people, and can be quite judgmental. Instead of struggling, do some charity work and tap in to your benevolent royal side that will want to help others less fortunate than yourself.

Mostly Es – lover

If you answered with a majority of Es you have had a past life where you were a great lover, geisha or courtesan, trained in the arts of love and sensual to a fault. This time around you may need to become more dependable as a partner, and learn to place more value on friendship, creating a family and making a commitment without feeling you're going to have your wings clipped. You could have a tendency to use your wiles to get ahead, so explore your many other skills to become a more rounded person.

Lessons of the Tarot

Tarot cards are a great tool for divination and healing, and can reveal many hidden aspects of your personality, your life, and the issues that are facing you.

Here are two wonderful spreads that you can use to help yourself and your loved ones understand current issues in the context of your past life themes, and discover the affect past life issues are having on your current life.

Discovering your past lives

Shuffle your Oracle Tarot deck while you focus on the question of your past lives. Ask the God and the Goddess to help you receive clear and precise information on the subject – Isis is a great one to help with this quest. When you have finished shuffling lay out the first 17 cards from the top of the deck in this manner:

One... Two
Three... Four... Five
Six... Seven... Eight... Nine...
Ten... Eleven... Twelve... Thirteen... Fourteen
Fifteen... Sixteen... Seventeen.

The first two cards you put down at the top (cards one and two) will give you your soul's theme for its entire journey. In other words, the qualities of all your incarnations, past, present and future. This is what you are here to do and to learn.

Cards three, four and five show the major influences and

inspirations from past lives which you are currently working with in this incarnation.

Cards six, seven, eight and nine show the ramifications of choices you made in previous incarnations. These cards will also provide you with valuable guidance regarding who you were, what kind of life experiences you had, and the kinds of relationships and activities you engaged in those other lifetimes.

Cards 10, 11, 12, 13 and 14 show you the most important issues that came up for you in your past incarnations.

And the last three cards, 15, 16 and 17, show you what will come up for you in future incarnations – remembering though that as we all have free will, we can create and re-create our life experiences from this moment on. The most powerful thing in the entire universe is the power of now.

Please record this reading in your Book of Shadows and Light, with the date you did it, as you may start to see signs, have dreams and receive further information from Goddesses, guides, angels or elementals regarding the nature of your past lives. You can also repeat it in a year or so to see if anything has changed in the way the issues are affecting you.

Soulmate incarnations spread

This spread can give you information on the past lives you have shared with another person. It's an amazing spread to clarify past lives and the soul purpose of a kindred spirit, and is wonderful, powerful and especially insightful and healing, especially for those of us in what feels to be a fated relationship, or where one partner feels this way and the other does not!

First, remove the card known as the Fool from the deck. This card is going to help give you very important information about your significant other. Put it to one side, as you will soon be using it.

Ask, while shuffling and holding an image of your love in your mind's eye, "What past lives have I shared with this person?" See them standing before you, fairly neutral. Allow their energy to come through – see auras, hear messages, feel emotions.

When you have completed shuffling, pull nine cards from throughout the deck – do not take them from the top of the deck. Take these nine cards and add the Fool to them. Now you have 10 cards. Shuffle once again.

Start to lay out your cards from left to right, with the card revealed (the pattern facing upwards). The trick to this layout is that when the Fool appears, you place your next card over the top of it. This card, with the Fool underneath it, indicates the very first lifetime you have shared with this person. The cards following that indicate consecutive lifetimes. The very last card indicates your current lifetime together. The cards prior to the Fool indicate the themes of your journeying together and the reasons you chose to incarnate together and be with each other again in this lifetime. I know this can be a little confusing, but when you have the cards in your hands it will become clear.

So, if the Fool is card two, then you have had eight lifetimes with this person, and the final card is the one you're working on together now. The third card – the one that is now on top of the Fool card – reveals your first lifetime together, and the next seven show other lives you've shared and the issues you dealt with then. Card one, to the left of the Fool, reveals the reasons for you incarnating together now.

If the Fool is card five, then this current lifetime is your fifth life together, and there are four cards (cards one to four) to represent the issues you are dealing with now.

If the Fool is card nine, then this may be your first lifetime together, in which case card 10 shows you what this lifetime is about, and every card preceding it reveals the issues, lessons and gifts you are bringing to each other's lives now.

If the Fool is the first card you put down (card one), then this lifetime – represented by the last card – is your ninth incarnation together. To clarify your theme, the reason you have shared so much, pull a further card randomly from the deck. This card will give you a message regarding the deeper meaning of your soul journey together.

If the Fool is the very last card put down, card 10, then you may be nearing the completion of your incarnations. Your earlier cards represent what you are going through in the present lifetime in regards to the person you have sought more information about.

Non linear incarnations - Living dimensionally

As time is not linear, we have not only lived before, we may also have incarnated already – in the future. Thus some people are literally from the future, and literally, from another planet! So, when looked at from the perspective of this great truth, the term past life is really something of a misnomer. We may have already lived in what we may feel, from our current incarnation and evolutionary point of view, in the future. Because time is not linear, nor do we incarnate chronologically, in the neat, lined-up fashion. We incarnate cyclically. Thus our next life, for example, may be in the past! Our previous life may have already been lived in what we call the future. This exciting topic is one I am currently researching avidly!

Chapter eight ~
The Wheel of the Year

THE EIGHT FESTIVALS
OF WHITE MAGIC

White magical practitioners celebrate eight annual sabbats, or festivals, which make up the Wheel of the Year. They are as old as Mother Earth herself – truly ancient, yet not historical, as they were not created to commemorate human events. The difference between the eight festivals of the Wheel of the Year and any other holiday is that they are natural. It is significant that these festivals are unlike other holidays. Instead they are an essential part of how this beautiful planet actually works. Although the names of these ancient festivals have changed over time, the energies they celebrate have been with us since the very beginning of the planet, and imprinted in her consciousness and expressed by her every year.

The celebrations and rituals begin on the eve of the actual day, and go from sundown to sundown of the following day. Often our ancestors would stay up all night to honor the seasonal change and the transformation of the God and the Goddess. This sounds easy at Litha (pronounced Lee-tha), when the sun is high and long and rises early, and even at Beltane (pronounced Bel-tayne), when they would stay out all night celebrating in fields dotted with bonfires. But they would also stay up at Yule, the longest night of the year, and keep vigil throughout the cold and snowy darkness to witness the return of the sun and the new spark of life. The people were as linked to and in tune with these important days as the earth was.

While the dates are prescribed, they can vary by a day or two each year depending on the turning of the earth, its position in comparison to the sun and the cycles of the moon. Variations can be found in magazines and on the net, but if in doubt celebrate the festival as close to the set day as is practical for you.

Why we celebrate the celestial and the terrestrial
(or As Above, So Below)

Four of the festivals are astronomical – the summer and winter solstices, when we are in the process of imminent change, and the autumn and spring equinoxes, when we are in balance.

The other four festivals, the cross-quarter days (because they are the midpoints of the solstices and equinoxes) or Greater Sabbats, are agricultural, and celebrate the turning of the seasons and the natural cycles of the earth, the flowing in and the flowing out of natural energy – the sowing of crops, the growing, the harvesting and the renewing to start all over again.

Just as the planet has these energetic shifts, balances and changes, so do we as individuals. We begin a project, we manifest it, we contemplate the results, then we go within to renew in order to create again. By celebrating each sacred festival of the Wheel of the Year, you will reconnect with your own internal magical seasons – your true source of power and creativity. You'll become imbued with love and respect for yourself, and your healing, psychic and spellworking abilities will be magnified because you are in tune with the creative energy of the planet itself.

Why celebrate the Wheel of the Year today?

While some sabbats are based on traditional pagan Celtic celebrations of seasonal changes, like Samhain and Beltane, others are based on the pagan Nordic traditions, for example, Yule and Ostara. They may in fact bear little resemblance to the flow of the seasons where you live, however, by observing these festivals wherever you are, you will be charged with white light and magical power, able to naturally and greatly enhance your innate ability to manifest. Becoming in tune with the planet yourself means you are more likely to speak your truths clearly, powerfully and with ease. You will be less inclined to get your fix from addictive relationships, food, alcohol and nicotine. These natural energies rebalance you gently, thus helping you to detach from any addictive behaviors and thoughts. Likewise you will begin to attract new, kindred spirits into your life.

These festivals are both outside of you – in the warmth of the sun, the flowering plants, the tides of the ocean – and within you. They help you to celebrate the miracle of nature that you are – the miracle that you were born to be.

Think of these festivals of the Wheel of the Year as portals into other realms, portals to other dimensions. They are days that are out of time, which all have the unique quality of acting as a powerful doorway between the worlds. Although you can also access these realms on other days, the festivals are the most simple, the most effective and the most powerful times to be a walker between the worlds, to draw back the veil and to part the mists.

May you enjoy every turn of the Wheel of Life, and may your own magical powers be discovered within you.

Summer
Solstice
LITHA
June 20-23

Beltane
April 30/May 1

Lughnasad
August 1/2

Spring Equinox
OSTARA
March 20-23

Autumn Equinox
MABON
September 20-23

Imbolc
February 1/2

Samhain
October 31/November 1

Winter Solstice
YULE
December 20-23

Northern Hemisphere

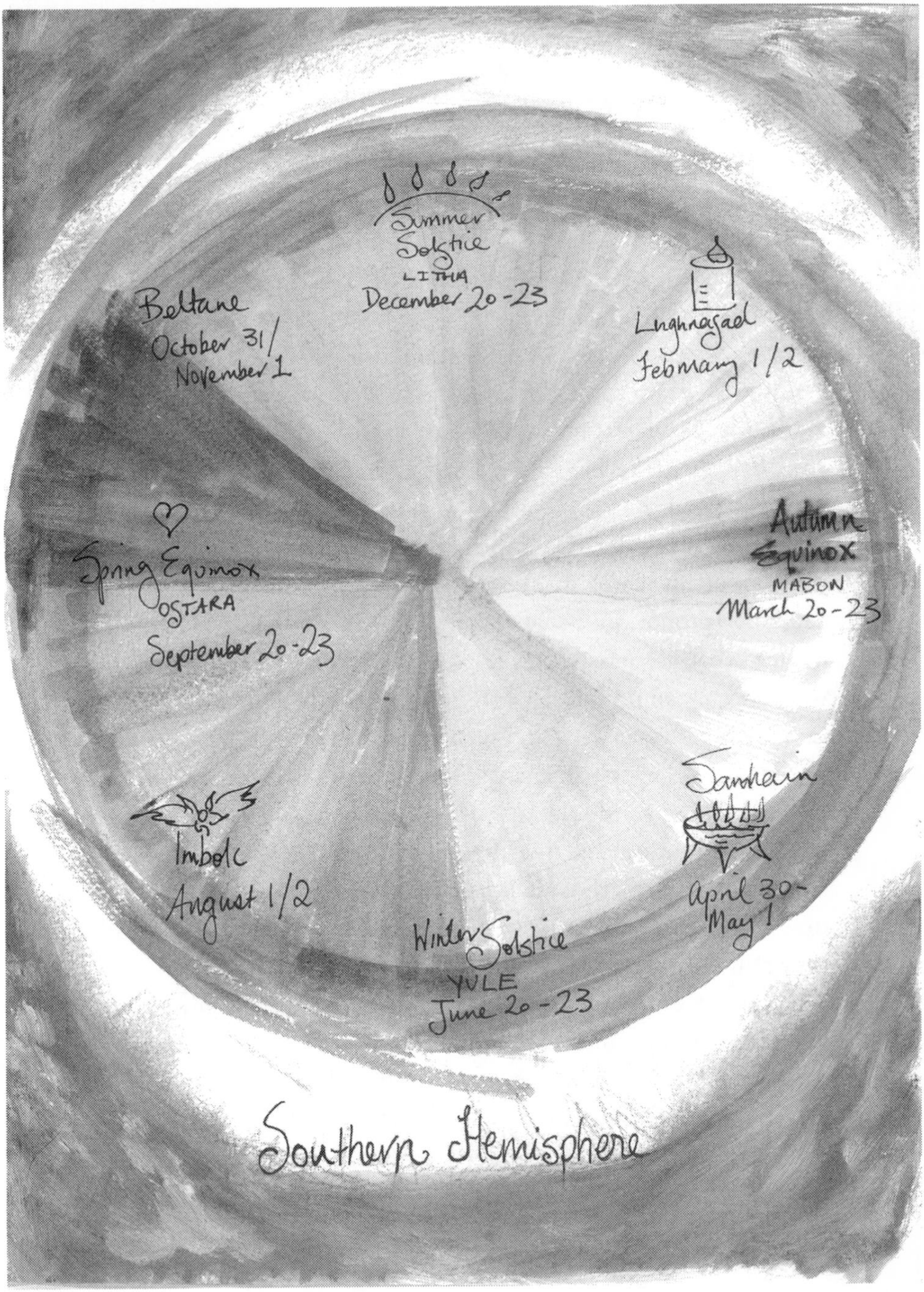
Summer Solstice
LITHA
December 20-23
Lughnasadh
February 1/2
Autumn Equinox
MABON
March 20-23
Samhain
April 30-
May 1
Winter Solstice
YULE
June 20-23
Imbolc
August 1/2
Spring Equinox
OSTARA
September 20-23
Beltane
October 31/
November 1
Southern Hemisphere

Samhain

The night that ghosts walk

Deeply magical, the festival of Samhain (pronounced Sow-en)is officially the start of the sacred energetic year. This beautiful festival acknowledges and honors all those who have gone before us. It is held October 31/November 1 in the northern hemisphere, and April 30/May 1 in the southern hemisphere.

Once a year comes a night when the dead do walk alongside us. They move through your memories, inspire your dreams, take hold of your imagination and illuminate your experience.

This night is called Halloween across the United States and the Day of the Dead in Mexico, but to white magicians it is Samhain (pronounced sow-en), the time when the dead teach us that what has passed can instruct us beyond death; that we who live can communicate with those who have gone from this incarnation if we just listen, watch and stay aware of the signs.

I've found myself in many countries, in many places, at this sacred time, and am always overwhelmed at the beauty of this celebration, the love and honor and respect which we as humans pay to those who have passed. So much of this urge is generated by the innate knowledge that not only are they still with us, but that our soul is indeed eternal.

This celebration – which starts, in the Celtic tradition, at sundown and continues for 24 hours – has led to many superstitions. Though exaggerated and made terrifying, which they are not, the spirits who populate horror films are in fact grounded in the symbolic truths of Samhain. This is the day which is set aside especially to honor our ancestors, to seek out their advice and insights, to reconnect with the souls that are no longer in their physical form. Samhain is about taking the time to respect death, and to revere life, and to welcome the cycle of life, death and rebirth. It's a chance to honor the memory of the friends and family members who have died and to celebrate their life and your love for them.

Your Samhain will not be complete without a ritual for those who have passed – this means candles, food and the power of your imagination. In pre-Burning Times, Celts were vocal about their belief that the souls of those who had already crossed over walked alongside those who were destined to pass over in the coming year. Others believed that the souls of those who were to yet be born also walked among the living.

This is the night when the veils between the worlds are at their thinnest. It is easy to slip into madness, delirium and trance-like states at this time, so it is important not to overindulge in any sort of substance at this time. At Samhain, anyone with any psychic ability at all will not need any extra help in contacting the other side or having "peculiar" experiences, which are of course completely natural. At any time, we white magical practitioners promise to work with clarity, coming from a healthy space that honors our bodies, minds and souls. Drugs or alcohol, or addictions to food, for example, will most likely create confusion and negativity in your crafting, most especially at Samhain.

A positive way to use this energy is to revere all those who have gone before you – friends, mentors, relatives, even people you never met who inspired you greatly. This is the night to remember them and honor their memories and their teachings.

On a symbolic and physical level, the three days before Samhain represent the triumph of the dark over the light.

Winter is approaching. It is another chance to celebrate the white magical' belief system of the rightness and natural harmony of seasonal transition – there is no good, no bad, no dominance – there is the light and the dark, and the shades in between, and all have their part to play in our lives.

Like the Wheel of Fortune card of the Oracle Tarot, the Wheel of the Year reminds us that the only constant is change – to attempt to dominate and enforce our will leads to corruption. Eternal summer is as bad for the land as the lifeless cold darkness of endless winter. For health and wealth and life, we must keep turning and changing, flowing in and out. Without the sun we cannot see our shadow. Without the dark we cannot see the stars.

All life comes from this marriage of dark and light. It is inescapable, wondrous, and what makes this journey called life so mysterious and rich.

Finally, don't forget that it's perfectly magically correct to enjoy and enhance the spine tingling feeling of Samhain. Getting together with a group of friends and watching horror classics until dawn, drinking cider (those magical apples!) and munching on corn on the cob is fun, spooky and spiritual too. Light candles, wear black, share scary stories and get ready to shiver. This night comes but once a year – get into the spirit and face your fears, because even death can enrich your life.

Candle magic

If you desire to open a portal between the worlds, the simplest spells work best at Samhain. This is because there is simply so much psychic activity taking place that to hold complicated rituals is not necessary – the best magic is that which will open your mind to the powerful energies and allow you to use them in a very direct and focused way. The energy itself is very dark and complex, so complicated magical recipes can make things very difficult. Don't be arcane and obscure just for the sake of it.

To seek wisdom from the past, try candle gazing. Light a black scented candle in a quiet, empty room, and stare into the flame. Allow your mind to linger on people and events of the past. This is the kind of ritual Pisceans, Scorpios and Cancerians (like myself) just adore – finally, permission to wallow in the past! And that's exactly what you should be doing at this time. Construct a family tree, contact living relatives, and communicate with those who have passed. Simply speak to them in your mind and ask for them to watch over you. I have chats to my darling Nanna and dream of my grandma, without fail, every Samhain.

Mirror to your soul

Mirror work is also very powerful at this time. In a softly lit room, preferably using flame or candles, gaze on your reflection with your eyes slightly unfocused. See your face merging with those of others you have known – the face of an aunt, a brother, a mother, a friend – and think of who you may have been to each other in a previous life, and what you have learned on your karmic path. Think of how fortunate we are to have the freedoms we do, to be magical. Never take this for granted. Spare a kind thought and a wish for peace and fulfillment for our fellow magical soul-sisters and brothers of yesteryear who suffered. Needless to say, Samhain works very well for any kind of past life therapy. It's a brilliant time to write automatically and simply allow what needs to come out to emerge, be discovered and then released.

Letting go

Samhain is also the most powerful time for letting go. Making amends with your own personal inventory of regrets is a compulsory exercise for this sabbat. If you need to forgive, or be forgiven, ask the universe and the Goddess and the God for this now. Warning – if you do choose to do this, be aware that it could have emotional and psychic side effects, not all of them necessarily pleasant. You may be troubled for the next 24 hours as you re-open old spiritual wounds, some of which may be centuries old, but ultimately the release is definitely worth the intensity of the process. Have a friend with you if you plan to use the energy of Samhain for this purpose. It is powerful, and you may need reassurance, protection and encouragement.

Releasing negativity

Samhain is also an excellent time for spellworking if you have experienced negative karmic residue or psychic attack. Confront your fears on this night, walk amongst them, then let them go. A salt water bath will help you release energetic forces and any build up of toxins that have occurred within your physical and etheric bodies. If you have had issues with someone or something, release its hold on you with love. Remember, this is not a dark, negative or evil festival, and hexing is completely out of the question. It is always a dubious and harmful practice: at this time full-force hexing will have the kind of karmic rebound that puts the law of the threefold return completely in the shade. Don't do it.

Celebrate!

It's lovely to get together with older relatives at this time and chat to them about their lives. Love them while they are with you – please don't wait until they've passed to honor them. A visit to any older person who may enjoy company or wish to share their time is another meaningful way to celebrate Samhain. Or have a feast with your friends and set a place for those who have passed on. Celebrate their memory rather than wallowing in sadness, and give thanks for the time you had together.

New Year's resolutions

Samhain marks the beginning of the energetic New Year, so it is the perfect time to look at what you want to improve or resolve in your life. Make a list of resolutions and things you want to achieve. You can also focus on mending relationships at this time. If you have any regrets or broken friendships, ask the Goddess and the God for help. At Samhain it will work magic. This may not mean that the next telephone call you get will be your long-lost love or broken-up-with best friend, but it does mean that peace will be in your heart, and that is always the best first step towards mending and healing the pain of broken relationships.

Supernatural signs

If relatives or people from your past who have died were associated with particular things, stay aware. You may hear an old song they loved, snatches of a conversation that has relevance to them or hear characters in films say lines that seem to come straight out of the mouth of a dead loved one. You may see a hat that reminds you of your mother, a car that a boyfriend used to drive, a tree that looks just like the one you used to climb at your aunt's house. A familiar perfume may mysteriously waft by, food may be served up that your grandpa ate. These are all signs that the spirits are near. Stay alert all Samhain evening for these moments. Even if you make no attempt to converse with the dead, they will try to reach you, so dreams may be a last resort for them. Better still, give over 15 minutes at sundown to say hello – it may save you some unsettling experiences!

Samhain altar

Apples – ruby red, sharp and sweet to taste.
Cider – made of apples.
A magical mirror (any mirror is fine, but a hand mirror is perfect).
Black scented candles.
Patchouli oil.
Fallen leaves.
Pictures of those loved and lost.

A Samhain spell for the beloved dead

Drape your altar with blood red fabric and light some black candles.

Cut three apples in half (cut horizontally to reveal the magical star at their heart).

Place pictures of those you have loved and lost (they need not have passed!) around you.

Open the magic circle.

Cut one more blood red apple in half with your boline. Cut it into nine – the number of completion – pieces.

Think of your loved ones who have passed, and write them a letter in purple ink. Give them your sorrow, your regrets, your ailments, your unfulfilled dreams. Give them your love, your respect, and express any sorrow you feel at their loss.

Spend some quiet time conversing with them. Ask them respectfully if they have anything they wish to share with you, and be ready to write down all that they tell you. Notice what happens.

Thank them for their messages or signs. Blow out the candles and close circle.

A Samhain spell for revealing the future

Go to an old well or source of water – a swimming pool, the sea, a bath or even a bowl of water will work well. Take with you a mirror. Stand with your back to the body of water and hold the scrying mirror up in front of you, so that the water is reflected in the surface of the mirror. This way you are scrying using both the reflective surfaces of the mirror and the water to gaze into, so you get a double whammy. Gaze into the mirror, focusing on the point over your left shoulder. Unfocus your eyes just a little and allow the images that come up in the mirror to form.

This form of scrying will allow you to see your future coming towards you. Remember that this is deeply symbolic. You may not literally see a vision, but whatever is there – a cloud in a specific shape, a telephone book opened to a page, a person walking by in a great hurry carrying yellow roses – all symbolize your coming year. Take the time to work out the meanings for yourself.

This is an old old Celtic spell that is still performed at wells in the Appalachian Mountains in the US. It's traditionally done at a well, and means leaning out over them. If you use a bowl of water, you can position it on the floor, then lie back to one side of it and hold the mirror so you can see both surfaces.

Samhain's names

Oidhche Shamna (pronounced Eee-uh How-nuh)
Feile na Marbh (pronounced Fay-na-Marbh)
Halloween
Day of the Dead
All Soul's Eve

Samhain's deities

Hecate

Lilith
Cerridwen
Morrigan
Kali
Calleach (pronounced Kal-eee-ach)
The Crone
Brigit

Samhain's sacred animals

Owl
Cat
Pig
Hawk
Eagle

Samhain's magical stones

Jet
Obsidian
Onyx
Smoky quartz
Spirit (fairy) quartz

Samhain's ritual plants

Apples
Corn
Mistletoe
Evergreen

Samhain's enchanted herbs

Rosemary
Sage
Mugwort
Allspice
Nightshade

Yule

The magic of the winter solstice

Yule (pronounced Yool), the festival to celebrate the rebirth of the sun, is held around December 20-23 each year in the northern hemisphere and around June 20-23 in the southern hemisphere, depending on the turning of the earth. It is the winter solstice, marking the longest night of the year.

The winter solstice is a magical time of energetic reawakening – both symbolically in our lives, and literally, as from this day forward the days start to lengthen and things begin to grow again. It is a time when the dark half of the year will start to recede, and the light half of the year is reborn.

These celestial truths are reflected in many ancient legends and myths – stories that contain archetypal truths, making mythology a kind of metaphorical repository of our sacred selves. When the sun God Lugh (pronounced Loo) is reborn, we too experience rebirth. These stories remind us of our connection to the earth's natural cycles, and how they are played out within our bodies, minds and souls. For our ancestors, these sacred tales kept them connected to the earth's cycles. From winter solstice night on, the sun rises just a little higher and stays in the sky just a little longer with each new day. What a relief this must have been to our ancestors, who sometimes must have felt that winter was eternal.

For us living in the world today, winter still has a profound impact on us. We too can feel unfit, chilly and less than motivated. But imagine how it must have felt for our ancestors – the hunger, the darkness, the lack of outdoor time, and wondering whether the sun God would come back to the tribe. With solstice night – the longest night of the year – came an outpouring of people's darkest fears – and simultaneously an outpouring of gratitude for the sun's return and the understanding that we are indeed divinely cared for. Winter solstice often heralded fervent thanks and uninhibited celebrations as it became clear that the sun God, known as Lugh to the Celts, had returned to help warm the frozen ground, and love the Goddess and the earth back to life once more.

So important were these ancient rites and festivals that pre-history's great architects were inspired to design and build powerful, magical astronomical observatories and sites of worship to mark them. Stonehenge, the powerful standing stone temple on Salisbury Plain in England, and Newgrange, an even more ancient site in Ireland, are just two examples of these ancient temples hewn from the earth to mark these special days. On the morning of the sabbat each one is aligned to, the first rays of the sun hit a certain spot, thus being not only a calendar to mark the turning of the year, but a repository of ancient wisdom.

But how does Yule manifest in the 21st century? Well, for starters, the winter solstice is still absolutely a time of renewal of the flow of energy. Think of how you feel at this time – like the blankets are your best friends, cozy and snug and maybe a little lazy, as if special projects, dreams and wishes belong on the back burner. You may still be holding on to relationships that need to be let go of, and sometimes you may find your material resources are stretched thin. Your rightful place has been in front of the fire, curled up with your Book of Shadows, a comforting familiar curled up next to you, enjoying a glass of red wine with hearty soups and stews.

If you find it difficult to motivate yourself or you think dark thoughts at this time, you may also be feeling the deep crone energy and her influence on the winter dark. But don't despair, soon the energy of the solstice will bring a lightening to your spirit and your energy, as the sun God and the maiden awaken across the land – and within you. As above, so below. The energy within has its cycle without, and you are connected to these cycles.

The energy of the wise, introverted crone will gently transform from this point forth – from the first sunrise following solstice night you'll feel a shift. Your attention will naturally be sparked by the world around you, and rather than feeling withdrawn, you will gradually become a little more outgoing with each day. Remember, this is all a gradual, natural process. Winter solstice is a particularly auspicious time to begin to work with a gathering of like-minded souls, in workshops, groups and covens. Even if you do nothing, consciously, unconsciously and naturally you will feel your energy start to flow anew, you'll begin to feel refreshed and re-energized and ready to take on the world – without actually having pushed or made an effort.

For those of us who are healing from the negative and twisted messages we have sometimes received regarding the white magical path, it can be challenging to keep Yule, especially in the northern hemisphere where the celebration of Christmas inundates our every sense. For those of us who are healing from having our natural beliefs rejected or reframed, dismissed and feared, it can be a challenge to celebrate a sabbat right in the midst of the feast of materialism that Christmas has become for many people.

However, remember that the roots of Christmas are in fact Yule – the forefathers of the Christian church proclaimed the birth of Christ to be at the same time as the birth of the sun God Lugh, overlaying ancient traditions with new. If we simply focus our attention on the rebirth of the sun, and of all that is new in our lives, and farewell with respect the wisdom of the crone, we will have a ceremony and a celebration that speaks to our hearts.

To really make the most of the solstice's powerful influence, try these simple, satisfying rituals. This is a superb time for rising early and gazing at the early morning rays, because they're going to be lengthening from now on. Turning your face to the sun means you are welcoming the new life it brings. Be prepared for changes after solstice time. Old habits, jobs and partners have a way of disappearing – reasonably painlessly, as it's the natural order of things – after this time. However if you're in the right place and with the right person, you will bloom and grow. It's all about moving into the most fertile patch possible, so you will really grow over the coming months.

Candle magic

Symbolically this solstice represents the power of light gently transforming the power of darkness, and in reality it means the darkest days of the year are definitely over. It's a time for wishing, for regeneration, rebirth, hope and the promise of the true growth of projects that are dear to you. And later, as you see the last days of winter leaving, feel the warmth in the air and see green shoots poking through the earth, you will realize that your fortunes have changed for the better. And you can really reap the benefits if you put a little magical intent into it. Intent is the very heart of spellworking. When combined with the planet's natural energy cycles, working with intent is a very powerful tool for manifesting.

On solstice night, light candles to the Goddess and the God. Here are some divine energies you may wish to honor.

Lugh The Celtic sun God, also known in some places as Llew, has very strong, powerful masculine energy. He is kind, vibrant, caring, nurturing and sexually passionate – just what many of us consider extremely desirable masculine traits. He can be invoked to help shift any negative experiences you have had with men, whether as partners or as friends. He assists in healing rifts between lovers and also shows men how to be balanced – how to be both masculine and caring, both strong and kind. With Lugh's help, men can show they care without feeling weak or threatened. He also loves laughter! He is a master of shapeshifting for personal safety too. He can show men how and when to shine, and when to change form in order to make it through lean times. Lugh was done some large injustices by those who wanted to diminish his strength and power and deny his Godliness. He became known as Lugh-chromain, or little stooping Lugh, and was thought of as simply a mischief maker. This name was Anglicized to Leprechaun, and he became a harmless figure of fun rather than the God of strength he really was. To me this symbolizes the loss of strength so many men felt as they were forbidden to reveal their wholeness, just as women have been too. But now Lugh is taking back his former shape, and once again coming into his beautiful, masculine power, as the wounded male energy on our planet heals, unfurls, and stands tall and strong once again.

Brigit As the Goddess of childbirth and a female warrior, Brigit helps the Goddess bring forth – or birth – the sun God. If you are wishing to conceive in the near future, or need assistance with childbirth or birthing new projects, simply ask for Brigit's assistance. Light a candle to her on solstice night and she will come to your side to aid you and help you find your inner source of strength.

Demeter The story of Demeter, the Greek Goddess of the grain, and her terrible grief at the loss of her daughter Persephone to the underworld for six months reflects the changes of the Wheel of the Year. Demeter's deep mourning creates the barren months of winter, when the earth lies fallow. Later, their joyful reunion brings with it the new life of spring in the form of abundant crops. The winter solstice is the time when Demeter would light a candle for her lost daughter, to give her strength and to guide her way home. Ask this mother Goddess for assistance and guidance regarding healing family issues, particularly in lifting and transforming any pain you may be feeling regarding your relationship with mothers, daughters or female relatives of any kind. Demeter will help bring you back together in gentle, natural ways.

Diana The huntress and Goddess of the moon, Diana really begins to show her strength come the winter solstice. If you are craving new challenges and desire to fulfill your ambitions, stand in your power and be who you truly are, call on her to assist you now. She will help you manifest your plans. She also helps us heal female friendships and to remain ourselves even when we are in a group of strong-minded friends.

Light your candles on solstice eve, and leave them burning throughout the evening. This little ritual symbolically welcomes the light. Our ancestors lit candles and kept fires burning on solstice eve as they felt it assisted the Goddess and gave her strength as she gave birth to the sun. Just as Brigit gained confidence and cheer from the light of the flame, you too will gain strength from your candles' soft light. As you light them, remember you are consciously aligning yourself with the power of gentle change in your own life – soon will come new ideas and fresh starts.

Yule healing

Powerful healing can occur before sunrise on the morning following solstice night. Some Witches keep vigil all night, as this can be a wonderful way to actually observe the rebirth taking place and to really reconnect that rebirth with your own personal plans and wishes. The amazing, wonderful feeling of those new rays on your face, your body and your skin will reinforce and revitalize you. Make sure you feel the magic – perhaps gather together with friends and celebrate this rebirth together by writing a list of things you wish to manifest as the sun's rays fall on your skin.

Hold your arms up to the sun as it rises, and draw down the newborn Lugh's rays to your physical and etheric bodies. Feel these rays gently healing any areas of hurt, darkness or sorrow within your body, and feel every cell reactivate with fresh golden energy. You may wish to picture the Sun card of your Oracle Tarot deck. Take this card out on the first morning after the solstice to assist you in focusing on this new energetic vibration.

On a practical, physical level, your body is craving sunshine and vitamin D after winter, and will thank you for this sun bath by providing you with increased vigor and an uplifted mood all day. And on a spiritual level, bathing in the new light is also very healing. This turning your face to the sun can be done every morning over the coming weeks – it is a way of welcoming in the new life it brings.

Although it is still the middle of winter, subtly you will begin, from this day forward, to feel the earth ready herself for change. This is the natural energy you will now be moving with.

The Yule log

On the eve of the solstice, decorate a log with pine cones, holly and mistletoe, and tie colorful ribbons around it. Later you can pop this in the fire and it will smell and look gorgeous – and of course you'll feel the magic. Afterwards take some ashes from the charred log, pop just the tiniest pinch into a glass of water and drink it down as you stand under the first rays of the morning sun. Keep a little part of your solstice log to rekindle next year's fire – it symbolically links your hopes as you move into this season of energy and growth with next season's new dreams and wishes.

Using mistletoe, a pagan symbol of regeneration and eternal life, is also a beautiful way of connecting with the fertile energy of this time of the year, but please do not ingest any, in any form, as it's a poisonous plant. Using it as a garland or to decorate your Yule log is safe however, and it will draw passion and potency to you. There's a reason we kiss under the mistletoe – in ancient times it was a fertility ritual. Mistletoe was considered a sacred plant by the druids and priestesses, and has long been associated with healing. The Romans also valued the plant as a symbol of peace, hence its current associations with Christmas.

A Yule spell for the future

If you have an open fireplace in your home, it is easy to cast this spell on solstice night. If not, light a mini-fire with twigs in your cauldron or create a mini-Yule log within the cauldron. I do feel compelled to persuade you to find a Yule log you can use – no matter how small, the energy is powerful.

This spell has its origins way, way back – it's literally prehistoric, and our ancestors worked this throughout the many years when the Wheel of the Year was in service to the Goddess, the God and the land.

You can cast this spell for any important area of your life. Just hold your question in your mind, charge it with intent, and say three times:

Fire red and burning well
Into your heart I cast this spell
Knowing that where I now dwell
My future soon to me you'll tell

Then, taking some ash wood, a wood sacred to this festival, gently poke the fire once, twice, three times.

Fast, plentiful sparking indicates a busy, almost hectic quality to the coming spring, with many demands on your time and seemingly little opportunity to fulfill your obligations. Affirm to yourself that you have enough time to complete all that you need to do. The Goddess will help you to prioritize if you ask her, and may even suggest those things that may be put aside as they are truly not your burdens to carry.

Several explosive pops indicates that you will soon experience some startling moments and surprises – there could be change, fast and unexpected, on the horizon this spring. If one of the pops is especially loud, this indicates that a new relationship, job or venture will really start with a bang!

Slow burning hisses and sizzles are telling you that you have time to further contemplate your life direction. The Goddess wishes you to know that once you have understood your part in the current manifestation that is your life, you will align yourself with a gentle shift in direction that will be fresh and wonderful for you.

Please do not put out your fire when you are done, but allow it to burn down safely.

This is a wonderful spell to work as a group. Declare your intentions and ask your magical questions out loud – or ask internally and keep the answers within, as sometimes silence is a powerful option. Either way, be sure to connect with the powerful magic of fire and newness via the Yule log.

Yule's names

Alban Arthur (Welsh), because King Arthur,
he of the Knights of the Round Table, Avalon and Camelot,
was born at Yule
Wassail (pronounced ves-hale, meaning be well!)
Festival of Dionysus

Yule's deities

Odin

Frigga

Freya

Skahdi (pronounced Skah-dee)

Cernunnos

Isis

Demeter

Dagda (pronounced DA-dah)

Brigit

The Oak king

Yule's sacred animals

Robin

Wren

Boar

Yule's magical stones

Ruby

Bloodstone

Carnelian

Citrine

Garnet

Yule's ritual plants

Ash

Yew

Laurel

Birch

Silver fir

Cranberries

Pine tree – for the Yule log

Cedar

Nuts

Yule's enchanted herbs

Sage

Bayberry

Thistle

Holly

Mistletoe

Sage

Imbolc

The joyful festival of the maiden

This wonderful festival is held on February 1/2 in the northern hemisphere, and is perfect for warming up and setting the mood for Saint Valentine's Day two weeks later.

In the southern hemisphere it is celebrated on August 1/2.

Imbolc (pronounced IM-bolk) is a festival that celebrates change – the change that heralds the approaching spring and all that takes place at this time of newness. Many animals give birth at this time, mother's milk begins to flow and the sun's warmth is stronger, for longer, each day.

And not a moment too soon. Sometimes, even for the most ardent lover of winter, there comes a time when you actually pine for warmth. When you long for the smell of jasmine. When you are tired of chapped lips, indoor spellworkings, log fires and mulled wine. You are craving the coming of the light. So while winter still holds you in its icy grasp, the sabbat of Imbolc comes along to remind us all that however dark the night, there will always be a dawn.

Winter can be cruel. Even in our deserts, which never know snow and frost, winter is a dormant time. All goes underground, and things can seem, especially after the drama and mystery of Samhain, kind of on hold. This is natural. Nature literally stops itself from moving forward until the time is right – we humans do too. It's natural to feel a little low, to lack energy, to eat more, to sleep more, to feel less enthused while the earth is sleeping.

And then comes Imbolc. Imbolc means, literally, "in the belly" (of the Mother), and its other name, Oimelc, means "ewe's milk", for Imbolc celebrates the coming of spring. And as soon as we've celebrated it everything seems to begin apace, so let your desires for the fresh new beginnings of spring slowly begin to take shape in your imagination.

This sabbat recognizes and honors the aspect of the triple goddess called the maiden – the fresh, the young, the naïve, the new, even a little unawakened, naïve and inexperienced. By embracing the aspects of this maiden energy, you can approach situations and people with open eyes and open heart. Coupled with wisdom and planning, this fresh approach to life can inspire your every moment to be happier and more energetic.

Her form is Bride (pronounced Brid-eee), although the Goddess Brigit is known by several names, which sometimes refer to her aspects or "ages" as either maiden, mother or crone – Bride being maiden, Brigit being Mother, Brigid being crone. This variation in her name can also come from cultural differences: for example, in Ireland she is most often known as Brigid, and in Glastonbury she is most often called Bridie.

Bride's energy gives you a chance for fresh starts and renewal – and much clearing of old debris can take place at this festival. Bride asks that you be fresh, new and independent. Think of the gardener, taking out the dead wood from winter, reworking and refreshing the soil prior to planting. Bride encourages you to replenish yourself, to feed and nourish your heart and soul, and clear away anything that is no longer for your own highest good. Bride also guides you to think of yourself – to be your own priority and to make your own growth take top position in your to-do list.

It's important to note that when we refer to the maiden aspect of the Goddess we are not saying "virgin". The maiden may be literally a virgin or she may not be – what the term means in this sense is unmarried and independent. And so issues of freedom, self-determination and identity within love relationships can come up for many of us at Imbolc. After the dark red crone energy of Samhain, the energy of Imbolc is blue and gold and young, which does not mean you have to feel 17 again – instead it's about rediscovering a time for hope and newness, which we all need.

We have less attachment to the past at Imbolc – we start to look forward once again. We can make decisions based on what feels right for who we are now, rather than working our way through a tangle of personal history and judgments. Imbolc allows us to move forward in unexpected ways that may feel awkward, but thus our habits are shed, and we rediscover who we truly are. It is all part of the natural cycle, and we can rediscover ourselves as tender, loving, beautiful creatures.

Imbolc is held in the northern hemisphere from the night of February and throughout the day of February 2 – the day known in the US as Groundhog Day. For a pop culture reference, the film Groundhog Day totally captures the somewhat stagnant energy preceding Imbolc. It is only by the fresh learnings and new approaches to the same old experiences that Bill Murray's character changes and grows and is able to break the spell he's caught in. And it's this shift, which breaks the spell of eternal winter, which is celebrated at Imbolc.

Spell for Imbolc

Imbolc is a fire festival, and this fire radiates warmth and light and reawakens us. To amplify this reawakening, take nine candles on Imbolc eve, and place them in a circle. Stand within the circle and light each candle in a deosil direction (clockwise in the northern hemisphere, counter-clockwise in the southern), welcoming in the new energy and allowing the candles' light to bathe away any old energy that no longer serves you.

This small, simple ritual clears away the hidden, the dark and any lingering sadness, grief or regret you may have experienced throughout winter's time of introspection. It is a wonderful practice to stay within this beautiful Bridie circle for nine minutes. After this you can simply move the candles to other areas of your home or place them safely on your altar to burn down.

From Imbolc to Beltane we can activate the new projects we wish to attract into our lives, so be sure to spend time on your projects in real terms – making calls, networking, paying attention to intuitive clues you receive – and allow anything that is no longer for your highest good to simply and gently dissolve and depart from your life.

Imbolc can bring change to us. Like a snake shedding its skin we ready ourselves for the new by letting go of things, but we can also feel exposed, tender and raw at this time. Instead of judging yourself for this sensitivity, understand that it will bring wonderful new experiences into your life.

Wake up your energy

Wash your face in the first dew on Imbolc morning. The dew will help refresh your looks, and tired eyes and sagging flesh will be firmed. This dew will cleanse you with its magical energies, and it is a very powerful energizing bath. It increases your self-love, which in turn increases your attractiveness and ability to draw love to you. See and feel yourself becoming more youthful with each drop you bathe your face in. This is not the time for the energy of the crone – no matter how old you are. Reinvigorate yourself.

Plant seedlings and bulbs. Daffodils and blue tulips represent the mood of Imbolc, and you will be reminded of your new wishes and rejuvenated hopes when they push through the soil closer to Beltane. In some climes, snow and frosts prevail throughout winter, and snowdrops and crocuses are among the first delicate harbingers of spring. To increase your own good fortune, tend your beautiful flowering plants carefully, and send them loving energy each day. This appreciation and gratitude will amplify your appreciation and gratitude for your own delicate new projects and your newfound sensitivity.

This is a wonderful time to space clear your home. Space clearing is all about finding, creating and maintaining an environment in which you feel safe, comfortable, stimulated and connected to the Goddess. Many people are sensitive to the atmosphere of their home, and will intuitively pick up on what is out of balance within an area without having had any formal training in esoteric or psychic matters. Space clearing is best conducted as regular spiritual maintenance – consider it at least as essential as regular cleaning. A house blessing is also a powerful and enjoyable way to celebrate Imbolc. This is a kind of energetic bath for your space that renews, invigorates and maintains the mental, physical and spiritual health of everyone within the home. It also increases the wonderful experiences, people and prosperity that are drawn to you. Your manifesting work can really take off once your space is healthy and cared for too.

Meditate in the early morning, and begin to rise earlier than you have been throughout winter. Meditation and early rising is the key to enriching your life. Bride's energy will be with you even more strongly the earlier you rise and bathe in the morning sun.

Plant a flowering shrub or tree. Make the soil ready, plant it with love, and adorn its branches with a ribbon upon which you have written a wish.

The Oracle Tarot and Imbolc

The Oracle Tarot cards most associated with this season are Change, the Star and the Empress. Put them on your altar and meditate on what they mean to you at this point in your life. Make notes in your Book of Shadows, then read the card meanings from the deck booklet. What does this combined reading mean to you? Over the years it will be fascinating to look back over what you have written and how you have changed from Imbolc to Imbolc.

You can also do a tarot spread for the coming year.

Shuffle the deck while thinking about the open space that is the year ahead of you. Clear your mind and meditate not on what you have done, but on what will come. Visualize fresh, green color and breathe in the scent of jasmine. When you are ready and have reached a state of calm and sweet joy, divide the pack into three. With your receiving hand (the one you don't write with), gather the pack together again. Then from the top of the deck draw five cards and lay them out in a row from left to right. Turn them over.

The first card represents the energy clinging from Samhain. The second card represents the current energy or influence. The third symbolizes upcoming fears, dreams and wishes. The fourth is the energy you need to balance. The fifth is your direction for the coming year.

Write up the results in your Book of Shadows and Light, interpreting the cards and their meanings to you right now.

Sensual Imbolc

Sensuality can be intense and powerful during Samhain – exciting, full of wisdom and teachings, yet energetically a little on the draining side. Come Imbolc, it's time to reacquaint yourself with tenderness, soft kisses and joy. While it is not as ecstatic in its sensual energy as Beltane, it is, like Beltane, a time of great fertility. Be mindful of this when having physical relationships in the green of the year, as women become pregnant very easily when the weather starts warming up.

Some of you may choose to practice celibacy and detach from relationships during the time between Imbolc and Beltane, because a hiatus from partnerships can assist in closely connecting us to our own maidenly, independent

Goddess and God aspects. However we need not go so far as to separate from wonderful, blissful relationships! Instead we can become more independent and really grow within our relationships at this time by using the wonderful qualities of the natural energies of Imbolc.

Imbolc's names

Imbolg
Oimelc (druidic) (Ewe-melk – literally, ewe-milk!)
Candlemas
Groundhog Day
Brigid's Day
Festival of Lights
Lupercus (festival of he-who-fends off the wolves,
pronounced Loopercoo)

Imbolc's deities

Bride
Brigid
Aradia
Athena
Inanna
Gaia
Oenghus
Eros

Imbolc's sacred animals

Swan
Ewes
All birthing animals
All lactating animals

Imbolc's magical stones

Clear quartz

Yellow tourmaline

Rose quartz

Hematite

Pearls

Imbolc's ritual plants

Ash tree – sacred to Brigit

Rowan tree

Oak tree

Heather

Violets

Sunflowers

Garlic

Imbolc's sacred herbs

Angelica

Basil

Bay laurel

Benzoin

Red clover

Dandelion

Dill

Ostara

The rites of spring

Ostara (pronounced Os-Tah-ra) – is the spring equinox festival named for the beautiful Goddess of fertility, Ostara – and is a time of balance and love. Day and night are of equal length, and all is in harmony. The exact time depends on the rotation of the earth and the sun each year, but Ostara is celebrated in the northern hemisphere around March 20-23, and in the southern hemisphere around September 20-23.

This is the magical, ancient and revered vernal, or spring, equinox. It is a truly sacred time, which signifies the coming of the light, of warmth, of the return of life itself. The myths of the Celts, Romans, Greeks, Norse and Egyptians all recognize the spring equinox as the new beginning. In old times it marked the festival of the fertility Goddess Ostara who, with her hare, brought fertility to the land and its people. People painted eggs and exchanged them in appreciation of her gifts – which later wand changed into Easter, keeping the symbols of the ancient worship and meaning. Interestingly, their Easter is celebrated each year on the first Sunday after the full moon following the vernal equinox.

In a physical sense, at the time of the spring and autumn equinoxes, our beautiful green and blue planet earth lies "flat" in her orbit of the sun. Neither her north nor her south poles are tilted into or away from the sun. She is fully facing it – there's no turning away. During the coming 24 hours she will rotate once on her axis, thus the sun's rays will have a unique opportunity to strike her surface equally from north to south poles, resulting in precisely twelve hours of day and twelve hours of night. From this day forward the light will increase with each day or degree she turns.

Spring in colder climates may seem to be more dramatic than in countries like Australia, but this is not so. In the Golden Bough, the 20th century bible of anthropology and myth by James Frazer, it recognizes that Australia has its own seasonal rebirth, even though the winters aren't as harsh as in many northern climes. "The natives of central Australia regularly practice magical ceremonies for the purpose of awakening the dormant energies of nature at what might be called the approach of the Australian spring. Nowhere apparently are the alterations of seasons more striking than in the deserts of central Australia, where at the end of a long period of drought the sandy and stony wilderness, over which the silence and desolation of death appeared to brood, is suddenly, after a few days of torrential rain, transformed into a landscape smiling with verdure and peopled with teeming multitudes of insects and lizards, of frogs and birds."

Even if the language is flowery, the point is well made. It is a sacred tradition to awaken spring through enacting sacred rites. The question is, what is the modern, often city-bound Witch to do?

To answer that, ask yourself what spring means to you. At its heart, it seems to me to be a natural revival, so ask yourself what needs reviving in your life. Hope? Passion? Health? Following your heart? Vocation?

The spring equinox is a time to celebrate the return of hope in your life. By connecting with the dance of nature, you connect to your own being. It's not a coincidence that humans become more sluggish during winter and that seasonal depression can take hold. We are creatures just as the blades of grass and small animals are – we need the light to live, and everything we live upon needs it too. We are reminded at this time to acknowledge our place in the web of life, not as some kind of winner at the top of a mythical food chain, but as a part of life, affecting it and absorbed by it, influencing it yes, but no more powerful than any other agent of life. If we honor our place in life, we will have many more years on this planet. By inhabiting nature gladly and fully, we will continue to live and be guardians of the planet. If we do not, we will bring about our own catastrophic destruction.

Ostara is an ideal time to make some kind of spiritual

pilgrimage. The solstices and equinoxes are times when people seeking a spiritual connection to the land visit landmarks like Stonehenge in England, Sedona in the US, Machu Picchu in Peru and Mount Warning in Australia.

Astronomically, we are witnessing our own promise of life. One way to commemorate the life force of the spring equinox is to take an egg and paint it with symbols of the God and the Goddess, who are in complete harmony at the time of the vernal equinox, just as they are at the autumn equinox. Thus it is a favored time to work out power balances in relationships, to handfast or marry, or to conceive a child.

It is also a great time to literally start again. At the basis of spring is creative growth and fertility – the energy that fuels the obvious displays of later spring and summer. But first the sap must rise and your energy increase. Your energy will naturally have been changing since the winter solstice – the sluggishness of the cold times becomes easier to shrug off once the shortest, darkest day is past. But now you need to reactivate your core energy.

Spring into spring

Here's a simple way to activate and increase your energy. Stand facing the sun each day. Feel its rays. Meditate on that which you desire to grow in your life. After doing this, take a colored ribbon and tie it to a branch of a flowering tree (jasmine, magnolia or fruit trees are perfect). If you have two areas you desire growth in, choose two ribbons. Choose the colors to correspond to that which needs stimulation – such as red for passion and courage, pink for love, green for prosperity and career, blue for healing. Weave your intent into the ribbons then tie them about your branch with care.

As the spring days advance, and as the sun lengthens its stay in the sky on your half of the planet, your plant will unfurl and reach towards the light – this is exactly the growth you need to emulate. There comes a time when staying dormant and static becomes far more uncomfortable than the pain we imagine there is in risk taking, growth and reaching out. Spring is the time for personal growth – the timing means that any chances you take are in harmony with the energy of the season and so your chances of success are magnified. You will literally be going with the flow.

If your plant flowers sooner than you expect, or if the flowers struggle to appear, these are all portents of your desires, and by reading the growth patterns of the flowers you can see where you need to focus your energies.

Ostara spell for new beginnings

This is based on the Spell for New Beginnings from my card deck Magical Spell Cards, a portable, wonderful way of always having a spell recipe available...

At Ostara, we celebrate the coming of spring and its healing energies, which refreshes our lives and reawakens us to creating optimum conditions for new projects, new energy and a sense of new self-love in our lives.

When we work this spell at Ostara, we participate in truly activating our own rebirth. Its magic will guide you to a place where you are welcoming your future and celebrating the new energy in your present.

You will need:

A feather gathered from a natural place.

A sea shell found along the shore.

Bergamot essential oil.

A small green candle.

The feather represents air, the seashell water, the oil earth and the candle fire – but you can find any other object that represents each element to you, depending on where you live – obviously a sea shell from the sea shore is going to be tricky if you live in the snowy mountains or near a desert. Don't ever stress about the ingredients being too literal – the point is to go out into nature and find an object that is meaningful to you, so just use your intuition and what feels right to you, because intent is always the most important thing.

Space cleanse your home with a new broom, then ground this cleansing with the ringing of a bell deosil (clockwise in the northern hemisphere, counter-clockwise in the southern) throughout your home. Consecrate the corners of each room with water you have blessed.

On your altar, burn the oil, light your candle, place your seashell and feather, and ask the Goddess Ostara for blessings and bounty as you enter this new season.

Connect with her during meditation, and be prepared to receive messages of inspiration from her. Always have your Book of Shadows and Light close by when spellworking so you can record these messages as soon as they come to you.

Once your candle has burned down, the spell is complete. Thank Ostara for her messages, and feel her beautiful energy flow through you, inspire you, fill you with love and the fresh, new, vital energy of spring.

Blessed be.

An Ostara ritual

Set up your springtime altar with the following:
Green cloth.
Green and golden candles, for the element of fire.
Seeds, for the element of earth.
A cone or stick of jasmine incense, for the element of air.

Spring water or dew collected on equinox morning, for the element of water.

Salt, for cleansing and purity of spirit and intent.

Cast the magic circle.

Light the candles and the incense and raise each of the four elemental objects one after the other, invoking the elements. Welcome the Goddess and the God.

Write three wishes down the length of three separate ribbons, and weave these together.

Place them on your magical altar. You can later use this charged magical binding at Beltane as part of the ribbon ritual.

Thank the elements and the God and the Goddess. Close the circle.

Make a magical wand for spring

As this is the season of air it is an auspicious time to make your own magical wand, which is the magical tool that corresponds to the element of air. It will have been created in the perfect season and will have great power. Again this can be as elaborate or as simple as you like. Some of you may wish to find a twig or small branch on the forest floor and use it just as it was gifted to you by nature herself. Or you can carve it, paint it or adorn it with crystals, ribbons or feathers. Be guided by your intuition to create the perfect magical tool for you.

Ostara's names

Alban Eiler (Welsh, pronounced Olbahn Isler, meaning light
of the earth)
The day of trees
Oestre
Lady Day
Easter
Gwyl Canol Gwenwynol

Ostara's deities

Persephone

Aphrodite

Ostara

Thoth

Blodeuwedd

Rhiannon

Ostara's sacred animals

The hare

All baby animals

Rabbits

Fauns

The chicken, duck, goose – all birds – for their sacred eggs

Ostara's magical stones

Moonstone

Aquamarine

Rose quartz

Moss agate

Green moonstone

Ostara's ritual plants

All bulbs

Jasmine

Daffodils

Narcissus

Anything that flowers/grows in your region at spring

Buttercups

Violets

Roses

Lilies

Ostara's enchanted herbs

Sage
Frankincense
Myrrh
Ginger
All herbs – this is the time to plant your
magical herb garden

Beltane

The sacred rites of love

Beltane (pronounced Bel-tayne) is the fire festival celebrating fertility, sensuality and bringing into balance the male and the female energies of our beautiful planet. It also celebrates passionate unions and commitments to soulmates. It is held in the northern hemisphere on April 30/May 1, and on October 31/November 1 in the southern hemisphere.

At Samhain and Beltane, the veil between the worlds is at its thinnest. Both these festivals merge the worlds of the spirit and magic with the world of men and women. But while the atmosphere and influences of Samhain are about the underworld and going into the earth, Beltane is about new life springing from it.

It is a celebration of fertility, both literal and metaphorical, so it is the perfect time to conceive of new ideas and new projects. The old Irish word Bealtaine means "bright fire", and in ancient times this festival was celebrated with the Beltane fires, which were thought to lend life to the springtime sun. One of the agricultural festivals, rituals were enacted to ensure the fertility of the land. Cattle were driven through the fires to purify them, and couples leaped across them and passed through the smoke for good luck. The Goddess would lie with the God to bring forth new life, and at night people made love outside in the fields as a symbolic re-enactment of this sacred marriage, this contract with the land.

In ancient times, under Celtic tradition, those who were joined at Beltane were in fact married in the eyes of the God and the Goddess – this was called a green marriage. If, however, either partner decided to end the union, this was permissible after one year and one day, if children had not been born. This is carried through both in Wiccan handfastings – where the union is renewed every year and a day – and in Christian wedding ceremonies, which are often held in springtime, at the very height of the fertile season.

The joy of this springtime festival was also represented with flowers. People would "bring in the May", hence its other name of May Day – going into the forest at dawn to pick flowers to decorate their homes, find a maypole to dance around and bathe their faces in the morning dew.

A woman would be chosen to represent the Goddess in this mystical marriage. In the northern hemisphere she is known as the May Queen, but in the southern hemisphere, where Beltane falls on November 1, she is the Beltane bride. Celebrate the Goddess's approach by weaving fresh flowers into your hair – her favourites are jasmine, gardenia and rose. And, for beauty, it is said that if you find dew under ivy or oak (although grass will do too) on this morning, bathe your face and eyes in it, to be beautiful all year long.

In Welsh mythology a lady was made from flowers to be the consort of the old king – her name was Blodeuwedd. But at night she transformed into an owl, to hunt, to be free, to learn of all the wild things and to find a lover – a younger man she chose for herself. Beltane is all about passion, love and the will of the Goddess.

Beltane and its rites have been played out from ancient times, in Celtic celebrations and Roman fertility festivals through to the pagan variations still celebrated today.

Despite all attempts to ban the celebration – it was almost extinguished in the fifth and sixth centuries when the Church took hold of the British Isles, and then banned, strictly, and distorted during the Burning Times of the 14th to 18th centuries in an attempt to stamp out the ancient and sacred customs – the purifying fires of Beltane were never truly put out. Beltane is ingrained in the consciousness of our culture.

Its disguises are manifold. Spring fever, summer holidays, all night parties, fires on the beach, flowers in the hair, jasmine in gardens, lovers pleasuring each other in the deep of the forest, marriages in high spring. Remember children's rhymes too, like "Jack be nimble, Jack be quick, Jack jump over the candlestick." Yes, that's referring to Jack o' the Green, a Beltane nature figure, and the jumping of the Beltane fires. All these things and more are Beltane.

At Beltane with Avalon's sacred, ancient oak.

Tracing the development of a ritual

Celtic culture: The late spring festival Beltane, on May 1, marked the movement of cattle and villagers to the summer fields. Fires were lit.

Ancient Roman times: Also at the beginning of May,

Romans celebrated the Flora festival, in honor of Flora, the Goddess of flowers.

Roman empire: Later the Flora festival merged with the Celtic Beltane traditions.

Christian: From around the 4th and 5th centuries, Beltane fires and the maypole were banned, and May Day became the celebration of the virgin.

Catholic May Day: Mary bedecked in wreaths.

Mother's Day: Held in May in western cultures in both southern and northern hemispheres, this is a direct descendant of the pagan May Day.

Beltane altar

Your altar should be covered in green cloth – silk if possible, as it is a natural fibre and a luxurious one.

Decorate your altar with green and white candles – in multiples of three to represent the God, the Goddess and the children they will bear.

If you can, move your altar out of doors, or set one up in a natural place.

If you wish to recreate this indoors, use flowers and branches of flowering trees.

Wear green, cherry or berry hues, to reflect the berries and fruits of the earth.

Wear a flower wreath in your hair – the Beltane crown – and flavour your wine or juice with the herb sweet woodruff – soak it in your wine or mead for 15 minutes. You can drink this potion with your lover if you wish, to enhance the Beltane ecstasy to come.

Adorn your altar and fill your cauldron with the following sacred tree twigs: oak, ash, thorn, rowan, apple, birch, alder, maple, elm and hawthorn. This will be tricky if you live in the southern hemisphere, so use native plants if you wish – gum, bottlebrush and wattle, or create your own sacred plants. Consult any of Ian White's bushflower books for more help, or use your imagination.

Ideal plants and herbs for your Beltane altar include: all-heal, daffodil, dogwood, marjoram, thistle, broom and rose.

A Beltane ritual

Bathe, and dress in your ceremonial garments.

Stand with your back to your altar and outstretch your right arm, pointing your index finger. Walk deosil, saying: "It is now the sacred space between the worlds is made."

Visualize a sacred shield of white light and etheric energy at the boundaries of your circle, then light your candles and incense.

Raise a candle, and say: "This circle is blessed by fire."

Hold up the incense and say: "This circle is blessed by air."

Hold up the bowl of salt or earth and say: "This circle is blessed by earth."

Last, hold up your bowl of water (dew, collected that morning, would be powerful) and say: "This circle is blessed by water."

Then chant the following invocation three times:

Oh Mother Goddess, queen of the night and of the earth

Oh Father God, king of the day and of the forests

We celebrate your union as nature blooms with bounty and hues

We anoint and worship thee.

Burn your twigs in the cauldron, and feel the fires burning away old cares, old worries and any disturbing elements. This is the new time, the blooming time, and the Goddess wishes you to resonate with the life force of the rich and splendid earth and the summer joy she brings.

Write down your wishes for the new season if you want to at this time.

Alow the fire to burn itself out, safely.

Close the circle.

Now it's time to celebrate!

Be with others tonight – stay up and watch the day come in if you can, a truly magical experience. It's also a great time to consummate a relationship.

Erotic rituals

For many people, Beltane is the most erotic festival of the year. Celebrate it by indulging your senses and feasting on your love – for yourself, and for each other.

* Strew rose petals on your bed, or in the garden, then make love on them on Beltane night.

* Drink wine flavoured with meadowsweet.

* Make love three times and stay up all night.

* Bathe in a bath scented with jasmine oil.

* Skyclad, leap over a lit bonfire, or a small green candle, together. Remember Jack be nimble?

Spell to find a lover at Beltane

Weave a garland of flowers, made from jasmine, ivy and rose (other flowers are fine –wildflowers are best), and hang it on the door of the one you desire on Beltane Day. You could email your intended an e-garland if they are a long way from you. You can be sure you will receive a sign over the next four weeks indicating their feelings for you.

If you wish to pledge your love, jump together over a Beltane fire!

Single at Beltane?

If you are single and wondering how to go about indulging in the Beltane erotic fever, remember, this is one time of the year when it is considered natural and right to have sex without strings. Or you can indulge in sex rites with yourself. Whether you are single and wish to have sex with another, or prefer to indulge yourself, there are no rules at Beltane – except to celebrate your sensual self, and to respect yourself and your partner.

You do need to be aware when celebrating Beltane that although it's a celebration of fertility, and although having sex outside, preferably on the grass, preferably covered in the Beltane dew, is a wonderful way to celebrate, it's also a time when you may be inclined to throw caution to the winds. Please be careful. Practice safe sex at all times, unless you fully intend to take the Beltane process all the way and have children in the following year.

The traditional maypole

Do you remember dancing around the maypole as a child, watching the ribbons weave in and out as you and your classmates wove amongst each other? Did you ever think then that you were performing a pagan rite?

In ancient times the maypole was a tall wooden pole of hawthorn or birch, or a tree, decorated with flowers and greenery and ribbons. It was set up on the village green, and symbolized springtime and fertility, the spirit of the forest entering the heart of the village. For many, the Tree of Winding represents our deep respect and worship of trees – we give thanks for the life they breathe into us. On another level the tree, or maypole, represents the God, and the ribbons the Goddess. The winding represents their coming together, joining and rebalancing at this sacred time of year. This activity is not only joyous and delightful, full of love and laughter, but it energetically rebalances the energies of masculine and feminine, both in the land, on the etheric plane, and within those who participate in the sacred dance.

The ancient Saxons had an oak pillar, the Irminsul, which was said to connect heaven and earth, reflecting the Nordic tale of Odin hanging from the Tree of Life upside down in order to gain knowledge. In Sweden and other northern countries the maypole represented the joining of male and female.

The maypole, which has its roots in the Flora festivals of ancient Roman times, has been a somewhat contentious symbol of Beltane. It has been banned and revived many times in cultures across Europe. In France it changed its name, the May Tree becoming the Tree of Liberty and the symbol of the French Revolution.

For many, this beautiful rite is all about tree worship, nothing more. For me, I choose to view the maypole as the great symbol of the Tree of Life, from which all life in all its forms can spring. Also, a maypole is incomplete without its winding ribbons, and so, should you see it as a symbol of the priapic God, you could address that perceived imbalance by viewing the ribbons as the blood ties of women. Some of you may even want to use white, red and black ribbons, to represent the maiden, mother and crone.

If you want to celebrate Beltane with a maypole you do not have to actually fell a tree. Some people find this not only impractical, but would rather celebrate with a live tree. Others use a male to literally be the pole, holding a circle tied with ribbons above his head, and dance around him, weaving the ribbons around him, until he is totally enveloped by them. If you do fell a small tree – birch is traditional – you can use the wood for burning during festival rites later in the year.

You will need lots of green ribbons, at least two metres in length. Find all hues of green, from sea green to spiky limes to soft greeny grays. Or if you would prefer, use different colors that are meaningful for you.

You can do this on your own, or you can gather together with others, and wind the ribbons around and around the winding tree, the Beltane pole or the maypole, whatever you wish to call it. It's traditional for men and women to stand facing each other and to dance through in a formation which causes the ribbons to intertwine. But you don't have to get worked up over this issue. Some covens allow their winding to be spontaneous, others like to create a formal pattern. Whichever way you do it, it is important that you keep a part of the braid from the Beltane pole for your altar and for use later in the year.

After you have finished with it for Beltane, breathe on the braid – for air. Lick it – for water. Wear it around one ankle for a day – for earth. For into it is woven the hopes and dreams and magical wishes for the new season of summer.

The fairy queen

Beltane is about new life, so it is at this time that we can engage with the elementals, or nature spirits. It is the time when you may go out at night and wait under an oak – a Moreton Bay fig or an old gum is also sacred – to hear the fairy bells ringing as the fairy queen passes.

Fire, fire, burning bright, in the forest, in the night.

There is a murmur of fairy voices, the jingling bells of the fairy queen's horse, the smell of fires across the land, the sight of lovers leaping the fire together, making love all night, coupling with who they choose, the sympathetic magic of fertility, to bring life and lusty crops, bountiful animals, strong young life, a future generation, a pole made of a sacred tree, with men and women weaving intricate patterns from the berry red and sea green ribbons, and the queen, a fair young woman crowned in flowers, dressed in white, her breasts exposed. The queen of the land, the Goddess, who will lie with the God to bring forth new life. And the fairy folk, intermingling and mating with menfolk, in order to merge our races and create new and magical life.

Upon all this gazes the fairy queen, who searches for a lover she can take for seven long years to her kingdom between the worlds. Don't look if you hear her bells, unless you wish to be chosen as her consort. As she looks upon your face she may choose you, and you could wander, lost, in the world between worlds for seven years.

Beltane's names

Beltaine
May Day
Celtic Flower Festival
Cetsamhain (the opposite of Samhain, pronounced Set-sowen)

Beltane's deities

Bel
The Horned God/Cernunnos
Flora
The Green Man
Minerva
Sheela na Gig
Rhiannon
Blodeuwedd

Aphrodite
Freya
Morgan le Fey

Beltane's sacred animals

Honey bees
Lambs
Deer
Calves

Beltane's magical stones

Citrine
Clear quartz
Golden tiger's eye
Amber
Topaz
Sunstone
Malachite
Orange calcite

Beltane's ritual plants

All nuts and seeds – anything that can grow (symbolizing
fertility)
Honey
Strawberries
Grapes
Daffodils
Roses
Twigs from each of these were burnt in the fires:
Oak
Ash

Thorn

Rowan

Apple

Birch

Alder

Maple

Elm

Gorse

Holly

Hawthorn

Beltane's enchanted herbs

Cinnamon

All-heal

Dogwood

Marjoram

Thistle

Vanilla

Litha

The magic of the summer solstice

Litha (pronounced Lee-tha) is the festival of the summer solstice, and is celebrated in the northern hemisphere around June 20-23, and in the southern hemisphere around December 20-23. It marks the longest day of the year, and is a time of midsummer madness and delight.

Litha is a wonderful festival – a time of joy tinged with regret as we greet the sun at its peak. Joy because it is the ultimate expression of sun power, and regret as this peak signifies that the sun will soon begin to turn its face away from us as the days shorten and the nights lengthen again

– but not until we have celebrated Litha's triumphant light.

Both symbolically and literally, the summer solstice is a time of celebration, ripeness, warmth, joy, heat and lust. It is the longest day of the year and the shortest night. It is a time for the God and the Goddess to reach fulfillment and perfect companionship. Relationships may have reached a peak over the past two months, and can now grow into maturity. Issues may come up over the next month as you feel your high priestess energy start to flow anew.

Litha represents the height of abundance, the fullness of beauty, a kind of peak experience. Its magic is flowing strongly, and we can make powerful connections with the fairy realm at this time. Litha also is the feast of the fairy, and at this time, doors between worlds open, and we can peek through and dwell for just a little time in the Otherworld of the fairies – a place where youth is everlasting, and enchantment, plenty, beauty, love and joy are ours for all time. For just a moment, Litha gives us a glimpse of life in all its perfection. It encourages us to seize the day, and to dwell completely in the magic of the present moment.

Litha is a time to consolidate your strengths and clear away negative thoughts and energies. It is a time to be joyful and full of life, while at the same time remaining mindful of the waning of the light from now until Yule. It is a time of beauty, love, strength, energy, rejoicing in the warmth of the sun, and the promise of the fruitfulness to come. Although the days begin to grow shorter after Litha, the time of abundance and harvest is still to come. It's also a great time to celebrate the bounty of the year – what you have achieved, what you have received – and is traditionally a time to meet up with friends and feast in celebration of life itself.

It is also a time when work may feel like an irrelevant

distraction, that being indoors is wrong. Maybe you've been finding it hard to concentrate on important issues, and have felt compelled to be social with friends as much as possible. You may also have been feeling a growing optimism, as though dreams and wishes can come true. Your rightful place has been with friends outside, on the beach, in the fields, eating the fruits of the land and sharing good times, talk and love. Summer romance is likely to have been on the agenda, as midsummer magic makes us feel warm and predisposed to love. You may, literally, have been burning the candle at both ends.

After Litha you may feel the need to cleanse, detox, rest and take time out from large gatherings. Drink a little fresh lemon juice in warm water each morning, and do 20 minutes of cleansing, stretching yoga or another physical discipline. This will help to battle the midsummer madness that may have taken its toll over the last two months. You'll need to do this too – otherwise you can run the risk of actually impairing your physical and mental health, so slow down a little, take some time out, refresh and re-energize as the sun begins to shorten its rays.

But now it is time to celebrate Litha, to celebrate the warmth, the ripeness, the time of your dreams coming to fruition. At Litha your creative powers are at their peak, so allow ideas to come to the surface, and begin to express them, to make them manifest in the world. Your imagination will flow, and your life will take on a more magical quality the more closely aligned you become to your instincts, your creativity and your spontaneity. Sensuality, living naturally, experiencing the world through your taste and touch, your sight, smell and hearing, is the gift of Litha.

This is a superb time for rising early and gazing at the

early morning rays – because they're going to be lessening in strength from now on. Turning your face to the sun also means you are prepared to farewell parts of the new life it has brought to you. Be prepared for changes after solstice time. Bad habits, bad jobs and bad relationships have a weird way of becoming difficult to deal with after this time – it's like some of the bloom has gone off the romance, and the hard work of getting to know each other intimately can begin.

However, if you're in the right place and with the right person, the trust and love you have built up during summer's days will sustain you in the more difficult times. It's all about moving through life's tests with a heart full of hope. Litha is definitely a fine time to gather what you need, while it is still there – which is why it is traditionally the harvesting time.

In ancient times it was the period of the year when you would harvest your magical and medicinal herbs, and this is still true today. In the old days, in the old way, we would cut them with a boline by the light of the moon. A boline is a small knife, like an athame, but this is used to cut magical herbs and food, while an athame is used only to cut and direct energy. Finding and picking herbs on the night of the summer solstice – midsummer night's eve – will render them even more magical. Make sure you leave two thirds of the bush for regeneration, and use what you have picked through the coming months.

Symbolically this solstice represents the power of the dark returning to triumph over the light, and in reality it means the brightest days of the year are soon to be over. As you begin to contemplate the days of summer leaving, feel the morning air start to cool and see flowers begin to fall and growth begin to slow, you will see that the time for gathering, preparing, contemplation and cleansing has begun. But that's all for contemplation after this fun festival. For now, enjoy the sunshine and feel yourself warmed by the sun God's rays. You can really benefit from its radiant energy with a little magical effort.

The Sun God

Litha is a sun ceremony, and as such, some White magical practitioners consider it to be primarily masculine in feel. The God and the Goddess can always be represented symbolically in ceremony, and for this ritual you may wish to emphasize the God more than you would at Samhain, for example. This is very much an individual choice, however, and all practitioners will have to think this issue through for themselves. Some spellcasters who feel very strongly that this is an Apollonian festival may choose to exclude the Goddess altogether.

For others who feel that without the Goddess there is no life, embrace the Goddess Kupala (pronounced Koo-pah-lah), a Slavonic Goddess associated with fire, sorcery and sex, whose festival, Kupala's Night, falls on the summer solstice. Her holy fires on this night have the power to cleanse both body and soul, and her followers formed chanting rings around her bonfires. Similar to Beltane, many would leap through the fires, enjoying the literal and symbolic effects for cleansing this time, rather than to stimulate the urge to mate and breed.

A Litha ceremony

You'll need:

A golden altar cloth.

Summertime herbs. Choose from whatever is growing vigorously in your region.

Summertime flowers. The sunflower is a great flower to

include, as its shape mirrors that of the sun, which this festival celebrates. Choose also a blooming night flower to honor the Goddess if you wish. Kupala is said to be the mistress of a mysterious night flower that blooms once a year – to pick it is to dispel lower energetic life forms from your auric field.

A cup of fresh spring water, for water.

Incense, for air. Choose one that evokes the fullness of summer.

Your cauldron, or a golden candle, for fire.

Sea salt – perfect for coastal dwellers – for earth.

Golden candles.

Flowers could also include rose, wisteria, plumeria or, if you live in an arid climate, even the smallest green thing that pushes its way through the earth. The Australian climate, long with many other countries, varies enormously, and as so much of the land is in drought, for some people fresh growing herbs will be impossible to find. I probably do not need to remind you to take great care with your cauldron or candle, especially if working out doors. Bushfires are a terrible thing for wildlife and the earth, so please, do not work anything more than symbolically out of doors – working on the beach is safe, but take great care in the bush, as the merest spark can ignite an enormous raging fire.

Remember we are working symbolically – so whatever you choose must work for the sabbat, and for you on a personal level. If a flower or object speaks to you, then use it. If you prefer sand or earth to sea salt, please substitute. If you wish to use grevillea instead of wisteria feel free, again, to choose what works for you. Nothing that grows from this earth is too humble to be recognized as sacred.

Prior to this ceremony starting, smudge your home or your altar's surroundings with a smudge stick, which are easily purchased from health stores or New Age outlets. This will allow you to focus, as the energy of this time of year can be quite scattered.

Emotionally, this can be a great ceremony for really releasing a great deal of energy. It is a very passionate and expressive time of year, so you can really benefit by letting go and expressing your energy. However, whispering is just as appropriate as making a lot of noise if you feel shy. Follow your heartsong.

Hold your bowl of spring water aloft and say: "I welcome the spirits of the water."

Hold your bowl of sea salt/earth/sand and say: "I welcome the spirits of the earth."

Hold your incense stick, alight, aloft and say: "I welcome the spirits of the air."

Hold your candle, aflame, aloft and say: "I welcome and rejoice in the spirits of the fire."

Then say three times:
Apollo's fires, Kupala's nights
The sun is highest, I see the night
Is coming fast and coming near
The summer's flames I do draw near
The beach, the sand, the sea, the earth
The growing time that gave me birth
I worship life at its full bloom
The wheel of life turns with the moon
The Horned God, the Midsummer King
The blessings of summer that you bring.

Raise you athame towards the sun, and say: "Great God and Goddess united now, I draw down your strength and warmth to me. We are one."

Replace your athame on the altar then, standing, close your eyes and feel, without judgment, any areas of your life that may have caused you or others harm. Allow the sun's healing energy to dissolve the dark spots in your own auric field, and breathe deeply.

Visualize the energy of the sun at its peak flowing into you, through you, around you. Talk with the God and the Goddess if you wish. Thank them for good times, and release to them your fears and worries.

Once you have finished reflecting, you may open your eyes, and cast a spell which you wish to see come to fruition over the coming months.

A midsummer night's eve

Litha is the time when the doors open between worlds, and through them flow the fairy folk, delighted to be able to connect with us. Enchanting, mischievous and naughty, teaching us how to play, revere nature and forget to clock-time. Our fairy-selves also come out to play. We may be inclined to make more mischief and merriment than at any other time!

Fairy influences at Litha can see us lose ourselves in daydreams, wander off, and experience the cyclic nature of reality in the land of the fae.

There are several ways to draw fairies to us at Litha. One is to smear pollen across our eyelids, allowing us to "see" them. Another is to carry a sprig of thyme on us, in a pocket or hanging from our neck or wrist. You can also leave out small saucers of mead, milk, honey and bread, food offerings for the fairy folk, or hang fairy lights from your home, trees and garden, creating a sparkling pathway for humans and fairy folk to follow and find each other.

A wonderful celebration for Litha is to invite friends and family around for a feast. Hang fairy lights, make food for both the human and the fairy guests, and stay up all night cavorting with your elemental friends, playing music, lighting a bonfire and farewelling the fullness of the sun.

It's also a wonderful night for skyclad workings – the weather is generally very conducive to disrobing and being at one with the universe. At this time we see ourselves as the perfect manifestations of the God and the Goddess that we are – and we won't shiver when we disrobe!

Also remember that whenever you see a ladybug, and when one alights on you, the fairies are sending you a message. If you can catch one – without hurting it! – whisper your message to the fairies and the ladybug will carry it off straight to fairyland.

Fairies love to play in gardens, so always leave a tiny bit of your garden untended. This gives them an area to play in and work with, and makes them feel that you are cultivating a little wild fairyland amidst the human realm, so they know you welcome them! It also helps you to cultivate the same wildness within yourself – reminding you to be free, to have fun, and to allow life to flow both within you and around you.

Litha's names

Alban Hefin or Alban Heruin (pronounced Al-bahn Heffin, and meaning Light of the Shore)
Midsummer
Feast of the Fairy
Celtic Oak Festival
Althing (All-thing)

Litha's deities

Lugh

Apollo

Aine – Queen of the Fae

Habondia

The Green Man

Kupala

Dana

Gwydion

Thor

Cerridwen (her cauldron is Litha's symbol)

Litha's sacred animals

The horse

Robins, larks, wrens – all songbirds

And it's a wonderful time to bring home a pet to care for
and bond with

Litha's magical stones

Amethyst

Malachite

Golden topaz

Opal

Lapis lazuli

Quartz

Azurite

Litha's ritual plants

Orange tree

Lemon tree

Daisy

Honeysuckle

Lavender

Carnation

Litha's enchanted herbs

Lemon verbena

Lemon vervain

Mugwort

Chamomile

Wild thyme

Lughnasadh

The feast of the shadowlands

Lughnasadh (pronounced Loo-nah-sah) is a beautiful harvest festival held each year on August 1/2 in the northern hemisphere and on February 1/2 in the southern hemisphere. It is a time to celebrate what you have harvested in your own life over the past year.

Lughnasadh is named after Lugh, the Celtic God of light and wisdom. At this special time, towards the end of summer, bread from the first harvest was eaten in thanks, Catherine wheels lit up the night, corn dollies were dressed and honored, bread was baked and sacrifices made – this is the mysterious and little-understood festival of Lughnasadh.

While the sun still shines strongly, this day marks the coming of the shadows and the lengthening of the dark – the nearing of the crone energy that will be fully expressed at Samhain. The maiden (Beltane) has become the mother (Litha) and the mother now faces growing older and the approach of her crone-time. At Lughnasadh we are reminded that even amidst bounty, the wheel turns; after the harvest, fruit falls. Personally it could mean your time has come to let go of people, to allow change to come, to accept growing older, and to understand that wisdom can be a challenge.

If you pay attention you'll notice signs of summer's passing – the lowering of the sun's arc in the sky, a lack of new growth, a slowing of the energy and a need to think of the future, while at the same time feeling reluctant to move on. It is the perfect time for industry and planning, to be busy and start planning for winter. This can be literal – you can conserve or can foods and harvest herbs for drying – or you can start to look at the next six months and think of where you would like to be when the Wheel of the Year has turned a further 180 degrees. Spend some time on this day thinking about what you need to do, personally, practically or professionally, to be ready for the cold, symbolically harsh times ahead. This is also a good time to banish fears.

Lughnasadh is a harvest festival too, a time to reap the bounty of summer's fruits and endeavors and to celebrate life. This makes it a time of thanksgiving for what you have received, and also a time of giving back to show your appreciation. Spend some time meditating on all the good things that have happened to you and the gifts you were given this year, be they more literal, like a birthday present, or more worldly, like the gift of a new friend, a newly learned characteristic, such as patience, or a hard-won realization about your life. You may wish to do volunteer work, help out a friend, donate to a charity or give back in some other way as a gesture of appreciation for all that you have and a thank you for your blessings.

A Lughnasadh ritual

A powerful ritual for Lughnasadh is to visit a farm and actually pick some produce yourself. One year, my daughter and I had been invited to a late New Year's picnic on a property outside of Byron Bay in north eastern Australia, which was held on a blueberry farm. We wandered amid the blueberry fields for half an hour before finding our companions, and while we wandered we plucked delicious blueberries and ate them standing in the fields – the life force of the berries was intense, and as I later studied more about this festival I learned that the blueberry is a sacred plant for this time of year. We'd spontaneously had our own Lughnasadh celebration.

It is also a great thing to share some of your bounty with others. Leave a basket of fruit for someone who will appreciate it, give a donation, count your blessings and share of them. As a human being, you have a link to every other person on this earth – give, and the Witches' law of the threefold return will be invoked.

A time for change

Some things to do at Lughnasadh:

* Declutter, then throw out or give away anything you do not need.
* Help a neighbor – one close by or one in another land.
* Save water, speak impeccably of others, recycle, mulch, be kind, start a savings plan – the energy of this day will support you in your efforts.
* Eat blueberries, blackberries and crab apples.
* Give up something you love and use the time and the money you save to help someone (chocolate, cigarettes, drinking expensive wine – it is only for one quarter of the year).
* Bake a gingerbread man to symbolize your sacrifice.
* The Oracle Tarot association for this sabbat is the Change card. This is a powerful card to meditate on for change, as our butterfly self emerges from the cocoon.

Letting go at Lughnasadh

Lughnasadh can also be a time of nostalgia and regret. It is the time when we tend to look back. We can feel pangs of regret for plans, dreams, ambitions and relationships that did not come, literally, to fruition. Feeling haunted by what we view as our failures can be overwhelming, but it is wise to see any "failure" as a test. To look back and to learn is worthwhile, however to be immobilized by regret is not only pointless, it can be destructive. And it is short sighted to assume that you know what is and isn't destined to be a failure – only with the wheel's turns will life's lessons be revealed. This is a time to practice patience, to learn that some things need more time to come to fruition, and to set your goals and intent and then let them grow as they should, for the good of all. It's a time for letting go and moving on.

One symbolic way is to make a corn dolly. Take a corn cob and decorate it – give her a face, make her a dress and a bonnet, and hang her in a conspicuous part of your home – she will serve to remind you of the plenty you have enjoyed, and will help to bring forth more after the fallow times.

Another traditional ritual for this holiday is the baking of bread, because not only does it reflect the harvest aspect of the time of year, but the rising of the dough symbolizes the cycle of life –the sun will soon weaken and go to the other side of the world, but it will rise again.

A sacred spell for Lughnasadh

You will need:
Your athame (pronounced Ath-AH-may) or boline (pronounced Bo-leen)
Gold and green candles.
A black pen.

Gold paper.

Sea salt.

Frankincense incense.

Spring water.

Cleanse your home. Follow with a smudge stick, then use a ceremonial broom to finish off. Sweep away sadness and feel and accept the gravity of winter's approach. Now you are ready for your ritual.

Open the magic circle with your athame, to represent the scythe of harvest. (It is appropriate to substitute your boline to open circle with at this sabbat, as it reflects the scythe of harvest more closely than even your athame)

Light and lift the candles, and say: "I welcome the spirits of fire."

Light and lift the incense, and say: "I welcome the spirits of air."

Take a sip of the water and say: "I welcome the spirits of water."

Lift the sea salt and say: "I welcome the spirits of the earth."

Reflect on anything you may regret – write these down with your black pen on your gold paper. As you write, sincerely farewell it. If there is anyone or anything you are holding on to now is the time for letting go.

Burn your list safely and say goodbye, with empathy and compassion. You will move forward.

Close the magic circle.

Letting go at Lughnasadh spell

This is a wonderful way to take your power back after a draining love affair or venture that didn't work out, which you just can't seem to move on from. It is perfect to do at Lughnasadh, so you can start to move forward with the new energy, but it can be performed at any time (if you miss this sabbat, a Saturday on a waning moon is also a very suitable time for letting go).

Run a warm bath into which you have scattered three handfuls of pure rock or sea salt. Then gently place one free-range egg into your tub. Light an indigo candle and bathe in its light. Rewind the tape of all your sad love stories or business disappointments, and allow any feelings that arise to come to the surface – any lingering pessimism, bitterness, anger, hurt or sadness. Feel it stream out of your feet, through the water and into the egg. When you pull the plug on the bath you will literally feel the pain of the past drain from your own body and mind. Then, just to be on the safe side, take your egg outside and bury it at least four inches deep in the earth. Sprinkle some water mixed with a few torn verbena leaves over it, then fill in the hole with the earth and thank it for transmuting your pain. Now you can move on with your new life.

A dear friend did this spell after a painful separation – even though I had felt it was a little too soon after the breakup and had advised her to give it more time. She went ahead though – then rang me, aghast, as several days later her carefully buried egg re-emerged from the earth! If you don't feel ready to let go you might need to ask the Goddess for help with that first.

Harvest Spell

This is from my Magical Spell Cards deck, and is simple and perfect for Lughnasadh.

Sitting at your altar, light a stick of vanilla incense. Take a silver coin and wrap it in an orange piece of fabric. Place this on your altar.

Put two green candles anointed with neroli essential oil on either side of the pouch. Light them. Concentrate on the silver coin and visualize your dream coming true in the present, not at a future time.

Say three times:
As the waves of the ocean are infinite
As the trees in the forest grow tall
Let my work now bring me to harvest
I'm ready to receive my all.

Shift your focus to the orange cloth and understand that harvest is coming. Blow out the candles, first right, then left, and place flowers and sprigs of fast-growing herbs around your magical space.

Catherine wheels

In ancient times at Lughnasadh, a large wheel would be taken to the top of a hill, covered in tar, set alight and rolled down. They were later called Catherine wheels, after Saint Catherine, to hide their Wiccan origins, but they actually symbolize the turning of the Wheel of the Year from summer towards the dark. Ignite your own Catherine wheel – they're gorgeous, great fun and remind us of time's passing and to relish today, every day.

Lughnasadh's names

Lunasa
Lammas
Harvest Mother's Day
Celtic Grain Festival

Lughnasadh's deities

Lugh
Tara – Irish Goddess of the land
The Green Man
The Corn Mother

Demeter
Cerridwen

Lughnasadh's sacred animals

Roosters
Calves
Pigs, particularly sows

Lughnasadh's magical stones

Aventurine
Peridot
Sardonyx
Tiger eye
Golden topaz
Ametrine

Lughnasadh's ritual plants

Berries
Grains
Corn
Blackberry
Oak
Sunflower
Aloes
Oak leaves

Lughnasadh's enchanted herbs

Sandalwood
Heather
Acacia
Cyclamen
Fenugreek

Mabon

The descent of Persephone

The bitter and the sweet collide at the festival of Mabon (pronounced Mah-bon)– the autumn equinox – which is held around September 20-23 in the northern hemisphere and around March 20-23 in the southern hemisphere. Day and night are of equal length and all things are in balance.

Mabon is at once a time to give thanks for the bounty you have created in your life and a time to grieve for the little deaths we all must endure to truly be alive.

When the Wheel of the Year turns to Mabon, the autumn equinox, it is time to give thanks for whatever has come to fruition over the past year. Be it a new relationship you nurtured from raw beginnings, something you made, built, studied or created or a goal once desired and now attained, all must be honored.

This is your chance to acknowledge the combination of your creative energy and the natural order, both of which helped you to grow this year. The purpose of paying this respect is twofold. Firstly, the acknowledgment of change brought about by the power of your will brings symbolic closure to a phase. That in turn will leave you free to move forward. Secondly, honoring your achievements establishes magical growth as a soul principle – and positive reinforcement will give you the incentive to make more positive changes in the future. Processing this soul development at Mabon means you are showing the Goddess that you actively value enriching and nurturing yourself as a spiritual being in the Craft. This in turn will bring you more blessings during the coming months.

Mabon brings equilibrium, both physically, of the days, and emotionally. It is the second time in the year that this happens – the other is at the spring equinox. Although Mabon's light is as long as its dark, with day and night of equal length, from this time forth the light begins to shorten.

And with the lengthening of the dark comes the increasing power of your own shadow self. Thus Mabon is the beginning of the wisdom of dark mysteries, of wise blood, of premonition, divination and facing your shadow.

Working through any negativity that arises is actively promoted at Mabon. Don't be afraid of working through your own darkness – it's important to honor and respect your anger, your mistrust, your depression, your guilt, your sorrows. We learn nothing from denial and repression – we need to engage with our shadow self and give it healthy expression.

But before your shadow self absorbs the light, it is vitally important for you to ready your psyche and your body for the intense crone energy that will grow more powerful each time the earth turns from Mabon forth.

Autumnal energy

How will you know when you are being affected by this energy? Even though you can pinpoint the turning of the earth into its flat zone with modern technology (and good astronomy websites!), there are plenty of seasonal signals that the sun God is dying. Watch for migrations of animals, particularly birds, falling leaves, the trees changing color, flowers becoming less abundant, the ground becoming colder and harder to the touch, and mornings having a distinct chill.

In nature, the energy begins to go within in order to preserve itself. Personally you may find you look back, withdraw, and feel aloof or confused regarding your relationships. You may feel less generous than you usually do, and you may also be nervous about any debt you may have accumulated over summer. You might feel it's time to clean up your act – both in terms of your health and in terms of who you are.

It can be hard to let go of summer's energy, its sensuous warmth and easy good times. Farewelling its carefree spirit is made easier by our sacred observation of the astronomical and agricultural seasonal sacred signposts. That's why, on a mundane level, Mabon is a wonderful time to:

* Start a savings plan.
* Set goals for the future.
* Make jams and preserves for winter.
* Restock your herbal medicine cabinet.
* Clean out any essential oils, flower remedies etc that have lost their energy.
* Completely clean out your fridge.
* Repair broken windows.
* Think of how best to make your home secure and snug and warm for the coming introspection of Samhain.
* Cook soups, stews and any slow cooked foods made with root vegetables.

It's a fortuitous time to clear the energy in your house – sort of the reverse of spring cleaning. This clean-up is to make yourself and your home ready for the colder nights coming, to acknowledge that the bare landscape has its own beauty and lessons, as well as a mental clarity and deep wisdom of experience that can be difficult to achieve during Beltane's sensuous haze and Litha's youthful joy. This is older, wiser, deeper, sadder – and somehow more beautiful. Prepare to snuggle into it and delve into your own shadow side in comfort.

A Mabon ritual

It's essential to give thanks for the bounty of your life. Write down on a piece of parchment all you have achieved. If you like, use russet-red ink on coppery autumn leaves – I love doing this. Write down on each leaf something you felt you really mastered. It can be a small thing (to others) or a great success. It can be a skill you learned, a debt you paid, a relationship you nurtured to fruition or even a relationship you gained closure with – this is also a good time to remember any pain you may have gone through, and is a time for letting go.

This is the phase of the natural year in which the earth goddess Demeter learned that, although her daughter Persephone would be with her on earth for six months of the year, she had eaten six seeds of the underworld fruit, the pomegranate, and would live underground for the other six months, forever linked to Hades. This is the beginning of Persephone's departure from her mother's home to return to her husband and the underworld, and thus the start of Demeter's wild grieving. It was her grief that turned the earth cold and brought winter, and it was this approaching winter that forced the people of the land to gather their second and last harvest of the year. Those who didn't would be forced to confront the realities of a barren earth, perhaps without enough stores to get them through.

The maiden and the mother spell

Here is a very special spell, which I developed over a period of a year, during which a very close friend endured a painful separation and divorce, which had many ramifications on her relationship with her daughter. This spell can also be adapted to suit any situation – a job ending, a friendship changing, a household breaking up or simply the end of summer. It can even be used for an actual death, though I sincerely wish that none of you will have need for it in that regard.

Whatever you use it for, remember it is a spell to help heal the pain of parting, to help you deal with the whirlwind of emotions separation can inspire. It will plug you in to the Goddess energies of Persephone and Demeter – mother and daughter deities who know all about leaving each other, and leaving lovers. It's also a great spell to perform if you're experiencing tension between your family and your lover. As a mother, I can imagine no greater suffering than the separation from a child. Even though Demeter knows Persephone will return, knowledge that she will be in the underworld for half of every year causes her such anguish that her mourning brings increasing cold to the earth. But it also means that the life energy goes underground to become strong again – which yours will do too.

Grieving takes time. But with this spell, we can be sure to be progressing through our sadness into a new era in our lives when the wheel next turns. It will help you avoid the tragic state of being stuck in a situation and in the emotions of a situation that is dead.

You will need:

Real clay – green or organic and able to decompose, enough for small figures which you will shape by hand.

One small lemon verbena plant, ample earth and a clay pot for it to be planted in. If you wish, you could tend it from a seedling prior to the spell so you feel confident it will survive. Lemon verbena has wonderful qualities, both healing and calming yet vigorously cleansing.

It is best to work this spell skyclad (naked), as anything you wear during the casting of it can retain the energy. So no jewelry either.

Don't bathe until after the spell is completed, after which

you will thoroughly cleanse yourself with lemon myrtle soap or a citrus-based cleanser. If you wish to take a natural approach, the fruit acids in a lemon will work just as well – grate up some rind and mix with one part olive oil and two parts sea salt. This will literally slough away any dead skin cells, leaving you energized and refreshed.

Water, blessed, in a ceremonial cup.

Pen and paper.

Casting the spell

On the morning of the autumn equinox, cast your circle in your usual manner.

Within the sacred circle, pour the earth into the pot and charge it with healing energy.

Still in the center of your circle, take your clay and forge two figures. These little people now represent you and the person or situation that you are moving away from. Pour your emotions into them. Do not judge them, do not hold back, but do not let them own you.

Bury your little people deep in the earth.

Now, connect with your crone energy and feel her power merge with your essence. Ask the crone to give you the wisdom to grieve well, and to move on when the wheel has turned.

Cover the figures completely with the earth, and feel the relationship moving into the past.

Now, move your energy back to that of the crone. Meditate on moving on, and how best you can manifest that goal. When you feel the power peak, take a pen and write down everything you would like to achieve over the following year.

Once this is completed, ask the crone to bless your plans and give you her wisdom to guide you in manifesting them.

Finally, take your little lemon verbena tree and plant it on top of the figures you have put in the earth. Water it with some water from your cup. Know that life is a circle, and that as there is sadness there will be joy. That as there is growth, there is the dying off. That the past, with all its sadness, can feed a better future.

Now say three times: "This wheel shall turn."

Close your circle by walking widdershins (counter-clockwise in the northern hemisphere, clockwise in the south) around it.

Place your magical pot plant somewhere you can see it, but not beside your bed. Somewhere you can see it but not obsess over it. Nurture the plant and notice its growth – this is your emotional and psychic progress made into a living green symbol. Over time, the clay figures will become one with the earth and nurture the roots of the plant. This is the symbol that signals to you that there can be a natural, organic end to a relationship. At some time it will become indistinguishable from the earth itself, and the earth can bring forth new life.

There is only one question. Are you ready to let go?

You will know you have absorbed this relationship's wisdom into your life, strengthening your very soul, when you can drink tea from the leaves of the verbena tree you planted.

You will know how hard you are holding on if you are tempted to dig up the clay figures. If you do dig them up, wait till the next waning moon and repeat the spell – but do not repeat your mistakes.

Blessed be.

Mabon's names

Alban Elfed (Welsh)
Second harvest festival
The feast of Avalon

Mabon's deities

Epona
Morgon, snake woman
Morgan le Fey
Modron
Persephone
Demeter
Hecate
The Crone

Mabon's sacred animals

The owl
The stag
The crow
The salmon
Dogs
Wolves
Birds of prey

Mabon's magical stones

Amethyst
Yellow topaz
Carnelian
Lapis lazuli
Sapphire
Yellow agate
Ruby

Mabon's ritual plants

Plants
Vines
Ivy

Hazel

Hops

Honeysuckle

Roses

Mabon's enchanted herbs

Sage

Benzoin

Marigold

Myrrh

Passionflower

Chapter Nine
Exploring the Mysteries

The path of white magic is bewitchingly beautiful, very safe and very healing. Its mysteries are those of the other dimensions, of other beings, of nature and of your own inner nature and self. White magic is a manifold path that never ceases to evolve and inspire. Its mysteries are constantly revealing deeper and deeper layers of wisdom to us, assisting and encouraging both men and women to live authentic, rich and loving lives full of an experience of the truth that everything is divine. At white magic's heart is the wonderful truth that you were born blessed, and its mysteries, detailed here, will reveal how you can rediscover the sense of your own innate divinity.

Magical names

Like me, and many other magical folks, you may wish to

take a magical name when you identify and acknowledge your bewitching magical self. Taking one is not strictly necessary, but there's a practical as well as a symbolic purpose behind adopting your own magical new name.

Firstly a little background. It is said that many of us worked our magic using a different name in the past primarily as a means of preserving secrecy and safety. The two, in the past, were inseparable. For example, during the Burning Times, if one of us was taken and tortured, she or he was often asked for names of others involved in their practices. One way of preserving the safety of a group was to have secret names and to meet in darkness so nobody could be identified. This is where the ritual use of masks may have come from too, as an aid to anonymity and for protection.

With a magical name, an extra degree of secrecy and thus safety came into being. Having a magical name became a little like being a resistance fighter in WWII, where only knowing the code names of your associates kept identities safe. We realised that working with their sacred names, not their own, would ensure not only their safety, but also preserve the old knowledge and deep magic from being destroyed.

However, in most places in the world today we no longer need to keep our power hidden, and bringing our magical names out in the open serves to create a more loving, powerful world in which we can speak the truth of who we are, and what we do, with no fear. Be it your magical name, birth name or fairy name, we need no longer go by cloak of darkness or mask our faces to keep our ways – and ourselves – alive.

For me, my magical name, Lucy Cavendish, is truly myself, at least as much myself as my birth name. While my birth name reflects the preferences of my family and my culture – my parents chose my first name, and my surname is that of my father's family – my magical name was a kind of blessing, or rebirthing, within my sacred path, a sign that I was ready to do my work, and to do it publicly.

To be clear, my own magical name in fact chose me. After my first year and a day, or thirteen moons, of working in the Craft, I was told my magical name in a truly enchanted experience. I was "woken up" during a deep meditation by a clear woman's voice, beautiful and resonant, bell like and clear. Perhaps it was my own voice, the voice of my soul. Perhaps it was the voice of the Lady who I often saw as a child, she of the soft hands and the kind, beautiful face, who has since returned to me, the more true to myself I became. Wherever the voice came from, it told me this: "Your name is Lucy Cavendish. By this name you will do my work."

Some of the babies born in recent time actually tell their parents their magical name prior to their birth, and as the vibration of this world shifts, parents are more and more likely to be sensitive and soulful enough to hear them. Many children are now being born with their magical names, whereas I and many others of my generation took on a magical name later. In some ancient cultures, mothers crooned to their children in the womb, then listened for their name. Recently a friend of mine told me that her daughter had told her her name before she was born. Her name is Avalon.

As nomenclature, the social practice of naming, becomes more in tune with who we are as beings, rather than who we are attached to, or considered to be owned by, we will eventually all be born into our true names.

Many of us who are now adults did not have the experience

of "telling" our parents our name prior to being born. Some of our parents were full of fear of magic, so they did not listen. Others were full of fear that they would be punished, so held back their true name. So after we were born, and after we had come to a greater understanding of our life path, and of our magical birthright, we adopted our true name for ourselves.

Some of those who have adopted magical names for their work include Dion Fortune (original name Violet Firth), Oberon Zell Ravenheart and Starhawk. All these names are beautiful, unique and powerful magical tools.

Some people ask: "If I change my name, will the Akashic records lose track of me?" They cannot. This magnificent etheric soul library know your soul's various names. Your birth name and your true name are all known on that level. They recorded the variations of our names when our ancestors moved across the world and changed their names in order to adapt to their new enviroment. Many women's birth names have been lost forever with the practice of children receiving only the father's name. Many women change their name when they marry. The Akashic record is wise and so knowledgeable that it records all your names in all directions of time, in all their variations. Do not fear disconnection. Choosing a sacred name only brings you closer to your truth.

How to find your magical name

It is not necessary to take a magical name, but if you would like to, how do you find this sacred name, this name which will help you raise energy and truly focus for workings and rituals, as well as establishing a deeper and more magical connection with your sacred work?

Many people take on the name of the Goddess or the God they have the most affinity with when they are working magically. Some other names are in regular use but have a particular meaning which could symbolize the style of the individual. Others are completely new and inventive. Some are of the earth, others of the stars. But all reflect your qualities and unique personality.

Many people, when seeking their magical name, may ask for it to be given to them during a meditation or spellworking. Some people do this intuitively, others consciously. One method is to team together images and objects that are sacred to you. For example Starhawk, considered by many to be the modern mother of Witchcraft, a pagan activist and heroic warrior woman figure to many, myself included, created her own name when she had a powerful meditation in which she was shown a hawk flying in a night sky filled with stars. It was deeply inspiring to her, and she has used this name for her work from that point on, and by that name she is publicly known.

Some of you may feel inspired most deeply by shamanistic names of aboriginal or American Indian origin, others take the name of their power or totem animal and incorporate it into their own name, along with a color or quality they feel drawn to. For some, this could be a species of tree – blackwood, hawthorn, oak or holly. It could be otherworldy beings from the realm of fairy who inspire your true name – those of us of the old blood are often drawn to name ourselves after our fairy relatives and ancestors. Stones, waterways, clouds and places may also inspire us. What is most right is the name that feels most perfect for you. Take your time with this process. It is a beautiful way of getting to know who you truly are and learning what it is you are longing for, drawn to, and already magically resonating with.

When I think about the name I have been given, Lucy Cavendish, when I feel its power flow through me and am at one with who I am, I am full of love and gratitude for the Lady. Lucy means light. And cave and dish are both sacred and mundane tools associated with water, the home and the feminine, at once mysterious and practical, receptive and sheltering – one a home hewn from the stone of the earth, the other something that can hold, receive and give in return. There are so many reasons why all this resonates for me. For a time I used this magical name only for things related to the Craft, but increasingly I became more truly my magical self, and use my magical name publicly.

And as I became more at one with my magical name, I began to feel curious about why the Lady had given it to me. I have since found many historical links to a 19th century social aristocrat who, rather than leading a life of privilege, devoted herself to social reform and women's right to education – a Lucy Cavendish. Her story is wonderful, and her work lives on in Lucy Cavendish College in Britain. I feel a strong association with her and with her work.

I was also fascinated and moved to discover a synchronicity with my names. I worked out the numerological value of my birth name, which is eleven. Then I calculated the equivalent value for my new magical name or, as I believe it to be, the name of my true nature.

It too is eleven. Or elven. Thank you Goddess.

Finding your inner self

Here are some names to stimulate some creativity and magic of your own!

Women's names

Ana (pronounced Ah-nah): Goddess of the land. (Celtic)
Arianrhod (Aree-AHN-rhod): Goddess of the silver wheel.

(Celtic)

Artemis (ARTemis): Goddess of the hunt, maiden huntress. (Greek)

Astrid: The name of many Scandinavian queens and princesses, meaning divine strength. (Old Norse)

Aurora: Fairy being of the dawn, her colors are that of sunrise. (Greek)

Calypso: A calm visage hides a woman's strong emotions. (Greek)

Danika (Dahn-ee-kah): Morning star, that which awakens. (Old Slavic)

Dido (DI-doe): Teacher, enlightener. Dido was an ancient priestess of the north African city of Carthage – her name has also come to mean that by teaching and serving others, you gain wisdom yourself.

Lilith: Lilith was the first wife of Adam in ancient mythology, and means belonging to the night. Lilitu and Lily are versions. (East Semitic)

Maeve: She who intoxicates. (Scots Gaelic)

Miranda: Admirable, extraordinary. (Latin)

Morgan: Woman of the sea. The name of one of the nine Morgens, or priestesses of Avalon. Variations include Morgaine, Morgen, Morgana and Morgan le Fey. (Welsh)

Rhiannon: Welsh moon Goddess, the name means able to communicate with nature, tamer of horses, bringer of love and birdsong. (Welsh)

Titania: After Shakespeare's Queen of the Fairies from A Midsummer Night's Dream. (English)

Urania: Meaning heavenly, as Urania was the Greek muse of astronomy. (Greek)

Wendy/Wanda: Wanderer. "A dream-led daughter, roaming over glen and dell and seeking violets in the snow." (Old

German)

Zeena: The welcoming one, from the Greek, Xenia. Some claim that names beginning with Z are more powerful than any other.

Zerlinda: Dawn, beautiful. (Hebrew/Spanish)

Men's names

Ailen (Ae-lahn): Rock, noble. (Scots Gaelic)

Ammon: The hidden. (Egyptian)

Anubis (AH-noo-bis): After the Egyptian God of the underworld. (Egyptian)

Beck: A lonesome brook looking for a river. (Celtic)

Cailean (Callan): Young warrior. (Scots Gaelic)

Conan: Intelligence, wisdom, high exalted. (Celtic)

Dion: After Dionysus, the Greek God of revelry, ectasy, and religious bliss. Famously used by a female, Dion Fortune. (Greek)

Forrest: Dweller in a forest. (Old French)

Frewin (Free-win): Free, noble, friend. (Old English)

Galen: Little bright one. (Irish Gaelic)

Llew (Lugh) Sun God, bringer of warmth and life. (Welsh, Celtic)

Marsden: Dweller in the marshy valley. (Old English)

Merlin: After the great wizard, King Arthur's mentor, the companion of the Lady of the Lake, also a general title for a druid leader. (Welsh)

Taraghlan (Tara-lan): White brow. (Scots gaelic)

Thoth (Toth): God of writing, scribes, inspiration. (Egyptian)

Taliesin (TAL-ee-ess-in): Radiant brow, after the druid bard who many believe is the same being as Merlin. (Welsh)

Ra: Sun God. (Egyptian)

Seth: The appointed one. (Hebrew)

An invocation of your magical name

Open your circle and call in the God and the Goddess, the quarters and any witnesses. You may wish to invite your ancestors to join you. You may also wish others to partake in this ceremony, to let all know and celebrate your rebirth in the sacred. Write your words beforehand – I have listed an example below, but find the words and meanings that really mean something to you. If you work with a group, you may wish someone else to anoint you with the water. This ritual can also be adapted for coven use or when we choose magical names when working in circle.

First, state all the names you have been known by – your birth name, married name, nicknames. Now state your magical name, and when and how you will be known by this name. Take some water you have charged (see the Beltane chapter for ways of creating your own sacred water), and say, for example:

I am Lucy
Daughter of Josephine
Granddaughter of Margaret and of Jessica
Sister of Mark
Mother of my daughter.
(Anoint yourself with the water at your throat)
I am Lucy
Daughter of Bruce
Granddaughter of Edward and of Edward.
(Anoint yourself with the water at your heart)
Dear God and Goddess, hear my name
Not born of this name, but known by it
Your daughter, God and Goddess
Your child in truth

Your child in light
Your child in the ancient ways
Your child of Atlantis
Of Avalon, of the lake and the wild woods, of the apple tree
For my name, and these gifts, and this path Lady, I thank thee.
(Anoint yourself with the water on your forehead)
Light a candle, stretch your arms out, and proclaim with
joy and reverence something along these lines:
I am Lucy
Dweller of the forest
Witch and mother
Dreamer and teacher
I walk between worlds
A friend to nature, her trees, her waterways,
to all her elements and to her creatures
As I do will, so mote it be
Blessed be.

Close your circle, leave an offering, and thank the God and
the Goddess for their presence, then ground yourself. If you
are with others, celebrate and ground with a naming feast!

Subtle, natural change
The magic of the five-pointed star

Along with other ritual jewelry, I often wear a pentacle on
a silver chain around my neck. It is a beautiful Nordic piece,
carved with runic symbols in a beautiful, uplifting shade of
blue. It is at once beguiling, mysterious, pretty, feminine and
powerful. But many people have mixed feelings about this
magical symbol, which was used by the wise Greek master
of magic and numbers, Pythagoras, to symbolize divine

protection. Misunderstanding the five-pointed star and viewing it through a lens of fear-based thinking sees some of us re-experiencing a kind of bigotry that still has an immense impact, triggering our fear, which holds many of us back.

It's important to understand what the pentacle, or pentagram, represents in order to offset the misinformation that abounds about this symbol. Let's embrace it for its magical significance and beauty of shape and spirit. Let's embrace our power!

The pentacle is an ancient figure of a five-pointed star within a circle, used ceremonially in magic to bless, protect and balance. The circle represents the truth that all energy is a cycle – it's almost the epitome of what goes around comes around, and is symbolic of the wheel of life. Always changing, yet always in perfect balance. The circle, which links all the points of the star, confirms the truth that there is no separation between the energies. There is perfect distance between each point – which creates a perfect circle joining all the elements. It can also be viewed as the womb, the eye, the center, and another spiritual truth – that we are all complete. The ancients gathered in circles of stone, and today we gather in circle together again, keeping this divine flow of energy moving throughout all dimensions, for all time.

The five rays represent the energy of the four elements – earth, air, fire and water – plus spirit, or ether, essence, soul. Thus the pentacle symbolizes the four great natural elements united in harmony with the spirit of humanity. Viewed another way, it resembles the human body, with our head as the top point, arms and legs outstretched, as we reach above and below for wholeness.

It is this harmonious relationship – spirit interacting with the power of the elemental forces of nature – from which we derive the ability to work magic. Some name it intent or emotion, but whatever the label, the spirit is the magical force that enables us to work with nature to will enchantments, to bless our work, to protect ourselves and balance the elements within spells and within our lives. But the five arms of the pentacle are not restricted to these representations – they can symbolize whatever elemental forces you wish, thus the pentacle's potency as a symbol is virtually limitless.

The five stages of life

Often the pentacle is said to represent the five stages of life – (re) Birth, Initiation, Love, Repose and Death – the cyclic nature of existence for all of us. These stages were identified by Starhawk, one of the leaders of the Wiccan revival, and her concepts are a wonderful starting point for deep wisdom and understanding of this symbol.

(Re) Birth: The first stage is about beginnings, the birthing of our projects and ideas, the impulse behind the start of something new. Sometimes this birth is metaphorical, sometimes it is literal, as in a soul returning to this world.

Initiation: The second stage of the life cycle is one of the most neglected areas of all for young people who no longer have the structure and power of ritual to guide them into the difficult, dazzling and sometimes dangerous world of adulthood. In the late 20th century, initiation is performed by young people in a haphazard and sometimes catastrophic fashion, resulting in violence and mayhem and a lack of love and respect between generations. Initiation is when we are learning. This can be a process of intensive study, formally or perhaps informally. It can also symbolize a time when we are mentored through life experiences. Whether or not we have a formal teacher, as Arthur did with Merlin and Morgan did with the priestesshood of Avalon, for example, we all are loved by the Goddess and the God, and we are never alone. Paradoxically, however, a part of this stage involves us sometimes feeling very alone.

Love: The third stage is when we learn to commune with another person externally. We fall in love, we physically join, and sometimes we create another life. There is a combining of energies, bodies and emotions. This is a time when we learn to love that which we can become like. It is also a time when the identity is more fluid, and when issues of independence can come up. Love is the station on the pentacle when we also fall in love with ourselves. Sometimes this process is sparked by falling in love with another, sometimes it is simply a process of falling in love with ourselves and our purpose.

Repose: The fourth stage is going within. We are resting, it seems, externally, but inside we are like the beautiful card in the Oracle Tarot of the Hermit – we need to go within to rediscover a part of ourselves, and to re-energize in order to grow again. Think of it as akin to a tree shedding leaves, withdrawing its external energy to become bare and silent during winter in order for the sap to run again in spring.

Death: The fifth stage is the time of change. This can be a time when we literally do pass from this realm into another, or it can be a death in the form of an ending in an aspect of our lives – the end of a job or a relationship, moving out of home or to another country, changing an aspect of your personality to become more truly how you want to be. These five stations of the star can be applied to many life experiences, so rather than thinking of the death stage as a literal death, think of it as change, akin to the Change card in the Oracle Tarot, when we need to go through a struggle, a change, in order to re-emerge.

Understanding the symbolic beauty and the power of

the links between these processes (Birth-Initiation, Death-Initiation, Love-Death, Birth-Repose and so on) will enable you to increase your own power to experience the five stages of life to their fullest. What are the associations between stages? Do we get stuck at a particular stage? Do we avoid a stage, finding it painful or fearful, only to find ourselves unable to move forward and progress as we would wish? Have we skipped through a stage without really integrating its lessons?

I know one of my own lessons is to embrace the stage known as Death. It can be painful for me to let go and to grieve, and the temptation in today's world is to simply "get over it" and move on. But sometimes we must allow ourselves the space and time for sadness, before true re-creation can begin.

Some of these stages may trigger particularly strong feelings – this is a wonderful sign that we are on track to learn something wonderful about ourselves. The pentacle as a therapeutic tool is truly magical indeed.

White Magic Sacred Star workshop

To connect more deeply with life, perform this magical exercise on a regular basis.

Draw a pentacle, and inscribe above each arm one of the five profound turnings of life. Meditate on the deep meanings of each of these processes, contemplate how they relate, one to the other, and reflect on the various thoughts, insights and emotions thrown up by this meditation.

This ritual is particularly enriching at significant turning points within one's life. It is enlightening and fulfilling when an individual encounters the joy and mystery of new life being born into the world, or the wrench and sorrow of death retrieving a soul for the Summerlands, the beautiful place where we go between our incarnations. It can also be used symbolically – when a birth has taken place in the form of a new job, house or philosophy, or a death such as the annihilation of a love bond or a business partnership that is no longer profitable.

The five-pointed star also corresponds to the five senses, so this diverse symbol can also be experienced as a metaphor for the physical realm. Other qualities that can be represented by the pentacle are Sex, Self, Passion, Pride and Power. Be imaginative and create your own meditations using five essential experiences or energies significant to you. I often work this way with Goddesses, sometimes with five of the Goddesses of the Holy Isle of Avalon – Branwen, Arianrhod, Rhiannon, Blodeuwedd and Cerridwen.

You may also wish to work with five stages of a relationship. And as five is the number of change, you can also use the pentacle as a wonderful symbol through which to manifest.

The five stages also resonate with the festivals of the Wheel of the Year – Birth is akin to Yule and Imbolc, Initiation to Lughnasadh and Ostara, Love to Beltane and Litha, Repose to Mabon and Death to Samhain – so when you are celebrating each sabbat, take a little time to draw a pentacle in your Book of Shadows, mark it with these significant phases, and ponder the significance of the relevant one and how it relates to your life.

Doing this at these times is a wonderful meditation tool, or it can be integrated into your festival ritual. It will intensify the experience of a sabbat while reminding you of the inevitability of the driving forces of the life cycle and of the utmost sanctity of spirit.

Manifesting with the pentacle

Birth: Visualize your project. See it being born. Give it detail, and activate it in your mind, seeing it working in the world and feeling the impact of this project on your life. Think about what kind of energy you wish to bring to it and what steps need to be taken to create it in reality.

Initiation: After extensive work on the birthing process, take your plan and gently begin working on it in the real world. Each day, take baby steps towards your goal. If it is prosperity, for example, decide what active, practical steps you are going to take to enable your goal to come to fruition, and take one every day. This stage represents the courage to test your visualized goal in the real world. Do not think that speaking of it is the same as acting on it – this stage is about practical work, which you will then learn from. It is an initiation into reality, and as such, practical, powerful steps need to be taken. Ninety per cent action, 10 per cent talking about it is a good goal. That 10 per cent can be very powerful – but we need the tangible steps to give it form and power.

Love: Who can help you? This is the time to accept input and help and get feedback. Are customers drawn to you? How can you reach them? If you are manifesting a lover, potential partners may be all around you at this stage, but perhaps you have not yet recognized them.

Repose: What are your results so far? How are things working? The repose stage gives you a moment to understand what must come next, and how to recreate your manifesting in order for it to gain power and be more closely aligned with your original intent. Compare your notes from the birth stage with where you are at now, and figure out what needs to happen at this stage. Give yourself time for contemplation and consideration of where you are going, and what it is that you are intending to create, energetically and in reality, with this manifestation.

Death: What do you need to alter about your original strategy? Letting go of some parts means you can breathe life into the areas of the project that are in most need. This can also be a time when we realize that in order to love, old attitudes must be released. Think of this stage as a kind of gentle purging or detoxing of the process so far, so you can go back to the first point of the star, Birth, and continue with the next, recreated stage.

By working with manifesting in this way we understand the natural processes that are part of bringing a project into life. By simply meditating on the points, and how they are manifesting in your day to day life, you will be naturally rebalancing yourself – the side effects of this process include developing an understanding as to which areas are your weak points, and thus becoming able to work to strengthen them, as well as developing an understanding of the transformational energies of life. This is not a linear process, but a cycle through which we endlessly transform, change and create sacred magic.

Your Book of Shadows and Light

A Book of Shadows and Light is every white magical practitioner's diary of the soul. It's also a lesson book, the keeper of their knowledge and experience of the Craft and sometimes their closest companion. Within this magical book we record our daily rituals and spellworkings, the results, original intent and eventual outcome. You can also keep spells, magical recipes, stories about the sabbats or other magical topics, information on healing or your Oracle Tarot divinations – anything that relates to your practise of white magic. Your Book of Shadows and Light is where you ponder, learn, reflect and grow.

A truly safe and sacred space, this book is guilt-free, honest and beautiful, a place to both wonder at your mysteries and darknesses, express the pain of your wounds, honor your gifts and express gratitude for the gift of life.

A Book of Shadows and Light can also be viewed as a way of working through and understanding your relationship with White Magic. It is the place for examining your intent, your ethics and your purpose – within its safe and sanctuary-like pages you can explore openly the many dilemmas a sorceress, priestess and white magical practitioner experiences when going deeply into the Craft. It is the place for your musings on the Craft, and the place to inscribe and ponder questions to which you seek answers from within and without. Any knowledge which you want to entrust and secure safely belongs in your Book of Shadows and Light.

It is also a wonderful way to preserve knowledge should you wish to pass on what you have learned and experienced, or share within a circle. Some hereditary Witches I am honoured to know are blessed to have their own family's Book of Shadows and Light which they pass on from generation to generation – with their own unique pages added, of course.

For a solitary practitioner, it is vital to keep this book. You are able to express within its pages confidentially, revise your understandings as you move to different levels of spiritual practice – for White Magic is a wonderful spiritual practice – and learn the lessons taught to you by the ritual workings and spellcastings and any gatherings you attend, all of which you will entrust to this record.

It is also a part of the chain of priestess-healers stretching back through the centuries – white magical practitioners have kept these books for many many years. In fact, the name comes from the prior need to keep the knowledge in the "shadows" in order to survive. Traditionally a Book of Shadows was something every Witch kept in secret. They never shared or even saw another's book of spellwork, rituals, herblore, joys, fears and epiphanies, due to the very real fear of being killed for their beliefs.

Please be very cautious about showing your book to another person before it is time, and when you do so, examine your intent thoroughly. This book must be kept safely – it is for you, and you are its guardian. It is, in a very real sense, your own white magical self. It more than symbolizes the sanctity of your relationship with your magical inner self – it is your own magical self, and is a repository and holder of your beautiful, energetic contribution to this planet and th Universe. Choose your book well, keep it faithfully and develop a strong relationship with it. You will find it a good and true magical friend.

Know that you are working powerful, healing white magic simply by keeping this book. This sacred tool will do so much for you – it will help you realize your magical workings, and will evoke the power of white magic in your daily life. White magic is about spellcraft in many ways – highly evolved and well-intentioned spellcraft. Spellcraft changes lives, and your Book of Shadows and Light is your place to reflect and respect your self and your Craft, and to see what you have manifested via your white magic.

Creating your own Book of Shadows

A Book of Shadows and Light can be made, gifted or purchased. It can be as minimalist as you wish, or as romantic and ornate as you desire. It can express your ancestry, or the path you are drawn to. Many Book of Shadows and Light have Celtic, Egyptian, Italian or fairy overtones. For some it's a beautiful book or journal, for others it's a folder that can be added to constantly, and some even keep theirs all on computer.

Many white magical practitioners decorate their Book of Shadows and Light symbolically. Making your own is wonderful, as is finding a book that declares who your inner self is becoming. Whatever you do, please ensure that your book reflects your own beautiful and unique magical identity.

Whatever its energy, it is best to feel as "at home" with it as possible. Your book is your unique and very personal expression of the Craft – it really is all about you.

Over time, with its every entry, with its musings, spontaneous artworks, thoughts, rituals and Oracle Tarot readings engraved on its pages, you are creating a living symbol of your own workings with white magic.

Dividing your book into sections – perhaps based on spells, rituals, readings, herbwork, psychic work and Goddess channeling, for example – may work best for you. Or you may wish to simply revere and preserve every single day through recording its significant happenings, magical and mundane. Remember they are both the same! Never neglect the ordinary white magic of your day to day life.

Keeping alive your Book of Shadows and Light by working with it each day will allow you to gradually peel back the layers, to draw back the veils between cause and effect in your life, enabling you to see more and more clearly the relationship between your inner magical self, your white magic. Know that both you, and your soul-book, are creating a better world for us all to be part of via your practise of white magic.

The magic of Avalon

Morgan le Fey, the Lady of the Lake, Merlin, Nimue, Viviane... All these names, and their stories, are as familiar to us as our own memories, yet as strange to us as our own dreams. These inhabitants of Avalon, the world between the worlds, have kept us enthralled for centuries, and their tales have been retold by bards, scholars, mystics and monks.

But Avalon is no mystical realm of imagination. The legends we are all familiar with have their roots in the Goddess worship religion that flourished throughout Wales, Cornwall, Somerset and Brittany in pre-Christian times. It's not too hyperbolic to claim that in fact the very roots of modern day magic reach right back to this Goddess faith, which centered around the belief that the embodiment of the Goddess was the land, the crops, her children, its seasons, her cycles. Thus the magic of Avalon is the magic of the British/ Celtic Goddess, in its purest and most sacred form.

Why are these tales and the characters in them so very embedded in our collective psyches? Some spiritual teachers believe that we have all lived before. Certainly this was the view of the priestesses of Avalon and their druidic counterparts – that the birth, death and rebirth cycle was repeated by each individual soul throughout lifetimes, until lessons were learned and destinies fulfilled. If it is in fact the case that we live several lives, then many of us who feel a strong pull or affinity to the myths and legends of Avalon may in fact be hearing our own stories told through the distant fog of half remembered lives. I am not suggesting that we have all been Merlin or Morgan, that we were the Lady of the Lake, but perhaps we lived at that time, and thus these tales resonate for us so strongly because we have in fact heard them before, around a campfire, sung to us by a traveling bard. Some of us may even have lived in that community, been witnesses. Or maybe instead of a past life we're experiencing a kind of genetic race memory, and we carry within our DNA the genetic trace memories of Celtic ancestors who lived at that time.

Where is Avalon?

While the original pre-Christian geo-physical location of Avalon is said to be found on the Tor of the town of Glastonbury in south west England, there is also compelling evidence for it being located in Brittany in France or in Wales. That most people, scholars and pilgrims alike, feel it to be in the heart of Glastonbury is no surprise.

However there is also an Avalon of the heart, a world between worlds that we all carry within – thus Avalon can be said to be the trance-like state of the spellmaker, the altered consciousness of the mystic, the between the worlds communications of the medium. Avalon as a mystic state within occurs when we communicate with the Goddess, when we invoke white magic, when we are at one with the five elements.

This notion of Avalon can be illustrated by the world between the worlds that white magical practitioners discover and treasure on those enchanted sabbat nights when the veils between the worlds are so thin that we communicate with spirits and elementals, we shapeshift, and we find a place where clock-time no longer exists but becomes its truly fluid self, bending and shifting at will. It is a place where we are at one with nature. In Avalon we can transcend our own physical matter and become one with our spirit.

Avalon, or the Isle of Priestesses, was inhabited by a Lady of the Lake and nine priestesses, who underwent years of training, initiation and service to their Lady, their community and the Goddess. These priestesses had very serious and very real medical and symbolic roles in the community. But they were not passive, all-benevolent beings. They did not simply share love and light – they embodied the vast range of the feminine sacred, from the powerful to the glorious to the tender. Thus they were strong and vulnerable, self-sacrificing yet magnificent manifesters, loving yet detached. The innate contradictions and quandaries of the natural cycles were lived out via these women – the magic of the earth and the Goddess was expressed via the sacred cycles, the priestesses' rites and their healings, teachings and guidance for the people of the land.

They bore children during the Great Rites of Beltane, making the Great Marriage with the earth, and bringing the rites to flower with children whose destinies were carved out on the pages of time: Mordred, Arthur and Lancelot were all part of such events.

Very importantly, the priestesses of Avalon were the medical sorority of their community – they were remarkable healers, and their healing consisted of all the myriad variations and permutations of sacred earth magic – the use of her plants, herbs and natural growing things; foods and massage; energetic healing; the movement of blood; the rich tapestry of ways in which healers can skillfully and carefully rebalance the five elements that reside within each human. The properties of stones, metals and minerals were also utilized in healing – Merlin himself is said to have been healed from dreadful battle injuries via a golden bed. Certainly this has metaphorical attributes, but the properties of metals and minerals to heal are also well documented.

Channelings of the Goddess and the Lady were also part of their rituals and healings, and altered states were often reached using sacred plants in order to communicate effectively across the veils to their guides. In this further world between the worlds, spirit communications and time shifting took place, with sendings, glamours and bi-location all within the realms of possibility for the highly skilled priestesses. Prophecy was another of their arts, and the people often looked to the priestesses for guidance regarding the seasons, which crops to plant, for advice before making a marriage or handfasting and which sacrifices to make. The priestesses were also called upon for their charms and potions – what many would call spells – for fertility, love, healing and luck.

The Goddesses of Avalon

There are many manifestations of the Goddess in the state of being we call Avalon. She comes through in the maiden form as Nimue, a young priestess with beguiling sexual power; in the mother form as Morgan, the misunderstood mother-warrioress, sister, lover and healer of Arthur; and in the crone form as Viviane, a strong, unwavering and sometimes cruel crone-wise woman manifestation. Skilled in healing and the magical arts of creation and death, they are the Keepers of the Mysteries of the Goddess.

Their names also come to us as those of the Goddesses Anu, Danu, Mab, Morrigu, Madron, Mary, Arianrhod, Cerridwen, Rhiannon, Epona, Rigantona, Bride, Brigit, Hecate, Magdalena, Gwenhwyfar. And these Goddess archetypes have a deep, innate setting within each of us.

Today in Glastonbury you can train again to be a priestess of Avalon. These women – and a few men – run a local Goddess temple which provides the local community with a neo-pagan Goddess worship center. Its roots are pre-Christian, and its effect is yet to be fully understood.

The key to Avalon's magic is truly that we are now in the process of rebalancing the feminine sacred. In Celtic pre-Christian history, a major shift took place, from a Goddess-oriented, female-validating religion to a God-oriented, woman-fearing religion. Now we are in the process of returning to the Mother. This is not an ideal that is foreign to Christian teachers – or any religion or creed.

And one place where that return is being played out, in a very real way each and every day, and at each and every sabbat, is in Glastonbury. This tiny town is without doubt a sacred place. On the grounds of the Abbey there's a stone commemorating that this has been a place of worship "since there were Christians in England". For centuries before that it flourished as a center for service to the Goddess and interactions with the fae. The holy nature of this land is far more ancient than even that stone commemorates. Pagan pilgrims can feel it. As Dion Fortune, who lived there for a time, said, places where mankind has been in the habit of reaching out toward the divine make a kind of track, making it easy to go in that direction.

Avalon is such a place. Whether we reach for its magic within, or whether we journey to a physical place held sacred for eons, tracing the footsteps of our foremothers through Glastonbury, Wales or Brittany, we are most able to visit Avalon when we accept and allow the experience of life as more than a physical, third dimensional experience. We are spirit. And that spirit is Avalon.

Avalon's magic

- Trance work.
- Scrying.
- Mirror work.
- Fairy traditions.
- Automatic channelings/speech.
- Sex magic.
- Handfasting.
- Cauldron work.
- Work with crystals, stones and animals such as the raven, the fox and the owl.
- Observing the Celtic Wheel of the Year.
- Working with plants.
- Herblore.
- Vegetarianism.
- Detoxing.
- Water.
- Ritual use of sacred plant medicine and other substances – only for the highly disciplined initiate.

Goddesses and Gods of Avalon

The Merlin: Bard, druid, doctor, healer, teacher, known as Taliesin.

Morgan: Seer, prophet, lover, sister, mother, rebel.

The Lady of the Lake: The fairy blood of the Old People ran through the Lady's veins – her daughter became priestess in her place. Viviane and Nimue were both Lady of the Lake.

Brigit: Celtic mother/warrior Goddess archetype.

Aine: Fairy of new beginnings and daring leaps.

Rhiannon: The sorceress.

Maiden/Mother/Crone: The three aspects of the Goddess, integral to Avalon and Celtic Goddess worship.

Chapter 10 ~ The Elementals

ENTER THE REALM OF WHITE MAGIC

Welcome to working safely, deeply with the white magical realm, inhabited by you, me and the beloved elementals. Unicorn, dragons, centaurs, mermaids, fairies and gnomes are not real or unreal as we understand and use those terms – they simply are, as magic is. They live on the etheric plane, and appear to us when we are ready, when we humans need to receive a message, and when their environment is safe. I have such passion and love for these creatures, and I hope that this inspires you to take the time to develop a relationship with them too.

The Unicorn

The unicorn is the original fabulous beast, to quote Lewis Carroll in his classic novel Alice, Through the Looking Glass. For those of us who adore the elementals, it seems very natural to begin to explore their energies through this marvelous creature, the wondrous unicorn.

More and more frequently now the unicorn is being mentioned, its image appearing in popular culture as well as in esoteric writings, its resurgence becoming more and more apparent. As we shift into this new, very magical age, where technology and ancient knowledge are coming together to create a holistic and sacred future, the doors between the worlds are being opened wider and wider. The hope is growing that a new world – one where peace and sensitivity to each other and to the earth, to the Goddess and the God and to our own psyches and psychic abilities – will soon be reborn.

It seems to be happening. More and more individuals are meditating and visualizing, turning to nature for soul retrieval and spiritual succor. The Goddess is rising and the Old Ways are being revived and revered. More and more people are engaging in ancient sacred activities, and many have reported seeing unicorns. In dreams, meditations and sometimes with eyes wide open, we are being joined once again by this beautiful, gentle animal.

When we look at the mythology of any creature, we can see its spiritual truths as well as the attitudes of the people who tell us the story. Myths are also our human way of telling ourselves our sacred truths. They can be codes for an older story, and interwoven with the storyteller's attitudes as well as natural connections, for example the discovery of fossils, and the blending and layering of oral history over time. We come to own these myths, and they us, in a unique relationship, in special and significant ways.

It is not so much what the myth can tell us that is precious and compelling – it is what the myth reveals about ourselves that is so resonant and so fascinating.

The unicorn has been written about by both esteemed Ancient Greek philosopher Aristotle and Genghis Khan, Mongolian conqueror of the 1100s, who, having seen one, believed it was a sign to halt an attack. He did so, withdrawing his troops, and thus adding to the folklore/truths of the unicorn as a harbinger of peace, stopping bloodshed and violence.

A nursery rhyme still doing the rounds of children's story times tells of the lion and unicorn. In it the lion, a primary symbol of Christianity, drives the unicorn, a symbol of forest and nature worship, from England. In the streets of Kensington in London today, the symbols of the lion and the unicorn in this eternal face off remain.

The myth still lives within us, and around us. And slowly, if we look closely enough, we can see, hear and feel the messages the unicorn is sending to us.

Greek physician and historian Ctesias reported seeing a unicorn in 416 BC, in the court of Darius II, the King of Persia. In 2800 BC, the Chinese emperor Fu Hsi wrote of seeing Qi Lin, the Chinese name for the unicorn. He saw symbols on the coat of the creature, and from these symbols he is said to have derived the source and inspiration for the development of Chinese characters, which went on to form the basis of the Oriental alphabet. Thus the Qi Lin, or unicorn, is said to be the basis of the Chinese written language. Today in China it is believed that this magical creature assists and guides those who rely on symbols, language and the imagination to express themselves and make a living. So if you wish to be assisted in written communication, simply ask for the help and guidance of Qi Lin, who will fill you with inspiration and help you through any block you may be having regarding writing.

The unicorn, like the dragon and the fairy, is a cultural constant. Despite the world's immense diversity, these beautiful elementals are told of in tales from China to Wales, and the belief in them has existed for thousands of years from east to west.

In China, the Qi Lin reportedly spoke to the ancients of a time when a sage-like leader would come to help the planet. As more and more of us are recording and reporting unicorn sightings in dreams, meditations and fleeting glimpses in magical landscapes, is that time upon us?

In the legends of Vietnam, a unicorn is a powerful sign that abundance and good fortune are on their way. Often the unicorn appears with a Goddess, Dia, who has the face of the moon, and who guides the unicorn as to where it needs to direct its blessings. The unicorn dance is still performed each year throughout Vietnam and in Vietnamese communities. Its power, it seems, is universally acknowledged.

The Alicorn and the Mystic Ruby

The unicorn's magnificent and distinguishing spiral horn is a sacred shape which recurs across nature, and which contains the code upon which life itself is based. The spiral is a perfect manifestation of the divine sequence, a numeric code discovered by ancient sages where each successive number equals the addition of those preceding it. This symbolizes the continuing growth of everything – that everything in this world exists as a result of everything that goes before. As it is above, so it is below.

The unicorn's horn emanates from the center of his brow, the region in which our third eye and third eye chakra are located. The third eye contains our capacity for intuition, for psychic abilities, for clairvoyance and for communion and communication between worlds. Underneath the unicorn's beautiful white horn, called the alicorn, is said to be a magnificent blood red ruby. This Mystic Ruby is said to give whoever possesses it the powers of invincibility and immortality. The power emanating through the horn could be directed by whoever possessed it. When in the possession of the beautiful unicorn, it was directed to benefit all those around him – to purify water, create a race of forest super beings who assisted the plant and animal life within the forest, and to purify food and the thinking of individuals who came in contact with the unicorn.

The Mystic Ruby also holds the key to knowing what it is that resides in our own hearts – when we hear of the healing property of the ruby and the horn, we must observe our reactions. Do we covet the precious ruby? Do we wish to obtain power? Do we long for its healing properties to be focused on our lives? Our reaction reveals so much to us about ourselves.

I feel that the unicorn is highly symbolic of the new generation being born as this is written – children born from 1997 to the present day all have the precious ruby energy of the unicorn. It is their totem, their power animal, to use the language of shaman and author Steven Farmer. When I was writing this chapter, my daughter came in to the office clutching a beautiful silver and mauve unicorn toy, and demanded that I speak with it. Rather than turn her away, I felt it was important to indeed do as she asked – because from the mouths of little children comes much wisdom.

The horn of the unicorn is said to have magical qualities. Specifically it is used to purify bodies of water, a prize of great value to the ancients, who observed unicorns dipping their magical alicorn into polluted or poisoned waters in order for all the creatures of the forest to drink safely. In this respect they are guardians of our natural resources, particularly lakes, rivers and inland bodies of fresh water. For the great deeds they do, they are respected and loved by all the wild creatures of the deep forest.

When humans discovered this quality, it was kept secret by the druids and priestesses in order to preserve the sacred nature of the gift, and to protect the unicorn from those who would seek to use its powers ignobly. Once the secret was discovered, greed and veneration resulted. Hunters were sent to find and kill the unicorns so their horns could be used. The horn itself was often reshaped into a chalice, used by those who obtained it to ensure their own food and drink was pure and that any poisons were neutralized.

Interestingly, the alicorn appears on many medical prescriptions and lists of apothecary ingredients with great frequency until the mid 17th century – a time when the unicorn was an endangered magical creature. Slowly, as the century unfolded, its alicorn disappeared from the lists kept by doctors and apothecaries. Given their rare, shy, wild nature, and helped by the Witches and wise ones who wished to protect them, the unicorns went deeper and deeper into the forest – until they were linked to the maiden, when they were once again able to be hunted.

The maiden and the unicorn

Virginity, as a word, did not take on its modern meaning until quite recently. Virgin, in British and Celtic lore, simply meant a woman who chose to be without a husband or children. It did not preclude sex itself, it just ruled out the state of marriage. The virgin also represents a state of the Goddess, who is represented by the maiden, the mother and the crone in her triple aspect. In her maiden aspect she may or may not be literally a virgin, but she is in a state of innocence, and has not yet borne a child.

The virgin, or maiden, who was used as bait for a unicorn is far more associated with the ancient Goddess worship than with modern notions of virginity. She was pure in intent, loving and innocent, wild and free – as is the unicorn. Thus this wild aspect of the divine feminine was the sole way to contact and have communication with the unicorn.

Many of the young women who established contact with the unicorns actually assisted them in escaping the hunters by fleeing with them deeper and deeper into the forest – a kind of magical metaphor for the fact that Goddess worship, particularly in the 17th century, a peak of the Burning Times, saw Goddess worship/Witchcraft hide deeper and deeper within the forest, with the wild things, and surface only under guises that Christian folk could bear. For example, the only acceptable way for many hundreds of years to worship the Goddess, the feminine aspect of the divine, was via the worship of Mary, the "virgin" mother of Jesus Christ.

Perhaps it is not surprising that the unicorn is reconnecting with us at a time when Goddess worship and the divine feminine is re-entering the mainstream. This is because we are being reconnected with our magical selves, with our own maiden, our own pure, wild qualities. Gentle and free, fierce and beloved – as is the magical creature, the beloved unicorn.

The Wondrous dragon
A being of white magic,
a being of power

They are called the Rakona by the Maori of New Zealand, the Werwe by the tribes of Ethiopia. In Denmark they are called Drage, in Japan, Testsu, and in ancient Babylon they were the Tiamet. All over this planet, the beautiful dragon is ubiquitous, considered by many to be an omnipotent beast whose fascinating abilities and magical powers, fierce intelligence and fascinating contradictions have led to humanity conducting a long, passionate and still burning love affair with this magical beloved creature.

Why are dragon lore, legends and sightings so universal?

I've meditated on this, researched it and explored the ideas available at present with wise ones and mentors, friends and workshop participants. Dragons are real. Elementals exist.

The dragon can signify royalty, fierce fighting, far sightedness, incredible courage, gentleness, strength, dreadful anger when aroused beyond that which they should bear, and tolerance – they can withstand a multitude of horrors before they turn and unleash their fiery fury.

The Celts and Picts of pre-invasion Britain called their kings dragons – Uther Pendragon, the father of King Arthur, is a famed example. Merlin worked closely with dragons, and knew of their whereabouts and their impact on the land. In China, dragons were understood to be the beloved and loving protectors of the royal line, and in Japan the emperor was said to be descended from a line of flying spirit dragons. In India the nagas, or dragons with a human head, brought knowledge, peace and harmony to the warring peoples fighting over natural resources.

Greek heroes slayed dragons, as did Christian saints like St George. In Scandinavia, the great hero-king Beowulf was said to have slaughtered a mighty fire-breathing dragon, Grendel, yet in the famous old English tale is himself slain by the dragon at the end.

Irish naturalist Robert Lloyd Praeger has said that the dragon was so much a part of Irish culture that "it was practically an accepted part of Irish zoology."

The dragon is definitely one of the most complex and misunderstood of all the glorious and fascinating elementals. Embodying contradictory qualities, it has been demonized due to its historical associations with Witchcraft and paganism.

In the west we associate the dragon as being a fierce, fire-breathing, maiden munching monster. But in the east, where they were not seen as a symbol to be corrupted, and thus to aid the crushing of the pagan roots of the Celtic belief system, they were and are still seen as beneficent creatures that guard families, helping them in gentle ways, nudging them towards honoring themselves and creating and protecting family wealth.

So while they are found, and spoken of in awe, in almost all human societies, the meanings we attribute to them vary wildly. This change in beliefs – from the protectors and symbols of kings to maiden devouring monsters, can be traced through the history of religious colonization in the west.

Reclaiming our dragon friends

The Celtic dragon was systematically discredited – and ultimately symbolically destroyed – by the Church, who distorted the tale of St George, who lived at the end of the third century CE. The dragon held within it the practices of the Old Ways, pagan thinking, tribal rites, seasonal energies and the treasures and magic of the minerals and stones of the earth. The treasure of the dragon's hoard is actual as well as metaphorical. The treasure represents the fragments of earth wisdom and power within the seasonal festivals. The dragon guarding this treasure metaphorically represents the struggle of the keepers of the Old Ways to preserve the truths and their heritage. St George's "defeat" of the dragon (they actually worked closely together!)symbolizes the defeat of the Old Ways by the Roman version of the Church, which "defeated" paganism, or at least drove it underground to the dragon's lair.

Dragons have long been associated with every element. There are different kinds of dragons, and each embodies a different quality. There are also dragons associated with the cosmos and its heavenly bodies. They are also linked with natural phenomena – the rainbow is said to be a form of naturally occurring dragon, because it bridges sea and sky and earth. Expectant mothers in some indigenous cultures of Australia were advised to look away from the rainbow serpent, as it was said to be the stairway to heaven, the way souls left this realm and traveled to the one beyond. Thus this dragon of the rainbow could "spirit" you off to the celestial realm, by the unborn simply observing its beauty and longing to return home.

In their earliest forms, dragons were associated with the Great Mother, and sometimes with a warrior God, and by other cultures with a water and/or sun God. They represent so many things because dragons have the capacity to be both compassionate and totally destructive – so the duality of the universe is contained within their very physiology and their actions.

Devotion to duty and to the natural order, their desire to protect and their ability to annihilate are all part of the same creature. Creator and destroyer. Cold-blooded reptile of the earth and sky and sun and moon and rainbow, yet breathing fire. Able to fly above the planets and throughout the heavens, yet resting underground in the earth's mineral and jewel-encrusted hollows and caverns.

Intelligent yet utterly instinctual, the dragon is indeed the symbol of the all-powerful spirit, embodying all that lies beyond the realm of the rational, representing magic itself. To have dragon energy, to be at one with it, is to understand the chaos of the world and be able to deal with the contradictions that typify the flux of life.

Flying with the Dragonkin

Sea dragons: Unknown territories on European navigational maps of the 16th and 17th centuries were marked: "Here be dragons." Could these sightings have simply been of enormous squid, octopus or whales? Or were they actually sea dragons? For believers, myself included, sea serpents protect the balance of power within the world's oceans, interacting with coastal dwelling humans and particularly with sea Witches. They often have long relationships with one clan or blood lineage.

Sky dragons: The amphitere, the most renowned of all the myriad sky dragons, is exemplified by the Mexican sky serpent God Quetzalcoatl, who oversees all that happens within all societies, particularly the human societies. This shimmering, powerful and wise serpent God is celebrated in much of Mexico's stunning indigenous art.

Wyrms: These dragons have no wings and no legs, and are told of most often in Britain, Brittany, Ireland, Germany and Spain. They are primarily forest dwellers, however sometimes they move in to towns, most often when their natural habitat has been destroyed by development. In Lambton, a town in England, there is a well in which, it is said, dwells the Lambton Wyrm. The story goes that the heir to Lambton Hall caught a small wyrm in the forest when it was a baby, and fed and kept it imprisoned, refusing to let it return to the forest, until the wyrm became enraged and monstrous with misery and anger. It escaped and fled to the town's well, terrifying the local inhabitants, leading to a long-term grudge against the family whose son caused this dragon's suffering. They say the Lambton Wyrm is still alive and wreaking havoc. Others believe that in fact the wyrm has been a blessing for the town, and in keeping the Old Ways alive.

Lindwyrms: Sightings of these dragons of the steppes of central Asia were recorded by the explorer Marco Polo, who noted that these dragons had two legs and were flightless.

Wyverns: Wyverns are often seen on the banners of royalty, as they are said to bring strength, courage, wisdom and clear sightedness to those who carry their image into battle. Within your own work environment or a distressing personal situation, the wyvern can assist you if you call on its energy and wisdom. They can give you their courage when politics are draining you of your fire, and can assist you in remaining cool and "flying" above the dilemmas to see solutions – dragon energy, especially that of the wyvern, can help you see what is actually happening within a situation. They can also help you release fears or guilty feelings you may have regarding prosperity, success and winning. The wyvern's inability to blink means they miss nothing. They are a precious, unstoppable guardian.

Nagas: These sub-continental dragons have the head of a human and the body of a serpent. They are typically depicted in Indian art and sacred texts as having no wings. Their role is to work with the Gods, and they are also the spirits of the water and the clouds. Nagas, as with dragons generally, can shapeshift to become either wholly dragon or wholly human, and interact undercover with both species. Some nagas have conducted love affairs with humans, resulting in amazing children who are an elemental blend of human and dragon.

Drakes: This Western dragon is small, with legs but no

wings. There are two varies of drake – water drakes and fire drakes. Fire drakes do as their name suggests, they breathe fire, and are red and scarlet in color. Water drakes breathe the frost and the snows of winter, and are white and light bluish in color. I have a frost drake as a companion from time to time. She turns up when I need her help, and is very fond of green tourmaline – crystals are a wonderful way to connect with your dragon. There are many townships throughout Britain named for the drake, including Drakesford and Drakeshill. They were often found living with families, and started their fires to warm their humans in their role as guardian and protector of the home.

Eastern dragons: The premier hexagram of the I-Ching, the sacred Chinese form of divination, is known as The Creative, or the Dragon. Taoists also hold the dragon sacred, seeing it as the creative force that brings forth change, gives spiritual protection and helps the person in need to maintain integrity and their true essence.

Properties of the dragon

Dragons are beloved of many of us already, wise women, wizards, alchemists, seers and sorcerers, as well as many philosophers, who have often held long and fascinating debates with the dragon. However, even those who have feared the dragon (and feared their own power!) are now coming to understand the precious friendship and teachings this beautiful elemental offers. The symbol of the magical land of Wales is also a dragon. It is always red, and represents the Welsh divinity, Dewi, who works closely with Merlin and King Arthur (whose sirname is Pendragon) and the Knights of the Round Table.

Dragons can give those who seek their knowledge an

ancient and uniquely elemental perspective on the history of this planet and its manifold citizens – animal, plant, human and elemental.

One of the many qualities Witches in particular attribute to the dragon is that of regeneration. Each Beltane the earth serpent Ouroboros is said to bellow a terrible cry, a scream that can be heard beneath every source of fire within the land – every hearth, every fire, every Beltane candle. It awakens the fire within us all with its cry of pain and joy intertwined together. It is often shown with its tail in its mouth, symbolizing completion, perfection and totality. The shadow and the light is represented by this dragon's anguished celebration of the return of the warmth of summer, and of procreative activity.

Calling forth your dragon guardian

Many white magical practitioners interact with the lung wang, or dragon king, a creature of great allure who can shapeshift at will into a handsome man of startling blue. We also call upon the obsidian thunder dragon for change in our lives, and the fu-ts'ang lung, the dragon that guards the treasures of the earth, for environmental issues.

Perhaps the most wondrous of all is the shun lung, or spirit dragon, who brings us all rain, and is the companion of humans wise enough and courageous enough to befriend this magical, wise, sacred beast.

Deciding to call forth dragons, as the druids say, is both a responsibility and an honor. While we refer to dragons and other elementals as "ours", they can never be possessed – we are simply honored by their choice to work with us for a time.

Your dragon may come to you as a guardian, a protector or as a teacher. He or she can come in many shapes and sizes and colors – and temperaments too! There are massive heraldic dragons of scarlet and black, and there are tiny sprite-like dragons that exist, the Chinese say, in every raindrop, every snowflake, every flicker of fire. There are even moon dragons that can be seen traveling across its face, like darting birds. If you sense dragon energy around you, you may want to invite the dragon into your life.

Dragons respond to all of the elements, so by activating the element of fire on your altar and calling for your dragon, either silently in your mind or aloud, you will call forth a fire dragon. A fire dragon can help you to activate that element in your own life, and assist you in many ways.

An air dragon can be called using feathers, simply by waving them gently in the air, or by lighting incense, the smoke from which activates the element of air.

Water dragons, of course, are called forth by activating the element of water, and dragons of the earth can be called forth by activating the element of earth on your altar.

When you have intuitively decided which dragon you wish to work with, or need to work with, activate that element on your altar, cast a magical circle, and say the following three times with arms out and palms up:

I call forth my dragon kin
My fire friend, my water love, my host of air and
earth's sacred keeper
I call you forth on this day
I seek your assistance in understanding, growth,
love, wisdom and the quest for my true self
May you honor me with your powerful energy,
and make yourself known to me from this day forth,
until it is time for us to part.

Then place a crystal on your altar. Semi-precious stones will help you connect with your dragon, and the stone itself will assist you in working with their energy. Focusing on the stone, say: "I call you forth now, dragon kin, and honor you with this gift."

A dragon's gifts can be shared by those who love, respect and honor them. Do this, and wisdom will be yours in return. Allow yourself to sit quietly and meditate on the crystal, or with eyes gently closed.

Your dragon will soon let you know, gently, lovingly, of its presence, with increased warmth, the flickering of a candle flame, the breath of air upon your cheek, or tears, signifying your water dragon is helping you release emotional blockages.

Thank your dragon for these signs, and ask for its name.

Thank it for revealing its name, and tell it yours in return.

Ask your dragon what it is it has to share with you.

Ask your three questions, and then allow your dragon to answer them.

Finally, thank your dragon, and feel it leave. Close circle.

Now you have activated this connection, the dragon can be with you at any time, to help and empower you, simply by calling your dragon's name.

Blessed be.

Swim with the mermaidens
Immerse your soul and your senses in the element of water

Merfolk – mermaidens and mermen – are among the most complex of the elementals. A magical creature with the head and torso of a man or woman and the body, or tail, of a fish, they live primarily beneath the sea and are the guardians and protectors of women's sexuality. They can predict storms and future events, and some can even grant wishes to humans who encounter them. They are great teachers of wisdom and knowledge, and they can also replenish our physical energy, as well as refreshing and renewing our spirits. They are associated with the Candomble Goddess Yemanja, Mother Mary, Mary Magdalene, Aphrodite, Neptune, prostitution, virginity, irresistible desire, and the yearning for a love so great that we transform our very physical selves.

Sometimes we feel we are on intimate terms with the merfolk, and we forget just how amazing they are. After all, they are among the most culturally and commercially appropriated of all magical creatures, stimulating our imaginations, intriguing us and, for some, provoking fear and lust in equal combinations.

They are the constant elemental visitors to our popular culture – a twin tailed mermaid graces the symbol of coffee chain Starbucks, Siren Tuna has a beautiful mermaid on its can, and women with their legs encased in synthetic fishtails swim in shows across the world at aquatic parks.

As a child, who has not swum, legs held tightly together, imitating the merfolk's manner of propelling themselves through the water? And who has not imagined what it would be like to be able to breathe underwater, to be able to live in that utterly familiar yet most foreign of elements? The freedom, the beauty and the wild innocence are so very beguiling.

It's interesting to note that until relatively recently, merfolk were utterly believed in, with sightings by Italy's Christopher Columbus and England's Henry Hudson, famed explorers who recorded their sightings meticulously, and other reports in various natural journals. In 1830 off the coast of Scotland, a mermaid's body was found washed up, and was buried after examination and verification by a local doctor. Desmond

Morris, a cultural anthropologist of our times, believes that they are indeed real – a kind of water ape, a missing link in the evolutionary chain.

The mermaid's siren song

We often do see mermaids, and they are indeed real. But they are elementals, not actual creatures, and they interact with us on an energetic level, using our auric field to manifest – but only when they choose to, and only when we are ready to have the experience.

Mermaids encapsulate all of our fears, desires, temptations and repressed feelings about sex. As such, they are wonderful indicators of where our psyches are at. When we look at the historical representations of the beautiful mermaids, we see that the way in which they are portrayed says so much more about the time and its attitudes than it tells the truth about mermaids themselves.

They have been portrayed as sexually rapacious and predatory, as flesh eating bisexual monsters (recent films such as She Creature, Peter Pan and Dagon are prime examples of this enduring world view of the mermaid) who are self-obsessed, indulgent, untrustworthy and utterly feminine.

They have also been castrated, such as in the Disneyfication of The Little Mermaid, the super-sanitized yet still so appealing animated version of Han Christian Andersen's terrifying fairytale of the mermaid who sacrifices her voice, her legs and her every comfort and family tie in order to fulfill her desire to be human so she could love a man. This sacrificial aspect to Ariel's tale is an echo of medieval dogma, in which mermaids were said to long for a soul, as they were stated by the church to possess none, an unsurprising conclusion given that at the time the debate was still raging as to whether women had souls!

In fact mermaids were used as a kind of cultural repository of every negative or frightening feminine quality – vanity, sexuality, desire and independence. Even our smell and our taste was given description through the mermaid, and in writing about them – and Witches – the church was able to express their fears of the feminine body, our ability to conceive, gestate another body, bleed and love deeply – which were seen as being profoundly disturbing, suspect qualities.

Even celebrated 20th century poet WB Yeats, a man who understood magic and was a member of the Order of the Golden Dawn, encapsulated the belief that mermaids purposefully lured men to their deaths in his poem A Man Young And Old: III. The Mermaid. Of course what Yeats is really writing about is men's fear of loving deeply – that such love will see them overwhelmed, consumed and ultimately drowned.

A mermaid found a swimming lad,
Picked him for her own,
Pressed her body to his body,
Laughed; and plunging down
Forgot in cruel happiness
That even lovers drown.

The kinship aspect between humans and merfolk is also a fascinating one. Again, as with other elementals, sexual interaction between humans and the merfolk has led to the merging of the two.

Some families in Scotland and Ireland still claim descent from mermaids. Families of the Orkney Isles, who often have a genetic trait of slightly webbed hands, claim it as theirs due to an ancestor who fled from her unhappy marriage into the arms of a handsome Selkie, a type of merman who is part seal. The Native American tribe called Penobscot also claims descent from a mermaid. Others believe that the mermaid or merman is our original Atlantean form, when we were both water and land creatures, able to breathe and live in both elements with ease.

How to work with the merfolk

Once we understand the cultural significance of these manifold myths and tales, and the subtext of the stories and the poetry, we can begin our own clear and unencumbered work with the merfolk. We can communicate with them easily, beautifully and safely, and they can teach us much about different forms of communication and enable us to develop telepathic skills. There are some ways to make the meetings more likely – simply by following these steps and incorporating the elemental merfolk into your magic, you will be able to more easily connect with their energy and work on healing many issues which they will help you with.

The direction associated with the mermaid is the west, and her colors are those of the ocean – blues, greens and even the colors of sunset. Water is a reflective surface, thus the mermaid shows us a magical mirror to ourselves. How you feel about them reveals more about yourself, as their magical mirror is a kind of scrying tool for your own state of mind, body and soul.

The times of day you are most likely to encounter them is twilight and dawn – they are also affected tidally. They can assist women with menstrual and fertility issues, and help us come to terms with the outsider status so many of us experience during our lives.

Working with mermaid magic can also mean they are suggesting to you that you need to change your diet to include more natural sea vegetables, fish, seafood, and to incorporate the omega 3 fatty acids present in so much seafood, particularly salmon, into your body. Omega 3 assists people with dietary problems, is anti-carcinogenic, improves our skin tone, color and collagen quantity and quality and stabilizes brain chemistry.

They also suggest that we swim more, play more and have sea salt baths, which help to clear our auric body of any negativity and stale, old energy and beliefs we may be holding on to, especially regarding sexuality and issues of who we are within our various relationships.

Merfolk are an in-between creature, and the season of autumn is their time. To represent the merfolk on your altar, you simply need to include a chalice, as the chalice is the symbol of the mermaid, and of women and the sea.

The salt water aspect of the mermaid is extremely important to their magic. While water is the element that symbolizes cleansing, purification and the quenching of thirst, salt water is a variation on this element. Its qualities are to cleanse, to purify, to draw out impurities, to flavor our lives, to harmonize us and to create the mineral richness that is the bedrock of fertility. Blood, in our wombs and at menstruation, is also salty.

Sea water also enables us to float – it is more buoyant than fresh water and more difficult to move through. It is more complex, cleansing and sometimes stronger than fresh water. We cannot drink it, so there is an element of mistrust between many humans and salt water, although it sustains the life of so many other creatures, and offers we humans so very much in the form of nourishment. This complexity and lack of clarity does not make the mermaids' element deceptive, as some think, rather it makes us question what we assume to be true, and to taste before we drink deeply. Water also represents the unconscious, our urges, desires, instincts and psychic abilities. Salt water represents these abilities taken to a very high vibratory degree.

The tools the mermaid has been gifted with also perfectly illustrate her gifts to us. Her comb represents the precious and sacred nature of caring for our own physical selves. In acknowledging that our bodies deserve time and reverence there is a ritualistic element to all beauty routines that can be lifted out of the mundane and commercial world and into the sacred, making of our bodies an honored temple which we love and respect and demonstrate gratitude for. By honoring it, we honor most deeply the God and the Goddess and the spark of life itself.

With her independence and fleeting attachments, the mermaid shows us how to maintain who we are within intimate physical relationships. Her unabashed beauty and sexuality and her unselfconscious allure shows us that we are desirable and powerful simply for being alive.

Conversely, if we feel repelled or fearful of the sexual mermaid who is happy in her skin, it is indicative that we have a wounded aspect to our sexuality. If we feel an affinity only with the mermaid who gives up her self in order to be joined with a lover, we should sincerely examine just how much of ourselves we change when we are with a partner. This mermaid syndrome can extend to women (or men!) who change their appearance, manners, interests or religion to be with a lover. The mermaid's presence in our lives requires that we become closer to who we truly are, and honor our own truths instead of adopting and adapting to another's, sacrificing who we are in order to be with another – another who may not require that we change at all!

The mermaid also suggests to us that we need to see the

strength in femininity and in being overtly female. Her long hair is an emblem of strength, her sexuality wondrously powerful. There is nothing faint hearted about her, yet she shows us the power in passivity, a magical paradox of sex magic.

A mermaid seduction spell

Mermaids are the mischievous sirens of the sea, laughing, sexy, delightful women who revel in their sexuality and their power. They're not punished for being who they are –desirable yet unattainable. Indeed, they're wanted all the more for it.

If this spell draws you, you are reminded that it is safe to play with your sexuality. The universe will never punish you for being who you are – a beautiful, desirable human being. You are not to be fearful or ashamed of the fact that the universe has gifted you with this precious sexual nature and aspect to your life. The universe knows that your sexuality is sacred, and to seduce is a natural part of being alive to your true nature. There's no shame in the fact that being in a body stimulates desire, and allows you to feel desire and yet remain independent.

You may also be aware that you have some issues with your sexuality that need healing. Many people feel guilt about their sexual natures and the expression of it – this is nothing new! But the truth is that you are magical and you are innocent. This spell will assist you to charm, delight and attract others to you, and to revel in your desirability without obligation or cost to your conscience or anyone else's. Be free, and be happy in your unique desirability.

When the moonlight is strong and clear, dance in its rays, singing these words softly three times before day:

Lover, I draw thee to me with this siren song of the sea
And by the power of three times three
As I do will
So mote it be.

Wear turquoise and silver throughout the next week. Paste a picture of a mermaid in a place where you can see her every day, and let her presence remind you of your own allure. The magical truth is that you too are a siren. And you are never more desirable than when you remember who you truly are. Innocent, powerful, sexual.

Repeat this affirmation to yourself in a mirror – the mermaid's magical tool: "I am a powerful, desirable woman (or man!)."

Healing the wounded masculine – the magnificent Centaur

According to Greek mythology the centaurs were a race half human and half animal – not dissimilar to the merfolk – with a man's head and torso but the body of a horse.

As an elemental and a magical creature who is currently working strongly with many of us, the centaur is the lord of all that is fine, humane, strong and healing about men. He represents the sacred masculine principle, as does Cernunnos, the Horned God of the Celtic tradition, or the Green Man, as does Apollo and Thoth, Mercury and Hermes and Merlin. But the centaur has something very different to offer to all of us who wish to embrace the sacred masculine energy that is being brought back into balance along with the divine feminine. The centaur helps us to understand, love, and heal each other, and to appreciate the love of a man who is good, wise and compassionate. Who does not wish that for ourselves, and for our children and those who will inherit this planet after us?

This masculine energy oversees, orders and delegates the realms of music and medicine, as well as the skills and sacrifices of the hunt, both sacred and mundane. Thus he is bard and healer, provider and hunter. He is the one who chooses what and who to sacrifice for the good of all, and the one who heals and teaches others how to work with the wounded, both in body and in soul. As such the centaur embodies all that is best about the archetypes of father, teacher, brother and doctor.

The centaur is the masculine principle. All that is potentially good and bad of men and masculinity is explored within the tales of the heroic and ignoble deeds of the centaurs. If we explore the literature of the Greeks, we find that they are – as are all elementals – typically paradoxical. Heroic, self-sacrificing, the greatest of teachers. And yet they are also drunken, abusive, boorish, driven by the basest of instincts. Within them we explore the nature of what it is to be a man, and the centaur is a gift to all men. Observe us, they say, and learn what it is you have the potential to be.

The centaur holds up to the healing light of the God and the Goddess the secrets of the wounded earthbound male. They represent all that is active, rooted to the earth, able to move swiftly, engaging in the flesh, able to connect deeply with the secrets of the earth and our ability to connect with and activate the wisdom of the animus. They embody the primal aspect of masculinity – they are said to be wild, debauched, impulsive, fearsome, violent, vulgar, although they are not.

This creature, who lives in the wild and is totally at home with his instincts, represents acting intuitively, trusting our desires and celebrating the flesh. The notion of the centaur as a lust-frenzied savage is the fear we have of the masculine principle in its negative aspect, for they are also healers, readers of the stars, wonderful hunters and providers, superb and skilled lovers, beautiful to gaze upon and the guardians of the gate of the forest.

The great wise centaur Chiron

"If the poet's tongue might breathe the prayer that is on the lips of all, I would pray that Chiron, who is dead and gone, were now alive again. I would want him to reign again in the glens, the rugged monster whose mind was friendly to men. That gentle craftsman who drove pain from the limbs, that hero who cured all types of diseases." So wrote the classical Greek poet and historian Pindar about the centaur Chiron, around 500BC.

Much of what is wonderful about the centaur is characterized by the courageous, honorable, loving, kind and strong magical being known as Chiron, the wisest of all centaurs. To the Greeks he was a revered and sacred being, one who was both respected and beloved, and who to this day teaches us the very best of what it is to be a man, a father, a leader, a hunter, a doctor and a brother.

Chiron's story is one we can all relate to. Abandoned, maligned and treated as an outcast, he ultimately grew in influence and wisdom, until he made the ultimate sacrifice – that of his life for mankind. There are many parallels with the story of Jesus in the life of Chiron.

The tale goes like this: The God Saturn fell in love with a sea nymph, Philyra, but Saturn was already married. To hide their trysts, Saturn and Philyra shapeshifted into a magnificent stallion and a beautiful mare, and met as lovers in their guise as horses. However Philyra fell pregnant, and when she gave birth to her child she was horrified to discover it had the head and torso of a man, but the body of a horse. She wept, abandoning her deformed child on Mount Pelion, where many other elementals lived, and begged the Gods to transform her into a tree.

But being immortal, the infant Chiron could not die. He grew up alone except for the God Apollo, his grandfather, who came to teach him the mysteries of prophecy, music and understanding the ways of men and love. Chiron studied and learned much, became a master musician – "Even the stones stopped to listen when he played," wrote Pindar – and became known as a wise and honorable being.

In time, the Gods sent their own, often illegitimate, sons to Chiron to be taught and trained. He was the teacher and father-figure to many of the great heroes, including Jason of Argonaut and Golden Fleece fame, Achilles, Hercules and Asclepius. His teachings focused on integrating the physical, spiritual/moral and intellectual natures, because only by developing and integrating all three can heroes realize their true nature.

Then came a turning point in Chiron's life. During a fierce, alcohol-fueled and terrible battle, Chiron was wounded by an arrow from the bow of his own beloved foster-son, Hercules. The wound would have been fatal to any mortal, but since he was immortal, he could not die from this wound. But its raging, burning pain led him to search for relief. In his desperation for a cure for his own wound, Chiron learned all the secrets of healing, which he taught to Asclepius, acclaimed as the father of medicine. After many years of learning and passing on this invaluable medical knowledge, Chiron gave up his immortality to Prometheus so that man could have the gift of fire.

It was Chiron's pain that led him to the very font of healing talents, and in realizing this we can see that our own wounds create the potential for healing, for knowledge, and the possibility of stopping such things ever happening again. But even if they do, thanks to Chiron, we can treat each other, give each other comfort and transform ourselves from simply flesh into a creature where spirit, flesh and intellect bring us closer to our divine source.

Working with their magic

The centaur's magical therapy, teachings and healings are unique for each of us, and much of how they will manifest to us depends on our attitudes towards masculinity, force and power. Our experiences come into play in a profound manner when we magically invoke the centaur. Do we fear, revere, desire, accept or respect masculinity? Do we personally use the masculine principle for good and positive power and change? How do we feel about being noticed, being powerful? If we struggle with this part of our life's story, the centaur can be of great assistance in showing us how to be who we truly are, and how to express that fearlessly and powerfully in a profoundly healing way that will make a great difference to all of those around us – especially our children. Remember, the centaur in his positive aspect is also the ultimate father, so he is ideal to magically invoke for men wondering about parenting, teaching and raising children, or for women wanting a man like that to help rear, teach and love their children.

For despite the magical truth that all centaurs are male, women too can benefit from the centaur's energy and strength. He represents the greatest potential of fatherhood, and as such can reveal where our relationships with our own fathers have left us saddened, hurt or wounded, and help us heal them. The centaur is also the protector of abused children, and oversees the protection of orphaned male children, helping them to succeed in what seems to be a harsh and indifferent world.

When we connect with the centaur in magic and meditation, we will be astounded at his capacity to assist in our healing. The centaur's esoteric teachings focus on the possibility and challenges of integrating the physical, spiritual and intellectual natures, because only by developing and successfully harmonizing all three can men become the heroes they innately are.

The centaur's impact on our life is that of teasing out the sacred meaning and special qualities of our own unique journey, and in this quest there are no more magical elementals than the mighty centaurs Nessus, Pholus and Chiron to call on to assist you. Each of them has a particular healing talent – individually and collectively they are helping us transform wounds into strengths. The mistakes of the past will slowly stop being repeated when we listen to their message, and ask for their assistance.

Chiron will assist you with long and slow transformations, career change, fatherhood, attracting a partner who is honorable, ethical and strong, as well as being a good provider. Chiron can help men express masculine strength and tenderness. He assists with healing diseases of the blood, injury, abandonment, alienation, being orphaned and male friendships.

Pholus will assist you with true change through the release of old, injured emotional, mental or physical patterns which have a basis in family history. He can open the locked doors of families, lovers, children, cultures and societies. What is hidden can be revealed, healed and released. Pholus tends to make things happen more suddenly – people can swiftly determine a new direction and attitude with his intercession, unlike Chiron whose impact is long-term. Pholus is especially loving and offers helpful guidance to those with addictive behaviors and harmful compulsions which keep us stuck in unhealthy old patterns.

Nessus will profoundly empower us when it comes to healing the impact of abuse – psychological, physical or sexual. He also oversees the realm of consequence, of the cause and effect of our actions in the long-term. Nessus reveals where we have been hurt and where we are most likely to hurt others in return. He also delivers antidotes to the poison of the past, and creates opportunities for healing through delivering to us situations where we can change our actions, and thus heal the impact of other people's actions towards us.

Gradually, with meditation, spellwork and integration, these creatures can become our valued friends – the wise, intuitive and healing voices of our soul. Already, they are waiting for us within, simply keeping still, until we learn to listen.

The centaur energy began surging through this universe again in 1977, when the planetoid known as Chiron – yes, named after Chiron himself – was discovered. It coincided (but there are no coincidences!) with the beginnings of the recharging of masculine energy on this planet. When we speak of the new energies we often speak of the return of the divine feminine. The centaur reminds us not to overlook the masculine aspect of divinity in our quest to honor the Goddess.

We are now undergoing a rapid transformation of the male/female dynamic, and by 2012 there will be new discoveries in healing, sexuality and the use of power that will see the politics, power structures and relationships between men and women, and men and children, rapidly evolving – for the better in all ways. The beautiful centaurs can help bring about this change.

Creating connection with the fae

Far from being imaginary beings, fairy folk are energetic earth spirits that are present at all times and in all places where there is any bit of natural flora, fauna or a single trace of one of the five magical elements – so therefore they are everywhere!

They are both able to interact with humans, and able to avoid us if they wish to. It takes a great deal of faith, love, patience and respect to entice these magical creatures from their secret and ingenious hiding places and have them show themselves to us.

Why are they so capricious when it comes to people? Because it has been necessary for their survival to learn to be careful about which human beings they trust. They have developed a shy nature quite unlike the friendly wild creatures who used to appear to the people of ancient times in any wild place, especially at festival times or at dawn or twilight, back in the days when the earth was closer to the Goddess.

Sadly, they now have far sharper instincts, which alert them to possible danger – and we humans often represent serious danger to the fairy folk, because while they are strong, they are also fragile creatures. But their self-preservation instinct has meant we are fortunate and honored enough to still share this world with them. We may even be lucky enough to feel them, glimpse them, even talk with them from time to time.

The fairies may test you time and again until they know you are sincere, so great patience is necessary in encountering them. Yet even when we don't see them, we sense them. We could hardly not do so, as they are all around us. They are in our gardens, our forests, our parks, in every drop of water, in the fires we light, under the ground and in the trees, in the air and the wind and even, if we are very fortunate, we may have a house fairy living with us – a wonderful gift indeed!

Fairies are all elemental in nature, and each type or category – not that we believe in labels! – relates specifically to their element. Earth, air, fire, water and spirit fairies all exist. Many are far more likely to emerge from their secret hideaways and hidden places during the festivals of Beltane and Samhain, when the veil between the worlds is at its thinnest, as well as the other magical seasons of the earth and the sacred moon days. So if we observe and keep and honor these blessed festivals of the Goddess and her celestial and earthly events, we will open ourselves up to wonderful, magical encounters and interactions with the fairies.

Many fairies and elementals associate with wise ones, reborn druids, priestesses and shamans, because we work with nature so closely and have such a sacred and magical appreciation of her gifts. Even those of us who live in crowded cities are likely to attract the elementals to us. It is not that they need us – it is that they wish to help reawaken us to the impact human beings have upon them, their kin and their sacred environment. In essence, they are also asking us for assistance in assuring their survival. As so many of us work with the worlds between worlds, the fairies, who are etheric in nature, can assist us in our dreamscape adventures, our pathworkings and our meditative inner journeyings.

Working with the fairies

It is really important to realize something when we are working with the fairies – and all of the elementals. So many people allow themselves to be drawn into arguments, debates and full on fights about what fairies and gnomes, elves and mermaids look like. Here is the truth. They look different to everybody. The elementals use whatever energetic forms are around them to manifest and become visible. So how a fairy appears to me will differ from fairy being to fairy being, and depending on my mood, the season and how I energetically interact with it, my health and wellbeing, and my vibration at the time. And the very same energetic beings may appear quite differently to you – because we have different energy, emotions, vibrations, intellects and souls. Whatever energy we emanate influences not only what we create and manifest in our lives, but also strongly affects the quality and the type of interactions we have with all elementals.

This is true of every spiritual visitation and manifestation we have, and why it is totally pointless arguing about whether a fairy has long red hair and green skin, or is short and stumpy, or tall and willow-graceful, or has wings like a dragonfly or a bee! They are as they are to you. Yes, they have particular characteristics, but they will appear in a unique way to you. No two people's fairy experiences are the same.

Once we can win the trust of the fairies and begin to journey with them, we will discover worlds within worlds. There are fairies who will work with us and teach us, there are also fairies who simply want to play with us, and reawaken us to sensual joy and simple, natural pleasures – thus they make us laugh and cry, and help us unblock the paths by which energy flows through our bodies.

There are also fairies who teach us sharp lessons if we approach them with arrogance and assumptions of superior knowledge, or wishing to harness their powers to use for our own. The issue of power is one fairies are very aware of. The fae do not subscribe to the value system of humans. To anthropomorphize them – to make them the same as humans – is to misunderstand their intense energy. They are themselves. They belong to no man or woman, to no path or belief system. They belong to themselves, and are under the protection of the Lady.

Where the fairies came from

Fairies must be approached with an innocent heart and with great respect. Not with fear, but with an understanding that it is up to them to decide whether they will come forward and speak and learn with us.

While they are not human, fairies have interacted with humans in all historical ages, as in ancient times when the fairies and humans spent time together at play, at learning and sometimes even falling in love. In fact, many of the fairy realm have interacted with humans in order to keep their line alive in the physical world, resulting in poets, dreamers, wildlife activists and spiritual teachers coming partially from this realm, whether they are aware of it or not.

The Tuatha de Danaan – the children or tribe of Danu, the primary Goddess-source of the land of Eire, now Ireland – did so, interacting and mingling with humans, living with us and forming relationships in order to survive invasions and the hostility of some members of the New Ways which swept the ancient isles. Many of these people of the New Ways fervently feared and mistrusted the fairies and their powers, seeing in both them and nature itself a threat to the establishment of churches, and a threat to the eradication of the Old Ways.

In Wales the Tylweth Teg, the fairy people of that magical land, also mingled their blood with that of humankind – resulting in a continuation of their kind through to this day.

In truth, many of you reading these words today may have traces of fairy blood.

To attempt to keep the Tuatha de Danaan and humans apart, to drive us from our love of the Tylweth Teg, many of us were told that the "underworld" in which these fairies dwelled on sacred sites such as the Tor of Avalon were terrifying and forbidden places. Gatherings at fairy circles were banned, as were those at stone circles, and when the priestesses and druids continued with their worship of spirit in nature, the groves were torn apart. Others, full of fear, broke and burnt the sacred stones in their attempt to exorcise the spirits, the fairies, and the Goddesses and the Gods that were there.

We humans were shepherded indoors to worship, although the Christ himself taught out of doors, went into the wild to meditate and communed with Spirit in the garden of Gethsemane. Despite these truths, fairies were mistrusted, and driven out of their homes by priests of the New Ways who deeply mistrusted the elementals.

Even today, unless we are highly discerning, people may mistake a fairy haven for a haunted place, and again attempt to drive them away from where they belong, and the very area they are protecting.

Some people have also spread tales of the fairies having a mischievous streak. Yes, they are playful. But there is nothing to fear from the fairies when we approach them with love, respect and understanding. Those of us with fairy blood are more likely to see, hear, feel and know the presence of the fairies and recognize their right to be here.

Now knowing a little of the history of fairy and human interaction, we can empathize with their extreme caution regarding humanity. Think of it. Many humans have taken the wild places that were once the homes of the fairies. We have sprayed these sacred places with poisonous pesticides, torn out the plants and exhausted the once rich loamy soils. It is part of the sacred path for many of us to spend some time restoring the balance, communicating with the fae without obvious rewards, and making amends. This way they can begin to trust some of us again, and together we can work on restoring the health of our mother, the earth.

Fairies now dwell mainly in the fairy realm, also known as the in-between, the dreamscape, the Otherworld. It is located whenever an etheric and natural world occurs due to the energetic overlapping of our dimension with that of the fairies' dimension. And we can, as we will see later, open a magical portal to the world of the fairies, so that we can once again work with them and their beautiful energy that has so much to teach us.

How to see fairies

When you wish to be in touch with the fairies and connect with them, you must be clear, open and honest. Fairies are easily able to discern anything otherwise – it will show up in your aura, or energetic field, which is how fairies can read humans so very well.

Be aware of the animals and the wild-growing plants, particularly butterflies, ladybirds, certain beetles, mushrooms and wildflowers, around you, as they are often the messengers of the fairies. All have a unique message for you.

As energetic beings, fairies rely on belief and your clear energy in order to be "seen" – they literally infuse their etheric bodies with the energy from your own in order to manifest before you in a shape you will recognize. Without clarity and faith you may well gain insights and hear their messages, but the last great adventure – seeing them – may not occur. Be aware that the health or otherwise of your own energy will attract, or repel, all energetic beings and entities.

Fairies can and do appear, rarely, as whole humanoid beings. They can also appear as though made of vapor, of a kind of ectoplasm, as if outlined with vivid light, or as tiny lights. The more fairy blood you have, the easier it is to see certain types of fairies.

To attract fairies and send them a message that you wish to communicate with them, hang sprigs of thyme in your window. This is how the ancient ones invited the fairies into their homes, and this tradition is still as powerful now as it has been for thousands of years. And if you grow this enchanted herb, the fairies may come to dwell in your garden.

Creating your own visionary art can be a wonderful way of bringing through your fairy companions, as this painting of Lucy's shows

Bush and flower fairies

You can attract helpful, loving fairies into your life by growing or having the following plants and flowers indoors. Energetically, these fairies are linked with these types of plants and flowers. So when you grow them or have cuttings in your home, the fairies will come to you via the flowers, and work with you for your highest good. Every plant has associated elemental beings, so growing anything will assist you in connecting with the fairies and being able to communicate with them. Here are just a few of the plants they work with.

Clover: These fairies can assist you in finding new love. Allowing patches of clover to spring up in lawns allows them to connect with you – please do not mow over them. If this cannot be avoided, alert the fairies by going to their clovers and informing them so they can move to safety and not be frightened or hurt while you mow.

Eucalyptus: These fairies are working on helping the world find the correct treatments for perfect healing methods. Eucalyptus is a very healing plant, but one which must be used in small doses, and very carefully and wisely. These fairies are encouraging humans to work with and use its properties.

Jasmine: For help with clarity in relationships, these fairies tell you the truth.

Rose: These fairies work with deep and abiding love and passion. These fairies love roses, and are drawn particularly by those that have a sweet, deep smell.

Bluebells: Any flowers that are bell shaped are loved by the fairies, who can create homes in their sweet cushiony petals. Bluebell fairies assist too with your own workings within your home – they help to literally create a home sweet home and good sleep.

Elder: Elder trees protect the fairies, and if grown in a circle, create a strong protective force for many miles around.

Hawthorn, oak, ash and thorn: These trees grown together create an energetic realm through which the fairies can appear more easily to you.

Apple: Apple trees attract the fey associated with Avalon. You can use the bark in spellworking. Simply use it as fuel for a fire – its smoke sends a message to the fairy realm all around and smudges you, clearing your energy field to raise your vibration, and thus allows you to see and work with the fairy realm. Particularly wonderful for those who are attracted to the Celtic path, the apple tree is especially sacred due to its fruit, which within holds a secret, the five-pointed star. Cutting open an apple horizontally to reveal the five-pointed star is a sacred act – leave an apple cut in this way out on a moonlit night to tell the fairies who you are.

Lilac: This pretty flower brings forth the fairies who can assist you with allowing life to have more sweetness and recognizing its sacred moments, even in the most everyday situations.

Mistletoe: This attracts fairies who can assist you in activating your magic and help you activate the sacred nature of the elements within. Because of this, and mistletoe's connection with the druids, fairies attracted to mistletoe help us reconnect safely with each element, and draw upon the magical tools of the druids and the fairies – the sword, the spear, the cauldron and the stone. (Note how these occur in the suits of the tarot – the swords, the wands, the cups and the coins. If you read tarot, simply by recognizing these deep meanings to these symbols, you will be able to give stronger readings and experience the magical world far more lucidly, as well as travel between the worlds more safely.) But back to mistletoe! This sacred plant and its fairies can also assist you to heal from past life trauma as a result of the abusive misuse of the power of these elements, for example if you were persecuted by fire or water during the Burning Times.

Thyme: This is perhaps the most magical and powerful of all herbs in terms of attracting and drawing loving fairy helpers. Thyme fairies make a safe haven for all other fairies to visit you within, and the aura of the thyme plant itself is cared for and cleansed by the fairies. By growing this herb – thankfully a hardy one that even not-very-green-Witches like me are able to grow! – you also invite the fairies to work with and cleanse your own energetic body, as thyme raises your vibration and assists you in feeling connected to other dimensions, allowing all to flow, and helping you understand and merge with concepts that are outside of logic and linear time – like the fairies themselves!

Creating and stepping through your own fairy portal

Setting up your altar outdoors will assist you in meeting and working with your fairy guide. The most auspicious times are at dusk and dawn, all the "between" times, as the fairies are able to live in the world between worlds. At Litha, Beltane and Samhain they are also most readily contacted. You may wish to do this each new moon, or full moon, to set up a regular energetic cycle with the fairies.

Where two streams meet in a forest, where a circle of trees grow together naturally, where a ring of mushrooms are, where butterflies have been seen – all these sorts of places will create a kind of magical world in which they will feel most ready to come to you. If this cannot be done outdoors, recreate such a place indoors, and ensure you have sprigs of thyme about, creating an energetic space which the fairies adore and know is safe for them.

For this spell we will use the elvenstar, or septagram. This seven-pointed star is said to open a portal to the fairyworld. When I work with it, I draw it in the air before me, and it is through the center that the fairies can come to me, or that I am drawn to them.

Each of the seven points has a meaning for this type of journeying to and from the fairy realm. Firstly, seven is a magical number, and sacred to many cultures and peoples. It symbolizes the seven chakras, the seven days of the week, the seven notes of the musical scale, the seven colors of the rainbow, the seven alchemical metals, the seven heavens. And seven is a number that is sacred to the fairies.

I often like to draw it with a wand, and as I do so, I see each point as having a meaning, much as you would if working with a five-pointed star. For example, as I draw, the points represent:

Earth

Air

Fire

Water

Spirit

Life

Magic

And each can correspond to a direction: for example:

North

East

South

West

Above

Below

Within

And, just as a five-pointed star resembles the human form with arms and legs outstretched, the seven-pointed star resembles the fairy form, alike to human, but with two more triangular forms and points representing their wings.

Begin by opening the circle and calling in the seven directions you will be working with for this rite. On your altar, light three green candles in the center. Place milk and honey on the altar as an offering. Place thyme there too.

Now, draw a seven-pointed star in one fluid motion with your wand, your athame or your finger.

Say out loud three times into the center of the fairy portal you have just opened:

I call to thee, my fairy guide
To allow me to see thee
Speak with thee
Know thee

Now, state your purpose, for example: "I ask you to come to me now, so that I may know more deeply who I am."

Allow your physical and etheric bodies to pour forth the motive behind this intent, that they may know you are pure of heart, one of the good folk yourself!

Now, see with your eyes or with your inner vision the center of this seven-pointed fairy star begin to glow, and watch as through the center a fairy being comes to you.

You may see lights, flickering or a soft glow. You may wish to close your eyes and use your inner vision completely. This is up to you.

Greet your fairy friend and guide, and thank them for answering your call.

Ask their name.

Tell them why you wish to develop a relationship with the fairies.

Ask them to assist you in your quest to learn, and ask what

you can do to help them.

Ask them three questions that you would like their insight on.

Thank them for their answers and ask them if you may talk with them again.

Say farewell. Close the fairy portal.

Remember to record your experiences and messages in your Book of Shadows and Light, best done before you reconnect completely with the "real" world.

Leave an offering, then ground yourself by placing both feet on the earth and raising your arms to the sky. Depart, clearing away all physical traces of your presence (ie pick up your rubbish!) but feel free to leave a crystal, seeds or flowers for the fairies.

Gnomes ~ Earth's Wisdom-keepers

Need magical assistance with abundance and earthing yourself? Get ready to meet the wonderful, very powerful gnomes!

Gnomes are the heroic dwellers of the earth element. They are a contradictory elemental, in that they are small yet extremely powerful and strong. They are simply dressed and wild looking, with massive gray beards and woven clothes made in the hues of the earth, but they are the creators and keepers of the earth's wealth. They appear jolly, due to our associating them with the Father Christmas archetype, but are wise and long lived.

When saddened, gnomes are inclined to melancholy, especially when their queen and ruler, the earth, is endangered. They are masculine, although they are associated with earth, and thus with femininity. They assist humans who approach and treat them with respect, but as this happens so rarely, we have never truly understood how much a relationship with these earth elementals can assist us.

For the gnomes are the keepers of the precious things of the earth – and they are able to awaken us to the treasures of the earth. Thus salt, crystals, quality soil, gemstones, minerals and ores all come under their domain. While they have often protected the miners who search for the veins of valuable minerals in the ground, they are also weary of the rapaciousness of human beings regarding the many wondrous geological gifts of the planet, and thus are doing their best at this point in our history to assist us in turning away from using what is left of the resources of the earth, and encouraging us to re-use, recycle and reinvent so that we can all help provide for the future.

Many of us who work with crystals, salt, metals and minerals are also working with the gnomes. In gnome lore, their Goddess is Cerridwen, the threefold maiden/mother/ crone Goddess of the cauldron, and their God, or king of the gnomes, is Ghob – which, entomologists say, is where the word goblin comes from.

The root of the word gnome is the Greek word gnoma, or knowledge and wisdom. For gnomes are extremely wise and very very knowledgeable about how all things of this earth work. Another theory regarding their naming is that the great 16th century scientist and wise one, Paracelsus, was the first to use "gnome" as a collective term for the spirits of the earth. It's believed that he probably based this usage on the Greek term ge-nomos, meaning earth-dweller.

What they can teach us

Gnomes have an interesting physiology – they are etheric, yet they are the most solid of all the elementals. They exist on the earth plane, as do we humans, and dwell in hollow trees, underground amidst the roots of the wild forests, preferring to live where humans rarely tread – although these areas are becoming more and more rare. They are found in many wild areas, and their role, apart from their primary one of caring for and assisting animals who are ailing, starving, injured or cruelly used, is to attempt to protect the earth itself, which is suffering due to over farming and the use of pesticides and species introduction, all of which have compromised the earth's very fertility. Working to counteract soil salination, mineral leaching and poisoning with heavy metals and leads is also under the domain of the gnomes, who are encouraging many of us to take steps to assist the earth, our mother, to heal.

Gnomes also teach us respect and reverence for the collective wisdom and traditions of old age. They wish us to learn from the knowledge of our elders, our crones and sages – knowledge garnered over a lifetime of travails and experiences. They represent respect for old and advanced age – they will not tolerate those of us who have no respect for the crone and the sage, the two stages of life they are upheld to protect and teach us the wisdom of.

Gnomes deal primarily with the sense of touch, being sensual creatures, and they protect those who work with their hands for healing, arts and laboring manually.

Ghob is king of the gnomes, and from him comes the humanesque God Goibniu in Celtic myth, a smith God involved in making highly powerful weapons, who also corresponds with healing energies and building abilities. He was eventually Christianized as Gobban the Joiner, builder of churches, a more palatable way for Christians to allow his worship and reverence to continue.

Gnomes are also strongly associated with the wisdom of the druids, who retreated to the world between worlds, but who are now returning to reactivate the sacred and ancient earth magic that may still save this planet when teamed with modern technological and scientific innovation and brilliance. So as the druid teachings make a resurgence, the true meaning of the gnomes will become more clear, accessible and apparent to us. They have many lessons to teach all of us who live here on Gaia, and wish to make it clear that we need to revere the earth for us all to continue to dwell here in health, prosperity and peace. It's also important to note that despite their appropriation in many technological and mythological war role-playing games, such as Warcraft, gnomes are peaceful creatures, steadfast and true, the creators of weapons for defence and honor, not wanton bloodshed.

On a personal level, gnomes, through their personalities, their arts and crafts and magic, teach us patience, stability, tenacity, endurance and balance. They are very thorough and organized, and can be invoked to help those of us who are more air, fire and water oriented – more scattered and ethereal, impulsive and emotional than situations and circumstance may warrant. Gnomes can also assist those of us who are jewelers, artisans and craftspeople working with the ores and stones of the earth in converting our ideas into reality, by revealing to us the practical elemental processes that need to take place in order for us to bring our visions into the material plane in an enduring and earthly fashion.

However gnomes can also be stubborn, inflexible and lacking in spontaneity. This is their negative aspect. All elementals have, just as we humans do, negative as well as positive aspects. If you are already patient and somewhat stuck in your ways, gnomes may not be the best elemental for you to invoke. Instead, working with the air, fire and water elementals will be of more benefit. But for those of us who find it hard to settle, who move too quickly from one project to another, who are unable to work well with our finances and who lack a feeling of being earthed, there is no more wondrous and helpful an elemental creature than the wise and learned gnome. When invoked with respect, goodwill and reverence, they will always assist you, as long as that which you work or cast for is in the best interests of mother earth and her creatures.

An excited Lucy, up close and personal with the magical beings of Gnomesville in Western Australia (yes, it's an actual place!) – Photo: Anita Ryan

Invoking the gnomes

It is best to invoke the gnomes using a wand made of crystal, linking to the earth kingdom, or an athame, as things of the earth such as iron and steel are also in direct contact with the gnomes. Draw a pentacle in the air with one of these tools, and you will indeed summon them for their assistance.

You may also have success connecting with them by utilizing a crystal grid formation of moss agate, peridot, coal, aventurine, obsidian and turquoise, as well as their favored stone, rock crystal. Rock crystal is a very powerful healing crystal – it works on your physical body to rebalance your health and to correct any imbalances in appetite. It makes sense then that it is favored by the gnomes, as they assist you in all matters of the material world, including being able to receive material help and deal with abundance and prosperity. And to enhance the clarity of your contact with them, use rock salt on your altar or as an offering on to the earth when you call upon them for assistance.

If you have an animal that is unwell, consider working with the gnomes in tandem with veterinary medicine. The gnomes will intuitively guide you and assist you in healing your creature using things of the earth – food, poultices and herbs.

A magical secret is that the gnomes are also associated with the Archangel Uriel. He is an authority figure type angel who disperses justice and is associated with the direction of the north, the direction with which the gnomes are also linked. He is quiet, possessed of the wisdom of the earth and the ages. He is also the patron of clairvoyants and psychics, and helps all people distinguish true visions from imaginations, desires and conditioned worries.

On an earthly level, gnomes also care for and oversee the breakdown and transmutation of material matter, of alchemy, and respect for the usefulness of all things, which so many of us cannot see. They are the antithesis of the disposable culture we live in now. They encourage us to recycle, re-use and to fertilize our soil using worms, manure and other organic matters. They have a strong association with dragons too.

Although they can be connected with at all times, in all places, in all seasons, some places and times are more conducive than others. They are, for example, easier to contact at midnight and throughout winter. Their colors are black, dark green, browns – the hues of the earth, of leaves and mushrooms and pumpkins. Wearing these colors will evoke the qualities of the gnomes within you, thus assisting you in many ways.

They associate strongly with ancient trees – the hawthorn and the oak, in whose roots they dwell, as well as Moreton Bay figs and ancient eucalyptus forests. Those of us with substantial amounts of earth signs – Taurus, Virgo and Capricorn – in our astrological makeup will have an exceptional affinity with the gnomes. But those of us who lack earth in our chart will benefit greatly from associating with them and learning their ways and values.

Call on the gnomes to assist you with money problems, crystals, healing animals, gardening issues, tree magic, knot magic, fertility, and any issues to do with twins – gnomes are always born as twins, one male and one female, although the female is rarely seen.

On a mundane but very practical level, they are also of great assistance when you wish to lose weight in a practical, sensible, healthful manner.

You can invite a gnome to dwell with you in your house. They will help protect it, keeping home and hearth safe from robbery, connect you with the stability of the earth, and ground the family as a united group who reveres the teachings of old age. They also help women bear children, and are wonderful helpers for those of us with our own herbal gardens and remedies.

The Oracle Tarot cards associated with the gnomes are the Empress, the Chariot, the Hermit, Judgment, the World and the Wheel of Fortune cards, plus all cards from the suit of coins.

Chapter 11 ~ The art of divination

READING METHODS FROM THE
ANCIENT TO THE FUTURISTIC

The longing for knowledge of what the "future" will hold is common to all societies and to all peoples, and traditions of divination run across cultures, nations and time itself. We all desire to know where our footsteps will fall next, long for the assurance that decisions we have made are the very best, and yearn to know that things will get better. These instinctual desires are as fundamental as the need to eat, to be sheltered and to be loved. White magical practitioners have long been sought out to divine what may come next – it's an ancient art that remains relevant, powerful and healing.

Divination is an act of faith, and faith is what makes us human. The tools by which we seek the portents of the future are many and varied – they can be as simple as seeing shapes in the clouds, or as complex as developing a lengthy ritual at the relevant moon phase, with all the accompanying tools working with you.

When we divine, we are not simply seeking to "know" what will happen next, we are connecting with the divine flow of universal energy. As time is non-linear, we can, by connecting into that flow, see the likely outcome of events based on the conditions being set up in the present. Science is currently speculating on the existence of a fourth dimension, that of time. Other scientists and physicists are convinced that there are in fact eleven dimensions. String theory account for these multi-dimensional realties by hypothesizing that our eleven dimensions as interconnected as a ball of string, overlaid and looping in and out, influencing each other with echoes. My guides speak to me of the Avalonian dimension being the eleventh, where our perfected crystalline selves await incarnation once we have vibrationally sufficiently to activate this form's energy.

If the theories prove to be right and past, present and future do all co-exist, as the druids and other wise traditions thought, there is certainly reason to believe that we too can part the veils between history, the present and the future – even the various planes and dimensions.

But no matter how powerful the divination, all futures can be written, and rewritten, to an extent. Our fate is a co-creation between ourselves and our destiny blueprint, our soul contract if you like. In the Norse magical tradition this concept of co-creation is known as wryd (pronounced Word), a system whereby we interact at all times with our destiny or fate via our behavior, our intent, our beliefs and our choices. There are many ways to live out this destiny. For example, you may be called to help others, but will that be as a nurse, a doctor, a natural healer, a counsellor or a loving parent?

Divination can assist us in living connected to this potential to create our own rich, magical destiny – and unblock the fears which may be holding us back from fully experiencing our potential as magical beings with wonderful lives to create.

It is true that we create our lives in conjunction with many other factors, however we always have an energetic part to play in the unfolding of our lives, and when we work magic, when we work at consciously weaving our lives, we can change many aspects of our existence for the better of ourselves, and for others too. When we live in divine flow we benefit, and so does everyone who comes into contact with us, and even the planet and the universe itself. We are all connected, so how can this not be true?

Living with awareness always creates powerful, sacred results. So, for your enjoyment and interest and possibly use, here is a dictionary of divination tools which you may wish to explore to increase your awareness and connection with the divine. However, before working with these sacred tools and secrets of divination, there are fundamental steps one must take to prepare.

It's all part of the process, a sacred act in itself! A sound body and mind are essential – the Witch or wizard attempting to mix alcohol or drugs with divination ends up with confused messages and an energetic body that is not at its maximum health. Trying to discern meaning through the pain and fog of a hangover is a self-defeating process – it is far better to raise psychic power through dance, chanting or meditation.

Some of us have a wealth of natural psychic ability, while others rely on keen intuition and sensitive appraisals of their surroundings, using their knowledge of human nature to make predictions to guide them through life. Either way, you can be of assistance to others and to yourself. By working with magical tools, your gifts and talents can become even more powerful, reliable and healing.

Unfinished matters from previous incarnations may also have an effect on your progress in this life. Seeing a past-life therapist who specializes in regressions can clear a blockage or help you to understand the nature of your karma.

Ultimately, deep self-knowledge will also help you divine the future. Then, if you add tools to the brew, you are raising the kind of consciousness necessary to tap in to the deep knowledge of the collective unconscious and the psychic ether.

The important element in all this work is your self and your intent. The power to divine the future is within you, and with the aid of the tool most empathetic to your needs and your character and with which you feel the most affinity, you are on your way to working in one of the oldest magical traditions there is. The tarot, a crystal ball, a roaring fire or the cool waters of a lake at midnight can all be as effective as each other.

Destiny, in tandem with will, personal choice and reflection, will decide how the wheel of fate will turn for you. Discovering your life direction may be as simple as preparing your psyche then applying any of the methods that are listed here. You merely need to practice, again and again, until the raising of destiny-consciousness becomes second nature.

Types of divination

Aeromancy

The art of foretelling the future via the atmosphere, by reading portents and signs in the weather itself. For example, the metaphysical meaning of great storms and hurricanes is symbolic of mother earth healing herself. Comets are cosmic symbols by which we can read of a great change. The most well known example of aeromancy is the Star of Bethlehem appearing in the night sky to tell of the birth of Jesus. In modern times, the appearance or discovery of asteroids, such as Chiron, and new planets, such as Sedna, reveal that the healing of the masculine and the feminine has truly begun. Chiron represents the wounded masculine principle, and Sedna is a transformational Inuit sea Goddess. When Sedna appears, she guides us to consider feminine natures as perfect, whole and complete, in all their shifts and changes. Eclipses and lights in the sky also fall into this category. For anyone who has seen bodies of light in the night sky that cannot be identified, this powerful experience reminds us that we are connected to not only this planet, but to the many other planets containing life forms which are a part of our universe.

Amniomancy

This rare method of divination is the study of the remnants of the caul – the membrane surrounding the amniotic fluid – over the head of the newborn baby. This membrane quite often covers parts of the child's body, and is cleaned away in modern times directly after the birth. However, in older times, particularly in the British Isles, the pattern or shape the membrane made was studied by the midwife or mother. The most famous amniomantic reading is featured in Charles Dickens' Great Expectations, when the main character, Pip, knows he will never drown because he was born with a caul completely covering his head. Cauls which cover the forehead and eyes were said to be a sign that the baby was born with the Sight, or the power of clairvoyance.

Astrology

The art of studying the destiny of an individual according to the placement of the heavenly bodies – planets, moon, sun – at the time of their birth. This allows for intricate analysis of personality as well as long and short-term predictions. It also enables the practitioner to predict the compatibility of partners, friends and professionals to the individual, as well as the timing of particular events. Studied in both the west and the east, astrology is a complex science with many variations, far more attuned to specific needs when seriously undertaken than the daily forecasts in newspapers hint at. Currently, my feeling is that lunar astrology is what we will next focus on. As the new energy of the divine feminine becomes stronger, we will look to her symbol, the moon, for wisdom. Lunar astrology is quite different to solar astrology, in that it is more attuned to our inner world than to its outer expression, as is solar astrology.

Austromancy

Testing the direction of the wind for clues of the future. This works by the attribution of qualities to the directions – a common feature of both arcane and contemporary spirituality. Related to the art of aeromancy and weather control, which in itself is associated with a deep and intimate knowledge of the elements. It involves examining the qualities of the four directions as they manifest in your area. For example to me, being by the Pacific Ocean and on the east coast of Australia, it feels right to consider water to be aligned with the east, so if I feel an easterly wind blowing I associate that with the emotional and spiritual qualities of water. Whispering a question to the wind then feeling its movements can also help us become more in tune with our natural environment and the elementals associated with it.

Automatic writing

This is often used in spellworking, and is a wonderful way to train yourself to bypass your conscious mind and ego and tap in to the divine energy flow of the universe. Have a pen and paper on hand. Take a few moments to breathe deeply, focusing on the breath and its movement, and allowing yourself to go into a light trance. Always be sure to surround yourself with white light, and ask for the protection of the Goddess and the God when working with this powerful tool. Then take your pen and begin to write whatever comes to mind. Don't think about it or edit your thoughts, just write everything you feel. Especially at first, it may help to ask a specific question. You may also wish to work with a partner, who can ask you a question that you auto write the answer to. This is also a powerful means of communicating with the deities and elementals, and is a powerful basis from which to build your skills in channelling.

Belomancy

An ancient form of divination where arrows are used to predict the outcome of an event. If the arrow hits the mark, the event will be a positive one, which will bring good fortune and happiness to the questioner. It is also performed by tossing or balancing arrows – one method involved throwing the arrows in the air, and the point in which the arrows inclined pointed out the direction to be taken.

Bibliomancy

The art of randomly selecting passages or paragraphs from books in order to detect portents of the future. It can be done with any book, from The Bible to The Da Vinci Code, but there are also many books published purely for this purpose, where sayings are printed on each page and the reader is instructed to open randomly to one and read those words in order to determine what to make of their current situation. A Guide For the Advanced Soul is one of many such books that have become New Age best sellers in recent years.

Botanomancy

A method of divination by which the future is foretold by

using plants – either judging time frames from the life cycle of the plant, taken as a good or ill omen, or by using the properties of herbs, oils and flower essences to bring on a psychic state of awareness. Speaking with trees is another ancient form of divination. Always approach a tree gently and introduce yourself before beginning to feel its energy. As you get to know your tree you can ask questions and listen for its wisdom. Another method is to burn particular kinds of woods, for both their qualities as space clearers and for their magical qualities. Apple tree branches can be burned, as can those of any tree, as all have wonderful qualities. Fallen wood is best – don't cut live wood from a tree without first asking permission. To do so can upset the magic of the tree and render your divination powerless. The fairy occupants also suffer from this kind of mistreatment.

Capnomancy

This involves reading the future in the shapes made in plumes from ritual fires – sometimes aided by handfuls of magical herbs being thrown on to the fire.

Cartomancy

Divination using cards, be they oracle cards, ordinary decks of playing cards, which developed from the tarot deck, or tarot itself. The latter are said to hold the secrets of druidic, Egyptian, Hebrew and Indian magic. The earliest tarot decks are thought to be Chinese and Korean; the earliest European decks were recorded in the 13th century. But within the ancient treasures of the Valley of the Kings in Egypt, cards resembling the major arcana were found. Influential magician Aleister Crowley believed they were derived from the Egyptian book of magic, The Book of Thoth, upon which he based his own tarot deck in the early 20th century. In a traditional tarot deck there are 22 major arcana, or major, cards, which represent the 22 Mysteries, and 56 minor arcana, or suits, cards, which represent earth, air, fire and water, people and material, and spiritual situations we encounter throughout life. According to some tarot scholars, the major arcana represent causes, while the minor arcana represent effects. For me, the tarot is a sacred book of knowledge, which led to my creating a new and powerful, loving deck, the Oracle Tarot, imbued with colors that vibrate with our own energy. Thus we can read it simply – just contemplating the images on the cards, or sitting in meditation with them, can help to heal us. See the end of the chapter for a white magic workshop on how to read the Oracle Tarot.

Catoptromancy

A type of scrying, this involves using mirrors to promote a trance-like state in order to see deep within the soul of the viewer. Visions of the future may then be produced. Mirrors are often believed to have magical powers, and are used in many spells and rituals to promote an altered state of mind. Generally speaking, any reflective surface may be used for this method. Remember "Mirror mirror on the wall, who is the fairest of them all?" The mirror, which allows not only reflection but also self-reflection, has always been special in magic. As a result there are many superstitions about them – that they must be covered or removed after a death to prevent the soul of the dead person from being stolen, and that it is bad luck to break one.

Ceromancy

This is divination through studying the shapes formed when molten wax is dropped into cool water, which is much the same as determining the future by the shape of tea leaves or coffee grounds left in a pot.

Cheiromancy

This involves using the hands. Usually it is the laying on of hands to promote visions, but it can also mean assessing the size, shape and qualities of the hands, in a similar way to palmistry, and analyzing hand shape, fingers, fingernails and the palms. According to legend, it is one of the oldest Witch skills, taught to mortals by Aradia, daughter of Lucifer and Diana.

Clairaudience

Literally meaning "clear hearing", this is the psychic ability to hear voices and sounds that speak of coming events or give you messages from the other side. It's literally listening in to the future – being something of a human radio and picking up the energy field of what has been destined. When a person has clairaudience, they are able to hear the thoughts of other people –these words, sounds, noises and other sound phenomena seem to be literally coming from inside your own head, or from out of nowhere. When practicing mediumship, the person communicating with those who have passed over sometimes hear their voices, or are sent messages via sound clues, ie the sound of bells chiming, children laughing, water falling or birdsong all have a meaning for the medium. The first experience of clairaudience may occur as you are falling asleep, when your conscious mind ceases its whirl of activity. If this is so, you will find that with meditation and practice you can reach this state at any time of day, fully conscious.

Claircognizance

Another of the five "clairs", claircognizance meaning clear knowingness. It is a form of intuition and having an inner knowing about things. The information, idea, concept or thought seems to just come to you, and has the feeling of "this is important". The knowledge you receive often flashes suddenly into your mind, seemingly out of nowhere. You may know who is on the phone before you answer it or know personal things about people you just met. It is often described as a "just knowing", without the psychic being able to explain how they know.

Clairgustance

Meaning "clear tasting", this is a form of extra sensory perception that allows a person to divine meaning through the sensation of taste, without literally putting anything in their mouth. For example, during a reading a taste may come to the psychic, and as each different taste will have its own meaning, they will understand the message coming to them. It is claimed that those who possess this ability are able to perceive the essence of a substance from the spiritual or ethereal realms through taste.

Clairsentience

The paranormal obtaining of information using faculties other than vision or hearing, literally meaning "clear sensing" or emotional layer sensing. It is divination via touch, feeling and sensation, and is similar to psychometry in that it can determine the history of an object and its owner by touch. It may also happen when brushing up against a person, for example you may suddenly feel how they feel, and feel what has happened to them. Clothing can be a very powerful holder of energy, and can be used by clairsentients to pick up information about the wearer. People with this gift may also feel the presence of angels, the Goddess, fairies and other beings by literally feeling them. At times, I feel the very real sensation of a "push in the back" from a being I call the Lady, who represents the sacred Goddess of Avalon to me. She nudges me like this to get me back on my path and to pay attention to something important. Sometimes this can also manifest as a tingling in the palms when in the presence of information, or the sensation of stroking, handholding or being embraced. It can also manifest in unpleasant ways, as it did when I was a child and experienced heavy entities who were unbalanced and feeding from my energy. Other sensations when in the presence of Otherworldly beings include your hair standing on end, temperature changes, sweating, eye fluttering, vision changing or literally feeling ill when in contact with someone who is unwell. Clairsentients often pick up and absorb the emotions of those around them. When working as a healer, a clairsentient needs a healthy, strong diet, energetic awareness, cleansing of chakras, space clearing for energetic harmony and to check in to see whether their feelings are their own or they are receiving a message. Conversely, the emotions a clairsentient experiences when in the presence of a guide, angel or Goddess can be almost unbelievably moving, blissful and joyous, and the clairsentient can resonate with this energy for days after their contact. As the clairsentient begins to connect more and more with these energies, their experience becomes more and more beautiful, pleasurable and loving.

Clairvoyance

Also known as second sight or the Sight, this involves being able to see a clear image or vision, like a film or scene being played out in the mind of the Witch, in which events of the future are revealed to the seer in a very visual way. It literally means "clear view". Parapsychologists generally regard it as a form of extra sensory perception, and it is one of the most accepted and common psychic abilities. It involves seeing the metaphysical with the third eye.

Cledomancy

Divination by interpreting random events or statements, and attributing significance to off-the-cuff comments or seemingly meaningless events. It refers to accidental insight, and to sometimes not knowing why one knows that something is meaningful. Not dissimilar to Freudian slips.

Dowsing

Divining rods are used to locate bodies of water, and sometimes are used over objects meaningful to the individual to assess the outcome of the future. You can ask it questions, much like a pendulum, and it will give a yes or no answer.

Dreams

Our dreams have long been held to contain fragments of our futures, and thousands of books and years of study have been devoted to attempting to understand and develop a universally coherent dictionary of symbology for dreams. It is my opinion that we are the best interpreters of our dreams, for it is within our own subconscious that the key to unlock the hidden meanings of our dreams lies. To rely too closely on rote interpretations could send us in meaningless or random directions that take us only a very little way down the path of understanding. Nevertheless there are common symbologies – water representing the emotions, for instance. Dream interpreters recommend the keeping of a dream diary to get intimate with the subterranean currents of your psyche, leading to a greater understanding of the self and therefore of what your dreams are telling you. One of the most wise dream coaches is author Leon Nacson, a friend of mine, who astounds me with his warm and precise readings for individuals. He literally coaches people in how to discover the meaning within their own dreams, using his intuition and knowledge to promote reconnection with our own dreaming selves and the messages we are being given.

Elemental divination

Divination via the four elements – aeromancy (air), pyromancy (fire), hydromancy (water) and geomancy (earth).

Floromancy

The art of divination by tuning in to the messages that flowers have to give us. This practice, which is strong across many of the spiritual churches, is based on the belief that flowers radiate vibrations and energy and can have a strong energetic reaction to a loving environment or a hostile one. You can also divine messages such as in the old game where people pluck each petal as they say a line of the rhyme, "He loves me, he loves me not," and whichever statement the last remaining petal coincides with gives you the answer to your question.

Gyromancy

This involves the raising of clairvoyant energy by whirling until you lose your balance. The Sufi dervishes use such whirling in their religious ceremonies to take them into another level of consciousness. It also includes interpreting the fall of a person who whirls until they are dizzy and fall down.

Haruspicy

Reading portents amidst the innards of sacrificed animals, which was common in rituals of the ancient world and practiced by priests in ancient Rome. Afterwards the entrails were burnt in a sacrificial fire, and sometimes the observation of how the flame burned the sacrifice was taken into account.

The theory was that when an animal – usually a sheep or an ox – was sacrificed, it was absorbed by the God to which it had been offered, creating a direct channel to the deity. By opening the carcass, the priest presumed to peek inside the God's mind and watch the future being created.

I Ching

This is the revered Chinese art of divination, which is also a complete philosophical system that takes a lifetime – or lifetimes – to truly master. Based on the principles of yin and yang (yin is the moon, the feminine, the passive, while yang is the sun, the masculine, the active), where yin is represented by a broken short line and yang by a straight line, it allows you to divine meaning by the tossing of coins or plant stalks. This combination of lines in various combinations (eight trigrams and 64 hexagrams) forms The Book of Changes, which contains the meanings of all combinations.

Lampadomancy

A form of divination using a single oil lamp or a torch flame, which was popular in ancient Egypt. Messages were divined from the movements and shapes of the flame. Pointing a certain way was said to point the seeker in their future direction. It was good fortune if the flame had a single point, however two points was considered a sign of bad luck. A flame that bent indicated illness, and sparks indicated news. Sudden extinction of a flame was considered an omen of sudden change and endings.

Moleosophy

This "reads" the moles on the body – their site, color and size dictate the meaning. Used infamously, and inaccurately, by the Witch hunters during the Burning Times, it claims moles are an indicator of a person's character and future indications.

Necromancy

This involves consulting the dead or a spirit to obtain secret knowledge and receive messages from the souls of the departed – mediums and ouija boards are commonly used for this. It reached fever pitch during the spiritualist movement led by Madame Blavatsky in the 1800s. The spirits of the dead are sought for information because they are able to access information beyond that available to the living.

Numerology

The use of the numbers in your birth date to divine your life purpose and path and future obstacles and strengths. There is also a system to convert the letters of your birth name to numbers, to learn more about different aspects of your personality and future.

Oinomancy

Divination using wine. This is done by pouring out wine as a libation and interpreting the patterns that it forms. It can also be done by interpreting the sediment in the bottom of a glass of wine after drinking, and interpreting patterns after spilling onto cloth or paper.

Oneiromancy

See "Dreams".

Onomancy

This involves using the letters of a person's name to divine their future. One of Linda Goodman's astrology texts makes great use of this method.

Ophiomancy

Using the behaviors of serpents to divine the future, by observing the appearance and behavior of these reptiles.

Divining meaning from their movement and their manner of coiling up or eating.

Palmistry

The palms of the hands are lined, and the art of palm reading relies on the Witch knowing the way in which to decode the meaning of each hand. The left indicates the individual's potential – the skills, qualities and stumbling blocks fate has dealt them. The right indicates the lessons being learned and the way in which the person is using their talents and being held back by their personal challenges. Fingers, the palm, the lines upon it, the hand's size, color and temperature are all linked in an intricate dance of meaning.

Pegomancy

Concerns itself with spring water and bubbling fountains and the omens contained therein. It is divination by interpreting sacred pools, springs, wells or fountains. Often used in conjunction with scrying. In this form of divination stones are sometimes dropped into water, then the movements and ripples they produce in the water are interpreted.

Phrenology

Finding meaning by examining the shape of a person's head and reading the lumps and bumps on it.

Psychometry

With this method, you use an item belonging to the person you wish to forecast the future for. Usually a piece of jewelry (not antique) is used, preferably one that is worn by the person at all times so it has soaked up their aura in which the seeds of the future are already sown. Some diviners get in touch with the person's guides via the jewelry – these guides then offer information on the questions put to them. Others simply deliver the messages they receive when handling an object, which may be received in the form of visions, voices or even sensations, depending on the particular talents of the psychic. See the end of the chapter for a White Magical Workshop on how to perform psychometry.

Pyromancy

Divination by fire. Seeing shapes and visions of the future within fire, often assisted by substances thrown on the flames. Leaves, twigs or incense are thrown in the fire, and changes in the color, shape and intensity of the flames are interpreted.

Rhabdomancy

Using a magical wand or stick to divine answers. This method was a forerunner of the divining or dowsing rod. It involves the interpretation of the position of rods, arrows or staffs for the purpose of divination.

Scatoscopy

The examination of dung to discover signs of the future.

Scrying

Using a crystal – the traditional crystal ball of the gypsies –a mirror, the surface of a lake or a bowl of water in which you can see images of the future and divine destiny. It is a general term for divination using such tools to induce future visions. Magician John Dee, who was Queen Elizabeth I's astrologer in the 1500s, and acclaimed 16th century prophet Nostradamus both used a scrying mirror to receive some of their information. See the end of the chapter for a White Magical Workshop on how to scry.

Tasseomancy

Divining meaning from the shape and formation of the tea leaves that remain in a cup once the beverage has been drunk.

The dregs of a cup of tea are swirled around inside the cup, then the cup is inverted on a saucer. The psychic interprets the patterns of the leaves remaining inside the cup, as each symbol has a meaning. It can also be done with coffee grounds.

Theomancy

The consulting of oracles, which are people who channel the God or the Goddess, ascended masters or entities and provide knowledge of the future. Typical of ancient cultures were oracles like the Delphic Oracle of ancient Greece, who people from all over the world would consult for wisdom, healing and future divination, or Cassandra, daughter of the king of Troy, who was granted the gift of prophecy but was condemned never to be believed.

Xylomancy

The tossing of magical sticks and the assessing of the patterns in which they fall. Also refers to divination from pieces of wood, either from their shape when collected or their appearance while burning.

Zoomancy

Examining the habits and appearance of animals to reveal the future path for human beings.

Three White Magical Workshops

Divination is a very powerful magical art. Some people will have a natural gift for all forms of divination, some are very strong in a one or two variations, and for others even beginning to work with one will seem more difficult,. However, everyone is psychic, and each one of us can get results if we find the tool, method or innate gift we have the most affinity for - and practice! In my workshops, I like to take people through these methods, simply, magically, step by step, until the mysterious process becomes second nature!

Workshop One: The art of scrying

Scrying is the art of using our actual physical vision to connect with our psychic or inner vision, and involves seeing images in crystal balls, pools of water, mirrors and other objects. It is a practical magical mystery, and is a beautiful, personal way of working with tools like crystals and elements like water and fire. Learning to scry can train us to "see" the patterns that are all around us, and activate our inner vision when we wish to use it. It also teaches us how to turn down this inner vision for when we wish to be fully present with family, friends or simply with ourselves.

The word scry has its roots in the old Anglo Saxon word descry, meaning to reveal, or to see. It is also the root of our word describe. When we scry, we are releasing the hold our conscious mind has over our abilities to see, and allowing the element we are working with to share its wisdom and insights on our question. When we scry we work with magical intuition and intention with one of the elements, thus it is a wonderful form of connection as well as of psychic work.

How to scry

Essentially scrying relies on the practitioner using a surface to gaze upon. What that surface is can vary according to what you prefer, what activates your Sight, and what you have available. Many people use a scrying mirror, a mirror whose glass is either imbued with smoky tones or which has a black backing, making the surface less reflective and with more depth. Others simply use a mirror by candlelight or moonlight.

It is advisable to keep your scrying mirror for magical use, as its magic can become strong, and when you wish to use it for everyday activities you could find its psychic purpose makes it difficult to stay in the present moment – even when applying lipstick!

Similarly, you may use a bowl of water and scry upon its surface. Bath scrying can be done too, however you may not wish to have an impromptu session in the bath, so contemplate using a tool kept specifically for this magical purpose, to keep your other bath times free of visions and to enhance the clarity of your work.

Each element offers you a scrying tool, for example:

Water scrying

A silver or black bowl of water.

The surface of a lake. Outdoor, night-time scrying is blissful, very magical and powerful – and it reconnects us to the priestesses of Avalon and the druids of Britain, who used natural bodies of water such as wells and lakes to scry.

The ocean.

A rock pool.

A cauldron brimming with water, which is powerful and practical.

Earth scrying

Natural rocks and crystal formations.

A crystal ball – the quintessential image of the "fortune teller" which has its roots in Atlantean divination and crystal work.

Crystal skulls.

A mirror. You may also use a mirror and water in conjunction, although this is a more advanced art.

The Oracle Tarot. Using tarot can be very powerful during scrying. Use the image on the card and the key words as triggers for your scrying journey to begin. You can choose the card that most suits the question you have, for example, the Change card for when you are facing transitions in your life or the Lovers when you have a relationship question. This can be a wonderful way to work, and with the Oracle Tarot's powerful yet positive and loving energy, you can go safely into the Otherworld.

Fire scrying

Candle flames.
Cauldron fire.
The hearth fire.
Plumes of smoke from fire or from incense burning.

Air scrying

The clouds and their movements across the sky.
Storms, and reading the movements of the sky.
Vapor from oil burners.

Preparing to scry

The dark of the moon is a wonderful time for scrying, as your inner vision is at its peak during this beautiful, soft, inward turning time of the Goddess. The phases of the moon can be worked with thus – full moon for revelations, new moon for how things may transpire, dark of the moon for inner knowledge and waning moon for how best to release.

Take your scrying tool. For the purposes of clarity, we will use a bowl of water in this example.

Clear space in the room in which you'll be working. Ensure you are clear, fit and well.

If working outside, be sure to be warm enough, and to have lantern-style candles to ensure they do not blow out.

Set up your altar simply, with something to represent each of the elements, and light a stick of incense.

On either side of your bowl, light a candle.

Dim the lights, turn off phones and soften external noises with ambient music. Lyrics can "feed" the process, so you may wish to avoid this, although some people prefer to work with music which has this impact as it assists them process.

Take nine deep, slow breaths with your eyes closed, and gently relax your muscles.

With your eyes closed, say: "When I open my eyes, I shall see with my inner vision." Making this statement is a powerful declaration of intent.

Open your eyes, and softly gaze upon the surface of your scrying tool. There are no right or wrong ways to scry – simply allow what happens to happen. Sometimes the visions will seem like simple outlines or etchings at first, figures shaping themselves together out of the element you are working with, and then, quite suddenly, the surface may transform into a super-real movie screen on which the images from your inner vision are projected. This can happen with your eyes open, or it can happen within – either way it is an indication that your psychic vision has been switched on.

Some people experience a mist rising before images begin to slowly appear then move, and others experience almost a complete Otherworld. This may simply take some time and practice, and finding the element which you are most compatible with.

To complete your practice, thank the God and the Goddess, close your eyes, and again take nine deep breaths. Say: "When I open my eyes I shall see what is there for me to see." Open your eyes. You may like to wave your hand over the bowl three times to shift the energy.

It is essential to ground after scrying. Simply have something simple to eat and drink, and place your feet and your palms on the earth to allow the energy to flow back into the earth.

The reason it is important to sever the scrying vision is simply that this inner vision, switched on at all times, can be tiring and burn you out, leading to visions at unexpected moments. It is likely that, as a psychic and magical person, you may experience these in any case, but it is important that you remain safe and clear when driving, navigating roads and doing equally sacred mundane activities – to be clear and present for yourself, and for your loved ones. Grounding assists you to be present too, and brings your energy back into the world.

When you are beginning to scry, only do it for a short period of time, and build up from there. Record your visions in your Book of Shadows. Over time, you will notice your skills blooming and taking shape. Have patience with yourself – we are not all wizards at first scrying!

Scrying can be subtle, and it is as much about training yourself to discern these subtle messages as it is about powerful visions.

Workshop Two: Psychometry Class

Psychometry is the art of discerning information via objects belonging to another person, by holding the object and noticing what we feel, see and hear, as all objects give off an energetic vibration. We can read a piece of jewelry, an article of clothing, car keys or even a hairbrush!

When we "read" using this process, it is important that the object has not had a previous owner. If you read a ring that is an antique or family heirloom, it is as likely that the images and messages you receive will be from the previous owner. This is a valid form of reading however, as you can be asked to interact with a deceased loved one via their jewelry, or find out about family mysteries. Many white magical practitioners who are working with police investigators are asked to read an item of clothing belonging to the person the police require information about.

Psychometry is a powerful and very personal tool. It links us directly to the energy of the person in an intimate way – we are able to pick up on standout moments in their life and what they are creating based on the current circumstances. It gives clear messages that come directly from that person, and provides a clear link to them and the knowledge stored about them in the Akashic records, the cosmic library where the infinite variety of information regarding our soul and its journeying through dimensions, directions and time is stored. Anything we wear or own with frequency becomes imbued with our energy – and, as stated, when we access the Akashic records, we access or are guided to information in all directions of time. Therefore, via psychometry's ability to connect with this Akashic records, it is possible to receive messages about a person's past lives, their forthcoming experiences and their future incarnation.

It is advisable, I feel, to ask the God and the Goddess to help separate the creation of the jewelry from its owner – be clear about asking for information about the person who is its keeper. The creator energy can sometimes be strong in jewelry, particularly pieces with gemstones that have been handmade. This is not at all tricky – simply clarify with your guides and with the God and the Goddess that it is the object's keeper you wish to be given messages for.

How to use psychometry

When you work with psychometry, you are being given permission to read another person's energy, which is an honor. It is most beneficial to use your receptive hand when reading. Your receptive hand is the less dominant hand. For example, I am right handed, and thus when working with psychometry I would hold the item in my left hand, which is my receptive hand.

My receptive hand is very sensitive to energy – it tends to buzz at times, and tingle when something is wanting my attention. It is also the hand with which I can powerfully sense energy and auras, and is the hand I am most protective of, although my right is so much more useful in practical terms.

Psychometry is a form of psychic touch, of lucid sensory information gathering that enables the person asking for feedback to stay in a very safe place. Often during certain types of bodywork, like massage for example, we can also pick up messages. Psychometry however is more controlled and feels safer, yet maintains its powerful nature.

Psychometry ritual

Set up your sacred space – your world between the worlds, your portal to the dimension of spirit, the God and the Goddess and guides. Light a candle and some incense on your altar, dim the lights, play ambient music and call in the God and the Goddess and ask that the information relayed be for the highest good of all concerned. Within this sacred space, all messages are meaningful.

It is important to begin to read objects from people who you have no previous information about, particularly when you are learning, in order to filter out the negating noise that can so often rise from our "logical" mind. This realm is one in which the magical mind takes precedence.

Take the object you are going to read. Let us say, for the purpose of this example, that it is a ring.

Hold the ring gently in your receptive hand and feel what it has to say to you. Some people working with this tool prefer to close their eyes, however I have "seen" material while holding an object. It is best to allow your vision to blur a little, however, so your inner vision can take over.

Breathe softly and deeply, and allow your inner vision, your inner wisdom, to start receiving messages. These may be images, they may be sounds, they may be smells, they may be physical sensations, words in your head or feelings.

Speak them aloud – censor nothing. Spirit is sending you these messages in this sacred space – trust that you are receiving the messages to pass on to the person you are reading for. You have set up a sacred space, and within this all messages are meaningful. This is a very powerful tool in that it is the one that most leads to you trusting. It is the tool that requires you to leave your self-doubt to one side and relay the messages. In this exercise the Goddess will speak with you – allow her voice to be heard via the art of psychometry.

Workshop Three: Reading The Oracle Tarot

The secrets of the Oracle Tarot deck

The tarot is a deck of cards with words and images that can divine the future. They are as old as the written word, but gained popularity as a device for divination in the 1400s, when many wealthy Italian families actually had their own family decks made. Faces of the relatives were used as the models for cards such as the Hierophant (renamed Tradition in the Oracle Tarot deck), the Empress or Justice, completely depending on the family's self image and what they wished to convey about their dynasty. The Visconti deck illustrates this tendency perfectly, and is the deck from which the notion of the court cards – the king, queen, page and knight – sprang. The courts were a way for the Visconti to depict their patriarchs and female heads of family, which is why there are three male courts to only one female. This is one of the many reasons that I felt comfortable, happy and true removing them from my Oracle Tarot deck, which I co-created with my guides and the Goddess.

When the spiritualism movement flourished in the late 19th century, there were many magical groups who used the tarot for study, divination and meditation. They believed they had found links between the cards and the Kabbalah, the Jewish mystical tradition that has earned great respect. Indeed, the Kabbalah's Tree of Life can be seen as a metaphorical companion to the Fool's journey through the 22 cards of the tarot known as the major arcana. As the tombs of the pharaohs had just been discovered at this time, Egyptology was also all the rage, and many turn of the century occultists believed that the cards were in fact a lost book of Egyptian wisdom, The Book of Thoth.

I believe it is indeed true that valuable and sacred fragments of ancient knowledge have survived through to the present day due to them being encoded within the tarot. My Oracle Tarot deck, and tarot cards generally, are conduits of Egyptian, Persian, Hebrew, Atlantean and Avalonian energy. The information within them is indeed ancient, and is thought to have been taken from Atlantean survivors to Egypt, Greece and Rome, where the cards kept alive ancient wisdom and knowledge.

For me, the Avalonian connection is perhaps the strongest at the time of writing. The tarot deck contains each of the four pillars of druidry, the sacred symbols of the priestesses and druids, and the lore of the sacred isle of Avalon. The cards were the secret pathways to keep alive the information of Excalibur (the suit of swords), the Sacred Stones (the suit of coins), The Grail (the suit of cups) and the Staff of Merlin (the suit of wands). All these magical traditions are referenced in the Oracle Tarot. But most importantly, the Oracle Tarot interacts with your unique energetic blueprint, creating a one-off magical talking mirror of the soul, with a unique and beautiful language you can learn.

As you stretch outwards towards reading and interpreting the card you hold in your hand, you grow inwardly, reaching within for your own ancient and sacred connection to knowledge.

When I was younger and less experienced I was certainly attracted to "darker" decks. One of the first I saw I admired because it was deeply sensual and esoteric, but as I worked with it I felt nervous, negative and mistrusting of the cards. I put them aside, and thought more about what I could include in a tarot deck.

I felt a strong pull towards co-creating a new deck, as there have been some unbalanced, domineering and frightening individuals who have had the cards pass through their hands, and influence it in turn.

It was my absolute wish to take the cards to a true and honest place, where their wisdom could shine without fear, and be of service to people young and old, male and female, of all faiths – which is how the Oracle Tarot was born.

Changing the courts

Medieval society, quite literally, was the court of the king, and thus the court cards are king, queen, page and knight. But today, in a more equitable and less gender-stereotyped world, we do not have the same need for these cards. Considering that there are three male cards to only one female card, I felt it best to let the cards reveal what sort of people are playing a part in your life –we all have energies, so study the energy of the cards and you will know who they are speaking of. If you wish to know your life path with an individual, male or female, you simply need to ask the cards what that will be, and they will lovingly and clearly answer.

Changing the names

Over time, attitudes, titles and religious beliefs have altered, so I also revised the names of some of the cards within the Oracle Tarot deck. Names that were traditionally used for tarot cards reflected the cultures in which they were created, and thus they were a mirror of their time. As I do not believe in a Devil, having a card of that name did not work well for me – so it became Bondage in my new deck, which also reflects the meaning of the card far better. Likewise Death became Change, to better reflect its actual meaning, and the Hierophant became Tradition.

So why didn't the Hanged Man get a new name? The image of the card was changed instead, because people encountered so much fear when this card came up, but I retained the name because it refers to Odin's hanging on the Tree of Knowledge, and his coming to wisdom through patience and immobility. I wanted that reference to live on, but for the image to be less confrontational and to resonate more effectively with modern day lives.

My tarot deck has 62 cards. There are 22 of the major arcana, cards such as Justice, the Sun, the High Priestess and The Wheel of Fortune. They are the psychic powerhouses of the deck; the cards that indicate events and issues that are of the deepest significance to your soul and its journey. There are also 40 cards of the minor arcana, which are the four suits of the deck – the cups, swords, wands and coins. Cards such as the seven of swords and the three of wands reveal the narrative overview of your life.

Readings, rules and reversals

The cards, when they fall reversed in a reading, indicate a block in that area of your life. Don't be alarmed, because it is a wonderful message full of compassion from the deities and the universe which can open your eyes to an area that's causing difficulties for you, and give you wonderful insights into how best to let it go.

There is an old myth about tarot decks that does the spiritual rounds from time to time, which states that you should never read the tarot for yourself. Actually, I come from the opposite school of thought. I believe – and I believe this because I've seen it work time and time again – that it's definitely best to learn by reading for yourself. As you do this, over time, your psychic levels will increase. To develop this bond, simply handle respectfully and lovingly your Oracle Tarot each day, looking at cards, reading about them, gazing at the images on each of them and developing familiarity and trust.

A simple way to increase the power of your readings is to set aside a small part of your home where you can conduct a morning card meditation. This area is preferably one where you will have some privacy, can decorate as you wish, and feel safe and positive in. For many of us, this place is at your altar. Simply pick a card for the day, or go through the deck in order, and think about what the card represents to you at this point in your life. After that read the meaning in the accompanying booklet. Record your musings in your Book of Shadows.

The Oracle Tarot can bring you closer to your own spiritual insights, as well as guiding you along life's rocky roads. These cards are ultimately all about listening to your higher self, connecting to the universe and its abundant flow of cyclic energy, and trusting in your own inner wisdom. The Oracle Tarot can also help you make better choices and deal wisely with difficult situations. Best of all, they will re-introduce you to a sense of the sacred in your everyday life, which will raise your self-esteem and make every day just that little bit more magical.

After your readings, note down in your Book of Shadows and Light the cards your received, what you intuitively felt about each card, your response to the reading and its significance to you. Do this with both personal readings and when reading for clients.

Over time, you will begin to see patterns in your readings. For you personally, this is invaluable. You may notice that the Star comes up for you time and time again in varying positions. This is wonderful validation that, regardless of just how many cards and layout possibilities there are, we attract the cards that we need to us over and over again until we have incorporated its lesson and moved on.

This is also a very important practice to maintain when you are reading professionally. Just as a doctor takes and keeps notes on a patient's condition, you will be able to further help and guide your clients when you have a reference guide to their last reading with you. And if you study the Oracle Tarot in a group situation, the diary of your readings will be a wonderful way of structuring discussions and asking for feedback, thoughts and guidance from others.

Consecrating your deck

When you first receive your Oracle Tarot, one wonderful way of bonding with it is to consecrate it to its use, or to "charge" it. Any of you working with crystal healing will know about charging a crystal, and the same energetic work can attune your tarot deck to your own personal energy and intent.

Open your card deck up and handle each of the cards, with your eyes open. Touch each and every card, to infuse your own personal energy into every card of the deck, then fan the cards out into a manageable shape, place them to your heart and say: "I open my heart to you."

Next place them to your third eye and say: "I open my psychic vision to you."

Then hold them to your lips and say: "I open my love to you."

Place both hands on the deck and visualize a beautiful flame in your solar plexus region. Imagine this flame growing larger and larger. This is your very own divine spark. Feel the flame give off sparks, and see portions of your divine flame enter the heart of the deck. It is now yours. No matter who handles your deck, it is infused irreversibly with your own sacred energy.

Place your cards in front of you on a beautiful piece of fabric – silk is perfect, as it energetically works with the cards. You can choose one color or have different colors for different types of readings, for example if you are working with a relationship spread, pink silk will enhance that energy in you and the client. Enhance this further by burning rose oil, and even have beautiful flowers in a vase nearby. All these things help create a sacred space, and enhance the experience of the reading. Refer to the color section to see which colors work best for which readings. For past life readings use black fabric, as this is the magical, powerful color that contains all others. If you wish to do a general reading, use black also, as it will best bring out the energy of the cards.

Energetic integrity and reading

When you work with other people, you are always interacting with their energies, even when it's a job where you do not intentionally call on your intuition. When you work with a mystical system like the tarot, you become highly attuned and sensitive to energy. If you are reading this book it is likely that you are highly intuitive and sensitive. The form that sensitivity takes will vary from individual to individual, but we all have the ability to empathize with others. That is what makes us good psychics. However, the shadow side of this wonderful magical talent is that you can unknowingly accumulate the energies of other people.

Whether or not you are reading for others, please make it a daily practice to white light yourself. Simply visualize a ball of white light surrounding you, and ask the God, the Goddess, the angels or whoever you feel comfortable with to protect you. The white light will allow positive energies to filter through, while shielding you from unpleasant energies. This grounding white light is essential for you to maintain your own psychic stability.

After encountering people who seemingly drain you, take time to clear the energy by calling in angelic or Goddess entities to sweep your energetic field clean. Your own higher self can also assist with this. Imagine the Goddess pouring her healing light into your every cell. It is absolutely vital that you begin to connect with your own energy – feel it, understand it, raise it when the level is low, ground it when it is too flighty and excited to serve your purpose. When we read tarot, we are aiming to connect with the universal, elemental flow of energy, thus we do not drain ourselves. But even when we do connect with this endless flow of universal energy, it is wise to take time to cleanse your etheric body.

If you have several clients in a row, simply take one minute between them to literally smudge yourself in a wonderful essential oil you are burning, or a beautiful healing incense like nag champa. I cannot recommend nag champa too highly – it is a very high vibration incense that attracts wonderful people to you and cleanses negativity even more thoroughly, I feel, than sage, which is also terrifically powerful and very well known and widely used.

The purpose in every reading is to reunite the person coming to you with their own divine spark, and that is what the cards will assist you in doing. Please visualize this connection before they come to see you. If there are many clients coming one after the other, I sometimes use a spray made of pure water and rose essential oil, and spritz a little around the room to clarify the air and create an atmosphere of divine love.

This quick space spritz is ideal for when people are literally queuing up to see you, and it's amazing the difference it makes. But if you don't have anything on hand you can improvise. During one spiritual festival I was presenting at I was experiencing an enormous amount of energy leakage from client to client. With nothing handy, I simply visualized myself in a beautiful tower of light, connected to the celestials and rooted in the earth's core. I was exhausted, but maintained my focus and was able to give very clear readings.

Your own auric energy will also need to be cleansed regularly when doing this work. Make it a nightly practice, and become aware of the peace and serenity that is available to you when you simply, gently clean your energetic house.

Money is also an energy, and it is important to have your worth acknowledged by the exchange of energy when you read for someone. Whether it be money, a massage or simply some apples or herbs from their garden, the law of balance requires that energy investments must be reciprocated, and that the energy you give out in your reading must be returned on some way. People value what they must give something up for.

I also believe that you must be asked to read for someone. Don't go around telling people they need an Oracle Tarot reading, like psychic busybodies, or tell them what cards you pulled for them and what it means when they don't want to know. You can put the offer out there, for example by advertising your readings, and people who desire a reading from you and who will benefit from experiencing your particular energy, your healing signature, will be drawn to you.

Protecting yourself

When reading for people with a great deal of troubled, wounded energy:

* Use the stone black tourmaline.
* Cloak yourself, head to toe with not a single gap, in white light.
* Ask the Goddesses to stand at all four corners of the room, and be by your side too.
* Feel your aura each day for "holes". If you find any, psychically repair them.
* Maintain, or aim for, perfect health.
* Shamans recommend homeopathic remedies – they change the vibration of your subtle body and energies. Flower and/or etheric essences can be wonderful.
* Use humming/white noise/music as a shield.

If you feel you are under energetic attack during a reading, do not reflect or return the energy to the sender. Ground or transmute the energy instead. Stop the cycle, don't perpetuate it. And remember, often the person is not consciously attacking you, it is a deeply subconscious action that they are completely unaware of.

You will need to cleanse your energy more frequently if any of the following empathic points apply to you:
* You are sensitive.
* You find it hard to make a choice.
* You have chameleon tendencies – you pick up the habits and traits of dominant others.
* You have work to do on boundaries.
* You have recently suffered trauma (divorce, death, an accident in the family).
* You are in poor health, which can lead to auric field leakage.

If you answered yes to three or more of these questions, you may be more susceptible than others to negative energetic fields right now.

The secrets of the Oracle Tarot

There are so many layers to reading the Oracle Tarot. Here are the secret symbols in the images, which will reveal many important aspects of information to you, unveiling an even deeper meaning of each card to you.

Buds: The Goddess in her maiden aspect. New enterprises, growth. Immaturity, energy, fragility, impetuousness.

Roses: Mystic love, romantic love, self-love, fertility, natural sexual urges. The commitment of souls, the mystic rose, Mother Mary, the Goddess in her mother aspect.

Fallen petals: Disappointments in love, a feeling of abandonment, old issues regarding love coming up under unrelated circumstances. The Goddess in her crone aspect.

Tears. Elders. Deceased loved ones communicating with you through dreams, visions and intuitively. Look out for signs.

Cords: A symbol of an oath of office. Appears in cards like Tradition. Where you notice it is where it will have significance for you. It represents a responsibility that is obvious to others, that creates status and wealth but comes with a price, and many secrets too.

Spirals: These relate to the unicorn horn, DNA, and the changing genetic nature of humanity as we enter the New Age. The spiral is an ancient Celtic symbol for eternal life. Your soul, at the core of who you are, is this. It also represents the Goddess in her triple aspect and the God and male creative energy. A spiral in a reading is activating a soul-issue for you to examine, and you are being asked to truthfully ponder your relationship with the divine feminine. This could come up as body image, unpaid labor, respect for your sexuality. For men it also has many meanings. Please take the time to meditate on how this issue resonates in your life. There is no right or wrong. There is no judgment. There just is. Spirals going clockwise refer to events of the future – the seeds of which are being created in the present. You can change this by changing the present. Spirals going counter-clockwise refer to events of the past, and say that you can heal any remaining issues in the present.

Cracks in cups: Insecurity, issues around not believing that love lasts or that security is possible. Unresolved childhood issues regarding abandonment, love being taken away, love being finite in quantity. Feeling people can see through you. Auric leaking and a strong need to seal your aura, and protect and ground your energy. Susceptible to influence from others, rely on others for self-validation. Need to work on self-love and know you are perfect, whole and complete as you are. Covering up emotions. Self-healing is required. It is important to feel safe and express what you feel in order to heal.

The four-pointed star: Past-life issues of connecting with wisdom of the past, or issues from your own soul journeys many lifetimes ago. For example, if the Magician comes up in the first position, it is likely that you have had an experience as a wise woman or druid in a past life. The four-pointed star is also a symbol of the resurgence of the Goddess.

The six-pointed star: The symbol of the higher self connecting with astral spheres. It is futuristic in quality – a future that we are connecting with celestially. Indicates issues being revealed to you in the present. Knowledge about societies in the future, wisdom from conventionally inexplicable sources. A bigger issue than you as an individual is indicated – an event of tremendous power in which you have a role to play.

Color magic and the Oracle Tarot

Color has power – it is the source. Light creates color, and its different wavelengths stimulate energetic responses within your body and etheric self. Each of your seven energy centers, your chakras, vibrates at a different frequency, and color therapy can help them maintain balance and heath.

You have innate, intuitive abilities to recognize the colors you need. Within the reading, the cards that are chosen by the law of attraction will be perfect for your own healing.

Simply by gazing at a color and visualizing it, you reconnect with yourself at a very deep level. Each Oracle Tarot card is embedded with healing color energy, which you activate simply by using your cards. Thus handling them, and reading for yourself and others, is an innately healing experience on many levels.

Note the jewel-like intensity of color within the Oracle Tarot. This characteristic of this tarot deck is very deliberately there for your own energetic healing to be enhanced. Read on to discover why a particular color so attracts you. Please note that the color and cards you feel most affection for or attraction to will change over time, reflecting your changing energies and shifting circumstances, and of course your own personal journey back to the source – the divine spark that resides within you.

* Pink has the same vibration as divine love.
* Red empowers you to embrace your power fearlessly.
* Blue enables you to have faith in yourself, and speak your truth, gently and fearlessly.
* Black is the all-color – it is the color of change, learning and progression. You are creating your own truth.
* Brown grounds you, protects you and helps you trust your own discernment. It helps you identify with all of earth's creatures and connects you to healing animals.
* Orange stimulates your own talents, brings joy to relationships and creates an aura of positivity.
* Turquoise co-creates vitality in your physical and etheric bodies, and creates a strong immune system.
* Green is for health, vitality, rapid growth and natural source connections. You may need to literally get outside more.
* Violet is for your spirituality and for connecting with your higher self.

The secret meaning of numbers

Each number of the minor and major arcana has a meaning. The numbers of each of the minor arcana cards are actually printed on that card. The numbers of the major arcana are not. When assessing your spread for numbers and number sequences, look up your major arcana numbers in the deck guidebook until you have committed it to heart.

The symbology of numbers is an ancient art with numerous roots, including the Egyptian and Arabic schools of magic, through Pythagoras, continuing through to the Kabbalists, and even to controversial early 20th century magician Aleister Crowley's numerology, which borrowed heavily from the Kabbalists and Egyptians. These number meanings apply to any suit – coins, swords, cups or wands – and to both minor and major arcana.

There are many layers of meaning in your cards. The symbols, colors, numbers and inherent "code" of the card are all wonderful cues to activate your own natural psychic talents and enable you to read the cards easily, accurately and spiritually. Remember, there are no negatives in any reading – it may reveals blocks, and there may be issues, but we are all here to learn, and we will all have these lessons, and their joyful outcomes, cross our life path, if not in this lifetime then in one we have already experienced or are still to have. Being alive and being human is a wonderful gift, and the only way we can bring the soul to perfection and wisdom. Please clear your mind of the notion of "negatives". Emotions are not bad, they simply are. Sorrow teaches us compassion, if we learn the lesson well. Please see your lessons as gifts for the soul.

Ace (1)

These cards represent a powerful surge of new energy, and beginnings of tremendous significance.

Two

Represents opposing energies, yin and yang, female and male. It also represents the relationship between soul and matter.

Three

Represents expansion and the end of the first stage of a new project – this is a time to celebrate and acknowledge your journey and achievements so far.

Four

This reflects the outcome of sheer hard work, the use of logic to consolidate your enterprise, and a period of stability to come.

Five

Represents an important change, a shift in the energy of a situation. It's a card signifying change, and change, although it is the stuff of life itself, is a quality we resist. When we resist, it hurts. When it hurts we fear. Five can indicate a level of discomfort with changes and that these changes are not you idea, rather they are being imposed on you.

Six

Represents the urge to deal with the energies of others. It can signify the sharing of skills and knowledge and the development of talent for the betterment of all. It is a card of connection with family, work partners and community.

Seven

Represents the Mysteries, the growth of wisdom and the understanding of the difference between spirit and ego, while respecting the role of each.

Eight

Relates to bringing together opposing forces – a spiritual balancing act where the yin/yang dichotomy, the black/white, is replaced by a holistic understanding. It is a stage of high integrity, of learning respect and courage. This understanding of universal truths is the stage through which we all pass on our journey to knowledge. It is a stage of advanced initiation, after which manifestation and intent work together to create your soul life.

Nine

You at the edge, the very verge, of completion. Savor achievements, look over them with a grateful eye and see what you have learned from this stage of life. Be grateful for all the lessons, good or bad. Then consider where you would like to create change in your life, and make plans for manifesting these wishes and desires. Work on healing any issue you feel may be holding you back, and release what you no longer need in your life. The universe and the Goddess will be there for you, all you need do is ask for their help.

Ten

This interesting number is at once the sign of reaping rewards, yet also new beginnings. Sometimes what you have already let go of can return to you refreshed under the influences of this fascinating, mystical number. Joyful moments are to be yours. Simply recognize the blessings you have all around you and celebrate them. Your new cycle will then be activated without fear or pain, and with enormous compassion and love.

Number sequences and suits

If a spread is laid out with 10 cards, and within that spread are four twos, each two simply amplifies the meaning of that number. As every suit is included, the meaning of that number – the dual nature of all things – is relevant in virtually every area of your life, and you will experience a time where you are working on harmoniously dealing with this natural law. If you experience a reversal of any of the twos, then you'll be more challenged by that area. If, for example, the two of swords is reversed, you may be having trouble working things out despite an apparent cease-fire with hostility in a relationship.

Timing and the Oracle Tarot

One question that is often asked is: "When will this happen?" In divine right time is one answer, but it doesn't necessarily satisfy. Here is a very helpful, very accurate way of discovering the timing with the cards.

There are different card spreads you can do. A very powerful one is the Celtic cross spread, which is detailed in the Oracle Tarot guidebook. Using that as an example, here's how you can work out the timing of the event shown within the spread. Count backwards from the last card you put down until you reach the first minor arcana card. The number of the card will reveal the number of days, months, weeks or years, while the suit will reveal what time frame you are looking at, giving you the key to timing events very accurately.

* The suit of coins represents years.
* The suit of swords represents months.
* The suit of wands represents weeks.
* The suit of cups represents days.

For example, if the first minor arcana card from the end is the three of wands, it will be three weeks. If your first minor arcana card from the end is the six of swords, it is six months, if it is the ace of cups it is tomorrow (one day).

Practice. It is simple and easy and very insightful. Your

clients, friends and you will love the messages the timing method brings you.

Past life indications

This is something that can be used for all your readings, and it can also be used for specific past life readings, do acknowledge when your particular past life occurred.

The suit of coins represents the period of Atlantis and Lemuria.

The suit of swords represents the period that spans the civilizations of Ancient Greece and Egypt.

The suit of wands represents the period from the birth of Christ through the Middle Ages, until around 1350 CE.

The suit of cups represents from the end of the Middle Ages to the modern day.

The number of the card in the suit is another indication of past life timing. For example, if you draw the two of coins this indicates a lifetime in very early Atlantean times, while the 10 of coins indicates that the life being examined was during the last days of Atlantis. It is important to note too that the suits indicate timing, not the country of origin. So, for example, if you draw a sword card, your life may have been lived in Norway, but it was during the historical period of Ancient Greece and Egypt. Intuition will guide you further with this reading, and note all the clues in the card, like the colors, symbols and so on, which will prompt your intuition to pinpoint further details.

Suits and readings

A card's meaning is always reinforced if it falls between two cards of the same suit in a spread. Likewise, its influence is diminished if it falls between two cards of the same different suit. For example, if the ace of cups falls between two other cup cards, this strongly backs up the qualities of the ace of cups, and indeed all the cup cards. However if the ace of cups falls between the three of swords and the 10 of swords, you would read your ace very differently.

When a major arcana card falls between two cards of the same suit, its interpretation should be closely aligned with the meaning of the surrounding cards. Oracle Tarot reading – and indeed all tarot reading – is not simply about each card, it is the story of their sequence and their influences on each other that really gives your reading its strength, its detail and its poetic truths.

Below is some insight into what the number sequences signify when appearing in a spread. This is highly significant. Please become familiar with these as the sequences add another dimension to your reading, giving it a soul depth and breadth that otherwise could be simple to overlook. These sequences enrich every reading when they appear.

Number sequences and the Oracle Tarot

Four aces

The God and the Goddess commend you on your wonderful manifestations. Keep up the good work, and may you feel connected to the strong forces within and without you that are working in your life.

Three aces

Prosperity and success are yours. You will have status and recognition from others, and shifts where you feel you have successfully stepped into a new phase of your life. Congratulations!

Four twos

Now is the time to find your place within a larger group, working out what you can contribute and how to truly stand in your own power even when surrounded with powerful individuals. You have particular talents and unique attributes which are exactly what an idea or project needs in order to grow and succeed – all that is necessary is for you to remain in contact with who you truly are. Resist attempts to influence or change you. It can also indicate tests of personal strength within larger groups.

Three twos

This indicates a restructuring of your life – there will be changes that are significant but which herald further internal change to come. This can include creating a beautiful environment for you to be more truly yourself within, or an urge to take on a partnership in making these changes. It can be a streamlining of business, a beautification of your office, or deep thinking about how you present yourself to the world and where you get your sense of self from. As you become more aware of what it is that says "this is me" to the world and to your family, you will begin to make small changes – in home decor, dress, hair and make-up, the food you eat and the people you spend time with. This is the first stage of many significant changes to come – and all are positive and for your highest good.

Four threes

This indicates decisions, commitments and resolutions involving like-minded souls, friends and partners. There will be joyful gatherings with people who are part of your karmic growth cycle, opportunities to manifest new opportunities through other people, joyous gatherings where new talents and skills are developed and applauded, blessings regarding new family members, babies, children, female friendship, Goddess energy and the coming together of generations in harmony, peace and respect for mutual joy and healing.

Three threes

Everything may not be what it seems. Look beneath the surface of issues and examine what is really happening. Ask your own internal self what the truth of a situation is, and believe in your intuition, no matter how illogical it seems or how others deny your thoughts. You know the truth of this situation, so do not allow yourself to be persuaded against your better judgment. Pay close attention to messages within dreams, and confide only in trustworthy friends. A time of great healing will soon be with you.

Four fours

This means a period of complete respite from fears, worries and anxiety, with harmonious activities and relationships, serene moments in nature, blissful connections with loved ones, kindness, serenity, improved communication and a gentle hand at work behind the scenes bringing a loving vibration to activities which were previously problematic. Withdraw from frenetic activity in order to heal with this beautiful energy surrounding you.

Three fours

It's a time of commitments to work, projects and ambitions, of making dreams come true through practical tasks and steps, reaching out to connect with the right people and following through intent with action and commitment. An active time of increase, gain and reconstruction of working identity.

Four fives

Change is upon you, but it is a great and steady change that occurs in the right place and at the right time, in steady streams and apparent coincidences, in being in the perfect place at the perfect time, and all is for your highest good.

Three fives

This indicates a fear of change, a feeling that too much is happening too quickly. But trying to hold on to what is meant to leave, dissipate, decay or die only causes painful feelings. Separation actually creates the space for healing to begin. This is a lesson in letting go, in being able to release. Let go and allow the Goddess and the God to take the burden of the "shoulds" from your shoulders. Everything is happening for your highest possible good.

Four sixes

This indicates material pleasure, which can sometimes lead to an almost obsessive amount of interest in the material at the expense of the emotional and spiritual. It is a time of rewards and gifts. Ensure you have some fun and keep your emotional and spiritual connections going. Don't be fearful, as this is a phase many of us must go through in order to truly understand the nature and importance of placing the heart and soul's true desire first. Then all abundance will flow, you will connect with loved ones and appreciate joy. Pleasure will abound, so spread it around.

Three sixes

This is a time of material gains, potential pay rises, financial increase, windfalls, attracting new sources of income and being able to manage money more successfully than in previous experiences with money. You are energetically attuned to being able to receive.

Four sevens

Changes in relationships bring you closer to achieving your true goals. Sometimes when you ask the Goddess to lend a hand, many things must change in order for you to go in the right direction. Relationships that are no longer serving your higher purpose will fall away, and you may even be left by those who are no longer good for you. Please know that this is a shift that needed to happen, especially if you have been yearning for a soulmate. The people who are no longer perfect for you will leave, and this process can be gentler than you imagined.

Three sevens

This indicates arrangements with like-minded souls, the attraction to others within your own soul group, people who can help you with spiritual growth and personal lessons, a time of new friendships and a kinship that seems deeper than blood. Maintain your faith in relationships, especially in the enduring love of friendship.

Four eights

There is a fountain of news and information from both the world and your own growth – you are moving away from old modes of thinking and changing rapidly. Others may not give you their wholehearted support on this progress, but please take heart. The Goddess and the God love you very much, and you are moving forward into a new era of blessings. Change is necessary for true life, growth and transformation to take place.

Three eights

Travel plans may need to be revised or organized, and there is movement, change and activity. You could be pulled towards an area or location previously not considered – this is a soul-calling for you, the place you are divinely meant to be in order to fulfill the next stage of the unraveling journey known as your destiny.

Four nines

Many projects are reaching culmination, and there may be a feeling of pressure as you juggle these deadlines and projects. Keep going, because you have made wonderful progress – the end is in sight and you will successfully reach completion.

Three nines

This combination represents completion in matters regarding communication, for the highest good of all concerned. So, for example, a letter may arrive, concluding a matter that has been of much concern.

Four 10s

You have a great deal of responsibility and perhaps some nerves regarding being able to meet your obligations. Never fear. Your divine inner guidance has been alerted to your needs and you are being protected and watched over. Serene calm is yours – simply ask for help from the Goddess Brigit.

Three 10s

There will be movement in the home area, buying and selling, activity in the job sector and re-creation of how you make your living. Work on prosperity and abundance issues is in order to release old negative patterns that no longer serve you. By doing this you will move easily into a new, prosperous lifestyle.

Shuffling and cutting

Please prepare your reading area, including cleaning and energetically cleansing the surface on which you will lay out your cards before a reading. Soft music, a bell rung three times to call in your intention, and burning pure essential oils (frankincense and sandalwood are very positive clearing agents) as well as a silk cloth and a candle all create a beautiful, special experience. However, the cards do not need this level of attention to be read. You can simply pull a card as you're running for the bus if that's what you have time for on a hectic day.

Your cards do not need to be worshipped, but when you make the time to create a sacred world between the worlds when you give readings, for yourself or others, you will benefit in many ways. Making time to honor yourself with a wonderful, special and transformational reading will bring you many benefits, physical, spiritual and emotional. Please make a regular date with yourself for this enriching ritual.

It is important to form a question in your mind when you begin a reading. If a clear question proves elusive, simply ask, "What do I need to know?" or "What would you like to tell me?" The law of attraction will ensure that the perfect cards – and thus all the deities, angels and energies within them – will communicate with you. You simply need to ask for their help.

Shuffle while you simply meditate on the question. You can shuffle the cards as you wish – whatever you feel most comfortable with. The more you handle them the more practiced and comfortable and intuitive you will feel.

There are several ways to allow the cards that wish to pass messages to you to come to you.

Method one – All purpose

One way that I use a great deal is to divide the well-shuffled deck into three, keeping the mind clear. Please use your non-writing hand, as this is the hand that is your energetic receiver – left if you are right-handed, right if you are left-hand dominant. Put the pile back together in any order you wish, and then deal out from the top.

Method two – Revealing blocks

This is ideal for revealing blocks in difficult situations, discovering patterns that may be hindering your growth, happiness and prosperity and so forth. You will get very clear results with this spread.

Do all as above, only this time divide the deck into four piles with your receiving hand. Then turn the top card on each pile around – not over so that the image is revealed, but upside down.

Place the piles back together again, in any fashion you wish, and deal from the top. If you have blocks in any areas they will be revealed.

Re-energizing the cards

Handling your cards regularly will help you establish a marvelous, magical intimacy with each and every individual card. Some you will feel more attracted to than others. These cards are significant to you – please take note of this and work with them. Over time this may change as you learn the lessons of the cards and integrate their messages.

The greater your intimacy with the cards, the more benefit you will receive from them. Some people even sleep with their cards under their pillow or near their heart. Do whatever feels comfortable to you.

It is sensible, practical and enjoyable to give your deck a special place where you will always find it easily. If you wish, place a beautiful crystal on top to amp up their energy, or clear them when you feel they may have picked up someone's emotional residue, which can happen after some readings as people's energetic fields can linger. This is why cord cutting, soothing baths and clearing your own energy is absolutely necessary when working with other people, particularly in this energetic way.

If, after numerous readings and handlings by clients, your cards feel stale, take each card and order them into their suits, and place the major arcana in order too. Do this under the new moon or during a waxing moon, never during a waning moon or a full moon, as the latter will imbue them with more energy but will not cleanse and renew them.

Simply leaving them be in their box in a cozy dark place can renew their energy too. If it does not harm them, do what you feel is right.

If an area you are reading in feels burnt out, wash it down with bergamot and water, burn sandalwood oil and light a tall white candle in a circle of sea salt and let it burn down, then scatter the remnants (which can also be used for divination). Crystals can also be used to clear your deck and your space.

If it is not the cards but in fact you who feels run down, see a holistic medical practitioner, contemplate a gentle and effective detox and begin an enjoyable and effective exercise program. Your health is very important, as your vibrant, radiant wellbeing is the greatest life enhancer of all, and will support you emotionally, physically and spiritually, giving you the energy for your lightwork. By this I mean that optimum health for you is the aim – there are only your own goals to meet, you are not competing with anyone else. Simply do what you can to improve your physical wellbeing and, as the mind and body are inseparable, you will be improving your thoughts and your spirit – as the body is indeed the temple it resides in – and will feel and look more cheerful and radiant, all of which makes your more and more profoundly in touch with your innate psychic power.

Layouts for specific purposes

Relationships layout

I call this Aphrodite's Love Spread. Choose carefully which aspect of Aphrodite to call on, considering her three aspects – divine love, passionate love and soul love – when making your decision.

Use red/pink fabric, red/pink candles and rose quartz to enhance this spread's effectiveness.

Shuffle while mulling over the question. When you feel it is the right time to cease shuffling, do so, and use your preferred method to cut the deck. If, for instance, you wish to uncover the blocks within a relationship, split the deck into four piles, turn the top card on each pile around and put them back together again. This method is very effective and accurate.

When you have put your deck together again, take three cards from the top of the deck and lay them out on the left in a line. Then take three cards and lay them out to the right, again in a line. Then take three more cards and lay the first above the lines, the second below the lines and the third to the right.

The set of three cards on the left represents your partner or the person you feel a connection with. The first card you put down indicates their true feelings, the second their public face and how they behave towards you and the third the direction in which their feelings will develop.

The set on the right represents you. The first card here, card four, indicates your true feelings, the second, card five, your public face and how you come across to this person, and the third, card six, the direction in which your own feelings will develop.

The card above these two groups, card seven, indicates the destination of this relationship. The card below, card eight, indicates the potential problems, blocks and challenges and the lessons from this union. The card to the right, card nine, will give you guidance regarding right action in this relationship.

Finally, please honor Aphrodite for her assistance. Place an apple on your altar, as apples are the fruit of Aphrodite, and remember to eat some over the coming three days to consolidate these lessons. If you wish to know where you stand with someone, simply offering them an apple can help you assess their interest.

The annual spread

Sometimes we would really appreciate some guidance as to where we may be over the next year. This spread is wonderful for identifying the themes of your coming year and how best to respond to these themes. By identifying areas of opportunity and challenge, we can maximize our chances for a wonderful year of growth and divine happiness.

Your inner and outer issues may often arise during this spread, so it may be necessary to do some releasing work to let go of any areas that you find difficult. Release them – you no longer need to hold on to old patterns.

While shuffling, using the method you feel is most appropriate to your aims and goals, allow yourself to be open to the divine guidance that will come through for you with this spread. Ask that you receive clear directions for the best of all possible years for you and your loved ones.

After shuffling and putting the deck back together, fan out the cards and select 12 at random. Then, in a clockwise direction, lay out the cards in a circular formation.

Each card represents one of the 12 coming months, starting from the present month and moving around the circle. Shuffle the remaining cards again, randomly pull one card and place it above the entire spread. This card gives you the key to understanding the major theme of the next year, and its vibration will resonate strongly with you on an inner level.

If you wish to ascertain further information about each month, pull another 12 cards and place them in the same way as the previous 12, then read the two cards per month in conjunction with each other.

You can have a lot of fun with this spread – it is simple and very insightful. Enjoy! And if you wish to understand the vibrations and energy of a particular week, you can use the same principles but in groups of seven, with each card representing a day of the week.

The soul purpose spread

Shuffle and put your deck together again while contemplating what the universe would like you to know about your soul purpose. Take three cards and lay them down from left to right.

Take three more and lay them below the first line of cards, left to right. Now you have two lines of three cards each.

The first line represents your inner self. Card one represents the core issue of your inner self, card two the conscious form this takes or the material ways in which this manifests, and card three card the possible ways in which you may manifest this soul purpose in future.

In the second line, card four represents your goal at the present time, card five the potential problems, challenges and lessons in the situation, and card six gives you direct guidance about where to go from here.

Exploring your inner self can be a powerful method to unblock emotions, old patterns and beliefs that no longer serve you. This spread can help you to let go of any behavior patterns, which are no longer serving your life's true purpose.

A spread to discover another person's impact on you

Use any of the above layouts, or any other you know, and simply hold the image of the person you would like more information about in your mind as you ask the cards what you want to know regarding their impact on your life.

It is also effective simply to ask: "What does this person mean to me? What role will this person play in my life? Is this person right for me to be in a love relationship with?" Then, after shuffling, simply draw one card. If you would like more information, ask for right action and clear guidance and draw another card. You will also receive messages in signs, songs and snippets of conversation you may overhear. When you ask for guidance, you will receive it. Your part is to simply stay alert, note what happens and be aware of its significance.

Heart meditation and the Oracle Tarot

This beautiful ritual brings solace to those whose hearts are aching. Consecrate it to Aphrodite and you will receive her help, energy and guidance during and after this meditative reading.

Please be aware that this ritual requires a peaceful and harmonious atmosphere for it to work its magic. If there is trouble and strife within your home, please choose a peaceful time, or alternatively, perform this ritual somewhere else you feel calm and secure.

Before the ritual, light your oil burner and add six drops of rosewood, an oil that grounds matters of the heart. It can help you see through to the actual issues, separate the true origins of emotions and gain clarity as to the origins of issues. Put the red cloth on the surface you are reading on, and place the lily there too. Throughout your reading, burn the blue candle for peace and clarity.

You will need:
Your Oracle Tarot deck.
Red cloth.
A lily or a photograph of a lily.
Rosewood incense or oil.
One red and one blue candle.

Open your magic circle.

Shuffle your deck, all the while reflecting on the issues that are causing you concern in matters of the heart. Divide the deck into three, then place them together again with your receiving hand.

Draw three cards at random, and place the first on your left. This card represents the underlying issues of this problem.

Place the second card in the center. This card represents the way of the heart – where you are now and what you are experiencing within the present moment.

Place the third card to the right. This indicates the correct path to take in light of the information you now have regarding this relationship block. Really engage with this card. If a piece of information strikes a true cord with you, allow it to guide this process. Now, by the light of your beautiful blue candle, gaze at this card, scrying its surface. Simply allow your eyes to lose a little focus, and imagine yourself as part of the scene on the card. Be aware of its imagery, and create yourself as a character within the environment. Let your imagination collude with your psychic skills, and interact with the characters on the card. Ask for their guidance. This journey, be it for a minute or an hour, will highlight the direction you are to go in. It will also creatively illustrate any further future pathworking you may need to do.

Gently come out of this meditative state.

Close the magic circle and thank Aphrodite.

Now, light the red candle in her honor, and thank her as she has already begun to assist you. The lily – representing harmonious, deep and serious love – should be kept with you, either at work on your desk or in your home in a place where you will see it often. It will trigger an unconscious memory of the magical work you have done, and prompt you to thank Aphrodite for the outcome you are both working on together.

This ritual can be worked at any time, but a Friday – Aphrodite's day – on a new or waxing moon is the most auspicious time.

Chapter 12 ~
A Week of White Magic

Imagine we were to escape your daily life, together, now, and go together deep into a forest full of enchanted elementals, by a magical lake, with seven pure days to exercise your magical muscles... what would you learn?

You'll be happy to know that although you may not have that seven days, you can easily incorporate these magical exercises into your routine. This seven-day program is so powerful, yet so simple, you'll be able to carry on with business (only not quite as usual!)

Not only will your intuition, your powers increase, your career, love life, health and prosperity will bloom from the magic of a week of self-initiation as a white magical practitioner.

Ground rules for your initiation week

1. For this week to really change your life, you have to put the energy in. Now, that doesn't mean it's going to be all hard work – what I'm asking you to do is pamper yourself, explore new ways to think, move and feel, and invest time in rediscovering who you truly are. After seven days of transformative work and self-initiation you will uncover who you really are. The layers of old beliefs and habits will be peeled away, until an authentic new magical you is revealed, ready to really live life and experience it as a spiritually activated Witch.

The most important moments of the day are the seconds after you awake – it's within these moments that you program your thoughts and set up your day. So purposefully start every morning with a stretch in bed, and thank the Goddess and the God for giving you another day in which to experience the wonders of life.

2. Reduce the amount of media you consume, and be discerning about what you allow into your world. This is not a week to encourage negative thinking or discussions. This week is a Mystery sanctuary, a process within which you can heal and grow, so limit your TV watching, your magazine reading and your big nights out with your friends.

3. Eat well each day. It is not necessary or advisable for you to radically change your diet, but try to eat foods that are fresh, in season and organic as often as possible, to help you connect to the earth. And be aware of how much caffeine, nicotine, chocolate and dairy you consume, and minimize these products, which can keep you stuck in behavioral habits and encourage mood swings and insomnia coupled with lethargy.

4. Write in your Book of Shadows and Light each day. This book is the sacred space where you record the results of your meditations, the messages you receive and any issues or insights you have throughout this powerful healing week. Drawings, clippings, stories, spells, ribbons, leaves can all find a loving home within its pages. Your beautiful Book of Shadows is like a magical mirror, storing everything you learn about the Craft and reflecting your own journey back to you along the way. It is one of your most sacred tools of power.

5. Complete every day with a healing bath and a gentle meditation before you sleep. Do not watch the news or consume media for at least two hours prior to sleeping, although peaceful, healing and relaxing music is fine. To really activate your spirit, it's absolutely vital to witness at least one sunrise and sunset. Sunrises activate new beginnings, and sunsets consolidate lessons in our bodies. This is a new behavioral pattern which you should adopt long term – the physical, mental and spiritual benefits are amazing.

Your healing shopping list

Now, let's see what you'll need to stock up on prior to kick-starting your new spiritual life. You will need:
Book of Shadows and Light.
Essential oils of bergamot and rose absolue.
An oil burner.
A pink candle.
Sea salt, coarsely ground.
An apple.
Items for your altar. These can be stones you find, crystals, flowers, fresh water, feathers, incense, fresh fruit,

images or items that represent aspects of the Goddess and the God – anything you are drawn to.

You will also need a hand mirror and loose white clothing, which you may already have. Energetically our clothes need cleansing from time to time, so please air, smudge or place your clothing in sun or moonlight before you wear it on Monday. Infusing clothing with intent is one of the most simple and powerful magical acts we can work.

Let's begin!

Monday – Empower your intuition

Monday is usually all about getting used to the fact that it's the working week – again. Right? Not today. You're going to ease yourself into its energy and take it just a little slower than you would normally. This is because Monday's ruling planet (and don't worry, we know it's not actually a planet) is the moon, and this is the day when dreams, intuitive hunches and imaginings can all be very very powerful. Monday is a great day to dream up ideas, make progress on working with your intuition, get in touch with your femininity and celebrate the Goddess within. This is why so many of us suffer from Monday-itis – it's just not natural to stress and worry and rush on a moon-ruled day. So a kind of serenity is the gift of this day.

To start with when you awake, stretch thoroughly, really feeling the life in your body. Thank your bed for the sleep you've just had, and give yourself a big hug. Allow yourself to jot down any dreams you may have had during the night. Then choose something silver, metallic or pastel to wear, to channel that lunar energy all day long.

Today's spiritual assignment is to get back in touch with the creative, imaginative side of yourself by doing some automatic writing. It may be helpful to ask a question first, such as: "Beloved universe, what is it that you want me to know about my intuition?" Then give yourself one minute to write down whatever occurs to you, anything and everything that comes to mind. For those of us who are very left-brained, this can be a struggle. Please persevere though – you'll be amazed at what your spirit is attempting to tell you. Keep a coincidence journal too, in which you record dreams, hunches and seemingly strange coincidences, which you can then follow up on in the future. This is also a wonderful place to record your dreams.

In the evening, note what stage the moon is at, and gaze upon its form. Moonlight is an essential ingredient in our makeup, and it's beneficial for our health to spend time out in the moonlight, as it also reconnects us to the natural world and to our imagination.

Monday's meditation: For five minutes, sit comfortably in loose white clothing either on the floor or on a chair. It can help to touch the tip of your pointer finger to the tip of your thumb, as this keeps your energy directed within. Notice how you are breathing. Allow yourself to simply breathe, and sit, and be, and gently allow your thoughts to happen, but do not indulge them or activate them.

Complete your spiritual awakening with a gentle, beautifully cleansing sea salt bath. This will drain away a great deal of negativity, as salt is the universal cleanser of mind, body and spirit. Epsom salts can be used, just be sure to moisturize liberally afterwards.

Tuesday – Activate your energy

This is action stations day – after the beautiful, feminine energy of Monday, today's Mars-inspired power is all about activating your energy centers. This is a wonderful day to investigate an activity that burns fat, raises endorphins, increases your serotonin levels and activates your spiritual side. There are many spiritual ways to work out, among them yoga, which cleanses and literally "wrings out" your chakras, and is a favorite of teachers like Deepak Chopra and Doreen Virtue, and chakra dancing, which is like chakra healing but with a twist. It's possible to dance these living energy centers within your body into full activity – the benefits being that you feel awakened, energized, cleansed and more alive. Chakra dance is an easy, fun, stimulating and spiritual exercise routine anyone can do, and it increases spontaneity and connects you with the energy of every chakra. If you don't have a class near you, there are wonderful step-by-step videos to learn from. Listening to music, with spirited dancing, can also help activate you.

The aim is to dance or train or run or skip – whatever – until you can see the blood flowing anew in your body, so we want red cheeks. This is extremely cleansing for the blood, and will enhance the psychic ability you innately have.

Tuesday's meditation: What does the universe want you to know about your body? Write down the thoughts you have regarding your body, good or bad, and begin to reconnect with its power and wonderful ability to move you through space and time. Pamper yourself with a massage or a facial today, to thank your body for all it does for you.

Wednesday – Spread the word

Wednesdays are about communication and speaking your truth. This is the day to set in motion spiritual discussions, and maybe even make agreements or arrangements regarding a class or a therapy you've been interested in pursuing. It's about thinking quickly and making associations, and the Wednesday of this spiritual seven-day turnaround is a great day to enter into a contract – with yourself, if you like. It's the day to sign up for a course, investigate joining a group or coven, be involved in online discussion groups, find answers to your questions about your spiritual path or learn a new skill – reiki, tarot, healing, silversmithing, aromatherapy, candle making – anything that you feel drawn to and that makes you feel closer to your authentic self and spirit. If you can go to an introductory evening about it, all the better. In the absence of a formal lecture, consider attending a one-off discussion group – many New Age stores hold gatherings and talks with a variety of different speakers. Wednesday is the day to go and investigate!

Wednesday's meditation: Meditate on the way you communicate – with yourself, your friends and the world – and ask your higher self (the part of you that is directly connected to what we call source, or the universe, or God) what it is that you need to know about communicating. Afterwards, write down a wish list of all the things you'd like to achieve over the coming year. Take your list and choose five things you can achieve over the next month, then plan dates for them. Continue this with your list and you will be amazed at how much can be achieved.

Just before bed, talk to yourself in a mirror. Now, don't panic! Mirror work can feel very confronting at first, but as long as you persevere, the benefits are well worth the first few moments of negative self talk and feeling silly! Simply gaze at your own image in a mirror. It can be full length for full body work (later, you may wish to try skyclad mirror work for its ability to shift negative beliefs about our bodies), or simply a hand mirror to start with. Gaze with love into your own eyes, and affirm to your own image "I love you."

When I first encountered mirror work, two powerful insights were given to me. Firstly, I realized I had spoken these loving thoughts aloud to myself as a little girl in the exact same way. I had sat before what I called my magical mirror and told myself that I would always be my very best friend and always take very good care of me. But years later, layers of conditioning had led to me forgetting – perhaps rejecting – this magical intuitive work. When I later read Louise L. Hay's beautiful book You Can Heal Your Life, suggested to me during the very first professional tarot reading I ever received, I recognized that Louise was recommending what I had already known how to do so many years before.(And how magical an event!)

When I did this again, as an adult, I had a second epiphany. Which was that I could still say it, and that while there was a degree of self-consciousness, soon it became one of the most powerful acts of magic I had ever engaged in. And it had been there the whole time, just waiting for me to rediscover it!

Thursday – Work on prosperity

Thursday is energetically powered by Jupiter, the planet of good fortune and expansion, making it a perfect day to work on your growth, both personal and in terms of your abundance. Many of us have been raised to believe that attracting money is a less than noble pursuit, but this is not true. Money is simply an energy – it enables us to do certain things like eat, live, study and enjoy life. As far as good and bad value judgments are concerned, money is utterly neutral – it is us who invest it with emotion and feelings of deserving it, or not. It is up to us to draw it to us, and to feel deserving of having it. When we start attracting abundance and wealth, we are simply attracting to us that which we manifest.

Take steps today to improve your life in a significant way, by improving your relationship with money. Work on your manifestation skills, and recognize that we all are co-creators of our reality. Once we realize this, we can intentionally begin to create what we want.

Thursday's meditation: So many of us know we have the capacity to make more money – but we have mixed feelings about it. Today, examine your own feelings about being prosperous and successful. What if being successful was just as valid spiritually as, well, struggling? The truth is, struggling keeps you in a low energetic state. Manifesting abundance attracts wealth to us, and with that wealth we are tapping in to the universal truth that there is always enough. That we are always cared for. It is empowering to activate our prosperity consciousness, because we can then care for ourselves, invest in ethical, spiritual pursuits, follow our dreams and inspire others to do the same.

This evening, have a beautiful bath with seven drops of bergamot added – this is an uplifting essential oil that magically attracts prosperity to us.

Friday – Self love and attracting a soulmate

Friday is romantic, so we're going to look at your love connections and see what may need healing in order to attract love into your life.

We're going to call on the Goddess of love, Aphrodite, today to help you work through any body issues you may have, and to help you love yourself more and more every day. This has nothing to do with vanity or conceit, and everything to do with valuing who you are and being thankful to the universe for creating you.

It's all about gratitude again. If we are full of self-criticism, we are unlikely to attract someone to us, as we will not be free to love. Or we may attract to us someone who will constantly criticize us, reflecting back to us our own feelings about ourselves.

Friday's meditation: Throughout today, please connect with your true feelings about sensuality and love. If there are any issues that you may have around these hot topics – and let's face it, who doesn't? – note them in your Book of Shadows and Light and be prepared to work on them. This is also a wonderful day, if you are in a relationship, to set aside time to give each other a sensual massage. Spend time gazing into each other's eyes and really connecting with each other. If your partner isn't able to do this comfortably, or if you are not in a loving partnership at present, simply do this on your own, and appreciate the qualities you have.

Friday nights are sacred to Aphrodite. Run yourself a warm bath, light a pink candle and sprinkle seven drops of rose absolue into the bath. While bathing by candlelight, think of all the qualities you would like in a partner – it's important, by the way, not to focus on anyone in particular, as the universe may have someone else in mind for you. It's essential to contemplate what you want, not who you want, in this exercise!

Afterwards, put on a glamorous dress, have a cocktail and eat an apple – they're sacred to Aphrodite. While sipping your cocktail (non-alcoholic!) you can write down all your musings about the relationship you want in your beautiful Book of Shadows and light. Thank Aphrodite for all these insights, then spend the evening watching romantic movies, listening to passionate music or indulging in romance!

Before you go to sleep, notice your good points and affirm to yourself that you are worth loving, and worthy of attracting a wonderful relationship into your life now.

Saturday – The big picture

Saturday, in a sense, is a tough day. It's ruled by Saturn, the stern taskmaster, and is the day for letting go of what no longer serves you to clear the way for a better future. It's very much a big picture day, and a day for making huge changes in your life, if you feel ready for this. Remember, the universe supports you, and only wants what is best for you. If you feel your way being blocked, this could be a gentle nudge from the God and the Goddess that you are struggling too hard in the wrong direction. Spend time listening to your inner voice to understand where you really want to head and what you want from life.

Saturday's meditation: Your task for today is to meditate for a little while, until you feel calm and still, then take your Book of Shadows and Light and write down the names of all the people who you feel have harmed, hurt or betrayed you in any way. No one is exempt from this list – you might even be on it! You are not to feel guilty about people's inclusion because this is not about blame, this is about forgiveness and gratitude.

After you have written the names down, start at the beginning of the list and go through and forgive each person. Really forgive them. Bless them for what they taught you, and release them. Please be aware that strong feelings can come up during this exercise, but it is important to move forward. Once you have started, it becomes simpler to actually forgive.

This exercise is not about justifying or excusing people's behavior, it's about releasing the hold they and their actions have over you! This is about you – clearing the pain of the past in order to create a new future. You may notice with each name that you feel lighter and lighter and lighter. This process can even, according to metaphysicians, assist you in issues like losing weight and improving your skin and your health, as hanging on to old hurts and resentments can manifest in the body as illness or pain. By working this forgiveness prayer, you are boosting your own chances of health and happiness enormously.

Take very good care of yourself this evening. Have another sea salt bath to release any further pain, and clear yourself energetically. Try not to go out into any harsh social environments – you will be a little fragile and open right now, and need to nurture yourself.

Sunday – Celebrate the new you!

Sunday is all about celebrating, rebirth and creating a new you. Today you're going to investigate what you want to do in the next stage of your life, and how you're going to bring it about by tapping in to your true desires. The way to do this is twofold – first you will build an altar to represent your magical practice, then you will celebrate your new insights with friends.

The morning is about building an altar, using objects that you have found or collected. Be intuitive about this process. While it's great to collect a symbol for each element – earth, air, fire, water, spirit – it's more important that everything on your altar says something about the true you, the new you. So it can be as simple as some beautiful flowers, herbs, clear fresh water in a pretty cup, salt, candles and images that evoke a feeling of the sacred and a true sense of who you are becoming. Remember, being spiritual simply means becoming who you truly are and connecting to the source. Your altar will reflect that.

To create an altar you simply need a space – it can be as large or as small as you wish. It's a beautiful place to keep oils, crystals and pictures of inspirational people, mythological archetypes and Gods and Goddesses. You can even incorporate images from your own belief system along with images of pop icons who move you if you wish. What is important is that your altar and everything on it speaks to you, about you. Rework your altar every week or so, depending on what is happening in your life, and what you are working on.

Later today, have some close friends around to celebrate the New Spiritual You. Invite people who share your beliefs or are at least empathetic and respectful, then gather around in a circle and take turns discussing your dreams and what set you on this path. Now you have gathered your own support group to help you through the tough times. Perhaps you can meet up regularly, each Wednesday, to take your discussions deeper.

Being spiritual and being a White magical practitioner is a very personal thing. It does not mean adhering to another person's ideology or beliefs, or trying to impress yours upon another. There is no right or wrong, as long as you harm no one, especially yourself. Ultimately, being a Witch is about seeking that sense of the sacred in every moment of every day – and of being reminded of how blessed we all are to be here on this planet, right now.

Days and their spiritual properties

Monday

Planet: The moon (well, it's a celestial orb – the Universe's most powerful crystal!).
Stone: Rock crystal, moonstone, pearl.
Wear: White, silver, gray, metallics and pastels – feminine flowing garments reactivate your yin energy.
Affirmation: "I am in touch with my intuition and I listen to my divine guidance."
Essential oils: Sandalwood for protection, jasmine for sensuality.

Action: Explore intuition, realms and psychic talents – it's a great day to purchase a deck of tarot or oracle cards and begin to explore using them.

Action: Jot down any creative inspirations you may have.

Energy: Dreamy, feminine, imaginative, intuitive, a world between worlds, and it's wonderful if you can maintain this dreamy quality all day long.

Tuesday

Planet: Mars.

Stone: Garnet and carnelian, for strength when opening the heart, justice in all situations and discernment.

Wear: Reds, for power, passion and strength.

Affirmation: "I love moving my body. It's wonderful to be fit and strong."

Essential oil: Ylang ylang, which is revitalizing and sensual, and also alleviates headaches and de-stresses you when energy levels become way too high, as they can on a Tuesday!

Action: Find a way that you love to energize your body every week – explore the possibilities of tai chi, yoga, chakra dance or even boxing classes to awaken your energy and power.

Energy: Very active – it's the one day each week when you can extend yourself physically and get the very best results.

Wednesday

Planet: Mercury.

Stone: Turquoise and lapis lazuli to help you open your throat chakra and communicate your wants and needs.

Wear: Blues, for harmony, communication and clarity.

Affirmation: "I enjoy expressing my ideas and beliefs."

Essential oils: Lime, orange or a blend with these in it, to spice up communication and get people chatting easily. These are great for discussions.

Action: Talk to like-minded souls about what you believe and where you're going. It's a great day to "get it out there" – to express out loud your dreams and wishes – and a fabulous time to join a group, engage in therapy or join an online forum.

Energy: Intellectual, witty, interactive – it's a great day for working in a group and finding the support we all need for our journey.

Thursday

Planet: Jupiter.

Stone: Smoky quartz to help ground you and clear negativity.

Wear: Earthy tones, to reconnect you to the earth's energy and give you a solid feeling from which to face challenges.

Affirmation: "It is safe for me to manifest my abundance."

Essential oil: Basil for clear, practical thinking and focus, because being spiritual also means being connected.

Action: Examine your attitudes about money and prosperity.

Energy: Supportive of change – you can make large, bold changes regarding your beliefs on a Thursday.

Friday

Planet: Venus.

Stone: Rose quartz to open your heart and nurture yourself.

Wear: Pink, rose, red tones – this is your day for expressing your inner Love Goddess, so don't hold back. Be a bombshell, because being a sensual woman is a spiritual experience.

Affirmation: "I am a powerful, desirable woman."

Essential oil: Rose absolue.

Action: Tell someone you love them. And tell yourself too.

Energy: Sensual, playful, flirtatious, open and receptive, so take advantage of this nurturing energy to open your heart.

Saturday

Planet: Saturn.

Stone: Amber, to manifest a new reality and achieve your goals.

Wear: Dark clothes, to help you release old patterns and energies.

Affirmation: "It is safe to change. I am now moving into a wonderful new stage of my life."

Essential oil: Frankincense, to heighten awareness on all levels and assist you to realize your own truths.

Action: Release the hurts of the past and emerge stronger and more at peace with yourself.

Energy: Strong, releasing, supportive of change. It is a great day to close one chapter of your life in preparation for tomorrow's celebration.

Sunday

Planet: The sun.

Stone: Citrine, for abundance, joy and vitality.

Wear: Golds, yellows and oranges for good cheer and to attract positive people to you.

Affirmation: "I am a powerful spiritual being."

Essential oils: Bergamot, peppermint and rosewood to invigorate and energize.

Action: Create an altar in the morning, then host a gathering to celebrate the new you in the afternoon. Today is the perfect time to meditate on, channel or create your own personal magical name – a sure sign of being a white magical practitioner!

Energy: Supportive of allowing you to shine. The sun's energy on Sunday helps you walk your talk and be more who you are, comfortable in your skin, and allows you to radiate success without feeling uncomfortable.

Other Titles by Lucy Cavendish

The Oracle Tarot Cards
Magical Spell Cards

*Hay House Titles
of Related Interest*

BOOKS

Adventures of a Psychic, by Sylvia Browne

A Stream of Dreams, by Leon Nacson

Born Knowing, by John Holland

Chakra Clearing, by Doreen Virtue, Ph.D.

Conversations with the Other Side, by Sylvia Browne

Diary of a Psychic, by Sonia Choquette

CARD DECKS

Archangel Oracle Cards, by Doreen Virtue, Ph.D.

Healing with the Angels Oracle Cards, by Doreen Virtue, Ph.D.

Heart and Soul, by Sylvia Browne

Messages from your Angels Oracle Cards,

by Doreen Virtue, Ph.D.

We hope you enjoyed this Hay House book.
If you'd like to receive a free catalogue featuring additional
Hay House books and products, or if you'd like information
about the Hay Foundation, please contact:

Hay House Australia Pty. Ltd.
18/36 Ralph St., Alexandria NSW 2015
Phone: 612-9669-4299 • *Fax:* 612-9669-4144
www.hayhouse.com.au

Published and distributed in the USA by:
Hay House, Inc., P.O. Box 5100, Carlsbad, CA 92018-5100
Phone: (760) 431-7695 • *Fax:* (760) 431-6948
www.hayhouse.com® • www.hayfoundation.org

Published and distributed in the United Kingdom by:
Hay House UK, Ltd., 292B Kensal Rd., London W10 5BE
Phone: 44-20-8962-1230 • *Fax:* 44-20-8962-1239
www.hayhouse.co.uk

Published and distributed in the Republic of South Africa by:
Hay House SA (Pty), Ltd., P.O. Box 990, Witkoppen 2068
Phone/Fax: 27-11-706-6612 • orders@psdprom.co.za

Published in India by: Hay House Publications (India) Pvt. Ltd.,
Muskaan Complex, Plot No. 3, B-2, Vasant Kunj, New Delhi 110 070
Phone: 91-11-4176-1620 • *Fax:* 91-11-4176-1630
www.hayhouseindia.co.in

Distributed in Canada by: Raincoast,
9050 Shaughnessy St., Vancouver, B.C. V6P 6E5
Phone: (604) 323-7100 • *Fax:* (604) 323-2600
www.raincoast.com

Tune in to **HayHouseRadio.com**® for the best in inspirational
talk radio featuring top Hay House authors! And, sign up via the
Hay House Australia Website to receive the Hay House online newsletter
and stay informed about what's going on with your favourite authors.
You'll receive announcements about: Discounts and Offers,
Special Events, Product Highlights, Giveaways, and more!
www.hayhouse.com.au